A CENTURY OF YORKSHIRE DIALECT

A Century of Yorkshire Dialect

Selections from the
Transactions of the Yorkshire Dialect Society

Compiled and edited by
Arnold Kellett and Ian Dewhirst

First published in 1997 by
Smith Settle Ltd
Ilkley Road
Otley
West Yorkshire
LS21 3JP

This selection © Yorkshire Dialect Society 1997
Editorial matter © Arnold Kellett and Ian Dewhirst 1997

ISBN   Paperback   1 85825 087 0
       Hardback   1 85825 088 9

British Library Cataloguing-in-Publication data:
A catalogue record for this book is available from the British Library.

Set in Monotype Bulmer

Designed, printed and bound by
SMITH SETTLE
Ilkley Road, Otley, West Yorkshire LS21 3JP

Contents

Introduction

This is an unusual book — a unique anthology selected from the past 100 years of a particular journal, the *Transactions of the Yorkshire Dialect Society*. As part of the celebrations of the centenary of the society — the oldest of its kind in the world — we are hereby making available to the general public a selection of what our members have researched and discussed and enjoyed over the years.

The Yorkshire Dialect Society was founded in Bradford in 1897 by a committee who had been collecting Yorkshire dialect material for Professor Joseph Wright's monumental *English Dialect Dictionary*, which eventually appeared in 1905. When the committee's work was done, the members decided it would be a pity to disband, and instead they founded a society dedicated to studying and promoting Yorkshire dialect in all its variety. The name *Transactions* was chosen for the journal because it was essentially a record of what took place at the society's

The editors, Arnold Kellett and Ian Dewhirst.

meetings, especially papers that had been read. To these were added original articles, and — from 1914, under the editorship of Professor F W Moorman — original dialect verse and prose. The range of topics covered is quite remarkable, and as the years have progressed there seems to have been no lack of interest or material. Indeed, the amount of creative dialect writing led to the society starting a companion journal in 1954, the *Summer Bulletin*, in which less academic writing appears. Dialect items have also been published by the East Riding Dialect Society, founded in 1984.

As editors of this anthology we have found our task far from easy — for two reasons. In the first place there is the problem of deciding what to select from such an *embarras de richesses*. Limited space means that, inevitably, we have had to leave out so much that is worthy of being republished. Our guiding principle has been to try to give a balanced picture of the work of the Yorkshire Dialect Society. So we have painstakingly trawled through the 100 years, reading and comparing, and finally produced what we believe to be a representative selection — the linguistics, specialised word-lists, and so forth, taking their place alongside lighter material, including humour. For those whose appetites are whetted, the *Transactions* as a whole can be consulted in reference libraries. Better still, you can become a member of the YDS and attend our meetings!

The second reason we have found our editing so difficult arises from the nature of the texts and the technical problems associated with reproducing them. It would have been easy to make a book based on a photographic reproduction of the actual pages of *Transactions*. But as the typeface and presentation has varied so much over the years, we decided it would be better to reprint in a uniform style. Rather than retyping everything, it was decided to use a scanner to transfer all the text to disk. Electronic gadgetry, however, has its limitations, and we have found the scanner frequently baffled by phonetics and dialect — even though we had invaluable assistance from our honorary secretary, Stanley Ellis, at the computer stage. The vast number of awkward words and strange spellings in a work such as this has been an editorial nightmare — and yet we trust that all is now in order, and that the reader's enjoyment will not be marred by misprints.

This brings us to the problem of how dialect should be written. Instead of changing all the dialect texts to a uniform system of spelling, we have decided to retain the original — even if only to show how individual writers have tackled the problem. Occasionally pronunciation is given in the IPA (International Phonetic Alphabet), but even this cannot convey the precise accent and intonation. Throughout this book we do well to remember that dialect is essentially something spoken or read aloud, and that all printed versions are to some extent inadequate.

As to what the dialect words and expressions mean, most are explained in the text. In the creative prose and verse, however, the reader will have to guess the meaning of words which differ mainly because of their pronunciation (eg *dooar*, *deear* door). Where we felt that comprehension would be impeded, we have given the meaning of unusual or difficult words. As readers might be puzzled by the differing kinds of dialect, we have identified the creative pieces throughout by adding the provenance — something which has become YDS standard practice in recent years. This may be a town, but more usually the dialect will be indicated by WR (West Riding), NR (North Riding), ER (East Riding).

As we launch this anthology we take heart from the fact that, even 100 years ago, as our first item shows, there was a general belief that dialect was rapidly dying out. It is true that even less — far less — is spoken or understood now, and that almost all of it has been replaced by regional speech, which retains the accent and intonation of dialect, but little else. Yet those enthusiasts of a century ago would be delighted to know that the Yorkshire Dialect Society is still a going concern and that a warm interest in what remains of our dialect is sure to be maintained — well into the next millennium.

Ian Dewhirst (Keighley)
Arnold Kellett (Knaresborough)

INAUGURAL ADDRESS
By the President,
The Most Noble the Marquis of Ripon, KG

Before I proceed further with the observations I have to offer, I hope you will allow me to express my thanks to the society for the honour they have done me in electing me as your president. As I came to York it struck me that I ought to address the meeting in one of the Yorkshire dialects, but unfortunately I am, I regret to say, unable to do so, though I understand the dialect a good deal better than many of my friends who come from the South. But I felt when called upon to accept the position of president of the society that it was my duty not to refuse, and to afford all the assistance I could in pursuing objects which meet entirely with my concurrence and approval.

We are not met together today for the purpose of forming the society; it is already in existence, and this is the first of its quarterly meetings. Some persons may think that the time has passed for any practical inquiry into the dialects of this or any other part of our country, because, by the rapid progress of education, by the various means which bind us all together much more closely than we used to be bound, and the greater facilities for locomotion and mutual intercourse, those dialects, as spoken dialects, are undoubtedly gradually dying out. I remember that my late friend Archdeacon Watkin, when he was an inspector of schools, used always to tell me that he had no hostility whatever to the Yorkshire dialects, and that he would be very glad that they should continue to be talked anywhere except in school. In spite of the wishes of that very agreeable and distingushed person, I am afraid that the operations of the department with which he was connected are very seriously impairing the extent to which those dialects are now spoken. There may be present some enthusiasts for dialectic speech who may regret that such should be the case, but whether we regret it or not, we cannot help it, the thing is inevitable. But those dialects have not altogether departed from us yet. There are amongst us, at all events in the dales of Yorkshire, many persons who speak a language which persons from the South find it still by no means easy to understand.

This state of things seems to call for the establishment of such a society as this, because there are reasons, which I will refer to in a minute, why it is very desirable that these dialects should be studied and mastered and understood, and it is a great advantage that we should still be able, if we chose to do so, to learn something from them as spoken dialects. Dead languages are learned in a very different way from languages that can still be heard, and consequently, though at the present moment they may be dying out, those who are desirous of mastering their meaning and studying their peculiarities have opportunities of doing so. Why should we make a study of those dialects which we admit are departing? The answer is very simple—because they are closely connected with the history of our country and the history of our language. The study of the ancient languages of any country is of the highest value in understanding the national history and the national character. If we want to understand the English language in the real meaning of the word 'understand', to make it fully our own in all its bearings, we must study it, among other things, in its origin, in the sources from which it has been derived, and in the various aspects which, from time to time, it has presented.

I feel therefore very strongly that it is a useful and valuable work that those dialects should be studied, that their full meaning should be brought before us, and that we should have the means of bearing them in our recollection and of seeing their connection with the literary language of our own day. If you look at varieties of dialect you will find that almost every dale in Yorkshire has some little difference from its adjoining neighbour. All these things, small though they may be, have their value. Everything which brings before us the past of our country, what its people were and what they have been, the lives they lived and the tongue they talked—all this is of the deepest interest, especially in days like these, when it has come to be recognised by students of history that the real history of a people does not consist merely in the doings of its sovereign or statesmen, its great soldiers or sailors, but also in all that concerns the lives, the progress, the speech, and the industry of the people.

I believe some persons doubt whether there is room for a society of this kind, and whether it would not have been better to have affiliated it with some existing society. I am not prepared to say that there is not something to be said for that view of the subject, but we live in a time of specialization. It has its disadvantages, I am quite aware, but if we want closely to study any subject, the general tendency seems to be that we should specialize it, and study it in itself. Therefore I think it is consistent with the practice of our time that this society should have constituted itself as a separate society, and I do not think that there is any ground for complaint that it is trenching on the province of any other society. I believe that the English Dialect Society has ceased to exist, and if that is so there is a special reason for the establishment of local dialect societies to carry out the study of local dialects, and to aid in that way not merely in laying the foundation of a portion of the historical knowledge we require for the understanding of our past history, but also to aid in the great work now going on of the preparation of the *Dialect Dictionary*.

I have no hesitation in saying that I think those who formed the society as a separate and distinct body were justified in doing so. In the report it is pointed out that the majority of the members of the society at present belong to the West Riding. The society was started in the West Riding, but it was not started as a

2

West Riding society, but as a Yorkshire society, and in proof of that fact the metropolis of the county was chosen for the first meeting. I am not unaware that there is a little jealousy, or wholesome rivalry between the different ridings. Personally I happen to be connected with at least two or perhaps all the three, so that I am free from any element of jealousy of this kind. I should be extremely sorry if this Yorkshire society were to become merely a West Riding society. There are dialects of great interest in the North and East Ridings whose history requires to be considered. It would be a great pity if the work of this society should be limited so as to exclude the study of those dialects. Yorkshire is quite big enough to satisfy the aspirations of any man, and therefore I do not want to go beyond its borders in this matter, but I hope that our friends in the North and East Ridings will come forward and give us assistance in a work in which they are as much interested as any of us. In conclusion I wish to express my hearty desire that the labours of this society may be crowned with success, and that it may be worthy of the name of those who have established it.

(The opening article in the first issue of Transactions, *July 1898)*

BEN PRESTON
William Scruton

It was with feelings of genuine sorrow that the sad tidings of the death of the author of *Natterin' Nan* were received on the morning of the 29th May, by the many admirers of this well-known poet. He died at his residence, Hammondale House, Eldwick, during the afternoon of the previous day, at the ripe age of eighty-two years, and 'his end was peace'.

It is now some thirty-five years since the first appearance, in a collected form, of Ben Preston's poems. The little book was entitled *The Dialect Poems of Benjamin Preston*, and was issued at the modest charge of a shilling. Besides a glossary of local dialect words, it contained a portrait of the poet and a short biographical sketch from the pen of his nephew, Mr J E Preston. Its publisher was the late Mr Abraham Holroyd.

The little book was a success in every sense, and had a rapid sale; but there were then, as there are now, some hypercritical *quidnuncs* who will persist in regarding the West Riding dialect as vulgar, and a corruption of the good King's English. By these, any poetic effusion, no matter what its merit, if written in the dialect, is to be despised. And yet many of these critics claim to be highly educated people. The pity is that they are not sufficiently educated to be able to distinguish that the majority of the words in this dialect form, are the survivals of many centuries, and are neither corruptions nor vulgarisms. Moreover, they are words that when handled by a poet like Ben Preston can be used, as no others may, for the expression of satire, sentiment, vivid description, or for the production of songs and ballads of the raciest or the most pathetic kind.

Since the appearance of the edition above mentioned, many of Mr Preston's effusions have adorned the 'Poet's Corner' of the *Bradford Observer*, and from this and other sources, a choice collection of his poems, dialect and other, was, in 1881, compiled by the late Mr Thomas Empsall and published by the late Mr Brear. 'An hour with this book', says the Rev S Baring-Gould, 'is an hour of un-clouded happiness, like many more I have spent on the Yorkshire Moors, with the scent of whins in the air, and the larks singing overhead.'

Ben Preston was born at Bradford, the 10th August 1819. He, however, removed with his parents to a sweet rural spot known as 'Waterside', some two miles up Bradford-dale, at so early a period in his life that he regarded this as all but his actual birth-place. One can hardly feel too thankful that the future poet was

Ben Preston.

privileged to spend his childhood amid surroundings so calculated to nurture poetic ideas, and that his earliest and most enduring memories were of 'green fields, of waving woods, of streams quivering in the sunlight, and of an ever-changing and gorgeous cloudland.'

Preston's father was a handloom weaver, but after a few years' residence at Waterside he abandoned the loom and entered the warehouse of a Bradford manu-

5

facturer—a change not all to the liking of the young poet, who dreaded the prospect of factory incarceration, and infinitely preferred, young as he was, the green fields and blossoming hedgerows of the country, to the noisy pavement of the town.

The limited space at my disposal forbids even the merest outline of Ben Preston's life story. In some of his prose compositions, contributed to *The Yorkshireman* when that journal was at its best, there are some charming glimpses given of his early life, his schooldays, and subsequent apprenticeship as a woolsorter. It was while plodding at this labour, day by day, that he became so familiar with the life of the factory operative as it existed ere legislation stepped in to put the curb on grasping, unscrupulous employers, who in their haste to be rich cared little for the lives of those whom they employed. Ben Preston has more than once told me that he was often the witness of glaring evils that stirred his soul to its depths until he could hold his tongue no longer. His sensitive spirit and tender heart could not tolerate oppression and cruelty in any shape, no matter what cloak or name might be given to disguise it, hence the full force of his genius was brought to bear on behalf of the weak and helpless, and the vials of his wrath were poured out in burning words that can never be quenched.

Ere I conclude I gladly turn to a pleasanter picture in Mr Preston's life, namely, that which he was pleased to call his existence as 'a country gentleman.' After a quarter of a century's town life the old love of country became strong within him, and he longed for the

… Rivers, woods, and skies,
The meadow and the moor

that had charmed him so much in the days of his childhood and youth. And so it happened that when the common lands of Bingley were enclosed several years ago, he bought an allotment of some two or three acres and built a house upon it, to which he and his family removed in May 1865. Afterwards he bought another piece of land in a sheltered nook at Eldwick, where he built the house in which he has resided for many years, where he kept himself happily employed either in cultivating his bit of ground or in painting those homely and truthful pictures of Yorkshire life and character which so much amused and edified his numerous readers and admirers for many years, and where at length he closed his long and well-spent life 'to join the gathered fathers of his race'.

(1902)

SOME RECENT PUBLICATIONS IN THE YORKSHIRE DIALECT

F W Moorman

Smook thru a Shevvield Chimla: By T' Stooaker (W McGowan, Stalwart Office, Pontefract). 6d.

John Hartley's *Original Clock Almanac for 1913* (W Nicholson & Sons, Wakefield). 3d.

Bob Stubbs' (W Saville) *Original Comic Yorksher Awmynack for 1913* ('Fur and Feather' Offices, Idle, Bradford). 3d.

The above publications will serve to give our readers some indication of the vitality of Yorkshire dialect literature in verse and prose at the present time. The dialect used in all of them is that of the West Riding, which scholars are wont to describe as the north-east-midland dialect. In forthcoming numbers we hope to draw attention to recently published literature written in the so-called east-northern dialect as represented by the speech of the North and East Ridings. Meanwhile, in reviewing these books and pamphlets, we desire to pay chief attention to the literary quality of the work which finds a place in them.

Smook thru a Shevvield Chimla is a little collection of lyrics, partly in dialect and partly in standard English, which interpret with great force and sympathy the life and thought of the Sheffield working engineer. We congratulate the author most warmly on the sincerity of his emotions and on his command of rhythm and poetic language. There is a directness of appeal in these poems, and a swift insight into the heart of the working-man, which, we are convinced, should secure for them a fuller hearing than they have as yet obtained. *Working 'On Nights', What the Engine Said* and *John Smith* come straight from the heart, but the lyric which will probably prove of chief interest to our readers is *The Filecutter's Lament to Liberty*, which we give in full.

THE FILECUTTER'S LAMENT TO LIBERTY

Nay, aw'm moithered, fairly maddled,
What's a 'nicker-peck' to do ?
Mah owd brain's a hegg that's addled,
Tryin' to see this matter through.

Here's a strappin' young Inspector—
Dacent lad 'e is, an' ole —
Sez all things mun be correct, or
Aw shall 'av to climb the pole.

Sez ez all mi bonny pigeons
Ez aw keep wi' me i' t' shop,
Mun be ta'en to other regions;
'Ere the law wayn't ler 'em stop.

Sez ez 'ow mi little terrier
Mun foind kennellin' elsewheer.
Aw expect awst 'av to bury 'er;
Shoo'll rest nowheer else but 'ere.

Sez ez aw mun wear a appron
Thru mi shoulder to mi knee;
An' (nah, listen! this put's t' capper on)
Sez how cleanly it mun be.

Each ten men mun 'av a basin,
Fastened, mark yer, fixed an sure,
For to wesh ther 'ands and face in —
Not to throw it aht o' doohr.

There's to be two ventilators,
In good order and repair —
Uz 'at's short o' beef an' taters,
'As to fatten on fresh air.

Each shop floohr mun be substantial —
Concrete, pavement, wood, or brick —
So that water from the branch'll
Keep the dust from lyin' thick.

An' for ivvry bloomin' stidda
There's sooa many cubic feet,
We'st ha' room to play at 'idda—
Uz 'at isn't aht i' t' street.

Eh, aw can't tell hofe o' t' tottle
Ov these Regulations steep;
Aw expect a suckin'-bottle
Ull be t' next we 'av to keep.

Eh, aw know, mun! who knows better?
It's for t' good ov all, is this.

Ivvrybody's teed to t' letter
'Cos o' t' few 'at's done amiss.

Eytin' leead-dust brings leead-colic,
Sure as mornin' brings the day.
Does ter think 'at iver aw'll lick
Thumb and fingers' dirt away ?

Well, good bye, mi good owd beauta —
Liberta, nah left to few!
Since the common weal's mi duta,
Dear owd Liberta — adieu!

awst, I shall; *stidda*, anvil; *teed*, tied

The name of John Hartley is deservedly familiar to all lovers of dialect literature; for many long years he has never failed to delight us with his tales and poems in the Halifax dialect, and we offer him our very hearty congratulations on the publication of his forty-seventh *Clock Almanac*. Similar in character to this is the *Yorksher Awmynack* of Bob Stubbs (W Saville), now in its seventh year of issue, and written in the dialect of the Bradford district. In noticing these two almanacs, we should like to make an earnest appeal to every one of our readers to become an annual subscriber to these publications. The dialect-almanac needs all the help it can receive. It is with genuine regret that we record the fact that the famous *Pogmoor Olmenack*, which started on its career early in the nineteenth century, came to an end three years ago owing to a lack of supporters. A careful study of a large number of these Yorkshire almanacs has brought with it the conviction that they offer the reader a rare intellectual feast. The humour is almost without exception wholesome and breezy; there are touches of pathos which go straight to the heart, and what is equally welcome is the absence of pose and pretentiousness. Here, too, is a literature which, with kindly good-nature and sure insight, interprets for us the thoughts, and reveals the heart, of the Yorkshireman of to-day. No other county in England possesses such a literature, and its disappearance, through lack of support, would be a genuine calamity. It is the habit of shallow minds to call these dialect almanacs vulgar: nothing could be less true. The contributors have learnt the art of writing in a homely, familiar fashion without allowing the least breath of vulgarity to soil their pages, and it would be difficult to find anywhere a literature which evinces more kindliness of feeling or more regard for wholesome thought.

Most of the contributions are in prose, and too long to quote, but we can most heartily commend to our readers the overbrimming merriment of such stories as 'Sammywell Grimes Keeps House' and 'Bachelor Ben' in the *Clock Almanack*, or 'Eethla or Keethla' and 'Nanny Stubbs' chase after a Duck' in the rival publication of Bob Stubbs. A feature of the latter almanac is the inclusion of Yorkshire proverbs and apophthegms, many of which are full of incisive force. We offer our readers one or two illustrations: 'Love blinds a man, and oppens a woman her e'es.' 'Better be too thickheeaded ner too thin-skinned.' 'Th' clouds dooan't fall aht o' t' sky: they rise up off o' t' eearth.'

Readers will, perhaps, desire to know with what measure of accuracy these dialect tales reproduce the speech of the district. It must be confessed that there is at times a notable lack of consistency in this matter. Thus, in the last of the three proverbs quoted above, we should expect that the vowel sound in 'clouds' would be rendered in the same way as the vowel-sound in *aht*; in either case what we hear in the speech of the district is the long *a* of 'father'. Another error is that the contributors are in the habit of placing an apostrophe before the relative pronoun *at* ('at), as though it were a reduced form of *that*. This is by no means the case; *at* is a genuine Scandinavian form, which has been in use in the north of England and Scotland, as a pronoun or conjunction, since the early Middle English period. Finally, we would urge Yorkshire dialect writers to be courageous enough to drop the initial *h* in all words. As they know quite well, it is not heard under normal conditions, and only pedants and half-educated people really believe that the dropping of it is a mark of vulgarity. It is dropped by most of the modern Latin nations, and by many Scandinavians.

(1914)

THE GOOD AWD TAHMES

The good awd tahmes? The good awd tahmes?
An yer think at yer'd like 'em back ? Then Ah'll tell yer what, by Gaw!
You just should a lived as a lad when Ah did, an then yer'd knaw
Better 'an ax for t' good awd tahmes.

They're better awaah is t' good awd tahmes,
Wi their opper an gallusies, lays, an flaals, it was ard dree wark;
Gerrin up i' t' morn afoor leet, an laabourin wharl lang efter dark!
Deean't tell me aboot t' good awd tahmes.

Me faather ee threshed, i' t' good awd tahmes,
At Towthrop, a fower mahle walk, an mebbe be there afore fahve.
An ee yance get yam afoor seven at neet, ee'd getten a drahve,
A rare thing that, i' t' good owd tahmes.

An what could ee addle, i' t' good awd tahmes?
Ah'll tell yer; ee addled eight shillin a week, an they gav im his meeat,
An wi six growin bairns at yam, you may bet there was monny a treeat
Oot o' that for us, i' t' good awd tahmes!

A laabourer's waage, i' them good awd tahmes,
Wad buy aboot tweea steean o' flooer i' t' week, if weeared it all,
And vi seven tahmes seven odd mooths agaape sike looance is small.
Bud we did wer best i' t' good awd tahmes.

Me muther she slaaved, i' t' good awd tahmes,
An scratted, an tewed, an rahved, an wrowt wer weeams te trig,
Oed tonnups, an wicked, an gethered, an' gleaaned, an' kept a pig.
A recklin she'd begged, i' t' good awd tahmes.

Ah went wiv er oft, i' them good awd tahmes,
Afoor Ah were ten year awd, agetherin flints off'n t' land;
A shillin' a tun we got, wiv a sad ceeak o' t' sahze o' me 'and
Tea for wer dinners, i' t' good awd tahmes.

Ungery ? Say yer ? i' t' good awd tahmes ?
Aye, bairn, Ah was ungery allus at yam when Ah was a lad.
Bud efter Ah went te farm pleeacin, yer knew, things wasn't se bad,
At ten year awd, i' t' good awd tahmes.

That was salvaation, i' t' good awd tahmes.
We reckoned nowt aboot wark if we nobbut ad plenty te eeat;
Suet pudden, an broth, an baacon, or butcher meeat;
Twas grand was that, i' t' good awd tahmes!

D'yer want em back, sike good awd tahmes ?
Nay, lad, just be content, an mahnd o' what Ah saah,
I' t' providence o' God things breetens ivvery daah.
They're better gone is t' good awd tahmes.

Walter F Turner (NR)

opper an gallusies, seed-holder and braces; *addle*, to earn;
weeams te trig, stomachs to fill; *yam*, home

HOME THOUGHTS FROM FRANCE

Bods is singin' upo'd bushes,
Larrocks up i' d skies,
Laatle cauves i' d cauf-hoose bealin',
Laatle pigs i' d styes.
Praise the Lord! ah knaw their language
Even over here
An' my thowts gans back ti Yorksher,
Land ah luv si dear.

Whea drahves Depper, Beaut an Farmer?
Diz ee dea 'em weel?
Is his pleughin' sthrite as mahn was ?
Can he show his heel
Tiv all d' wags fra Kelk ta Cowlam
On a pleughin' day ?
Diz he say, 'A rotten meat-spot!
Ah sall run away?'

Ah suppoase it's Sundah mornin
Wiv 'em ower there.
Ah can ommost hear oor choch bell,
See 'em kneel i' prayer.
Aud foaks, bairns, an wives, an mothers,
Prayin' God above,
Ti send back fra France an Flanthers,
Driffil' lads they love.

F Austin Hyde (ER)

(both 1916)

A GLOSSARY OF MINING TERMS IN COMMON USE AMONG THE MINERS OF GREENHOW HILL
H J L Bruff
(Abridged)

ARS FLAP, ARS LOOUP. The ars flap is a board to which is fixed a rope. The rope again was fastened to the rope of a jack-roll, in similar fashion to a 'bosun's chair'. It is used for lowering men into a shaft or stope or similar inaccessible places. Instead of a board, a simple loop of a rope is also used, secured round the waist of the man about to be lowered. This is called 'ars looup.'

BEAR. Part of a vein, which at this point carries ore.

BELLAMED or BELLONED. This word is pronounced either way. Cattle or fowls — in fact, any animals or human beings — may become 'bellamed', or suffer from lead-poisoning. It depends on whether it is caused by smelting fumes or drinking water containing lead salts. In rare cases, it may be through drinking water charged with fine lead ore in suspension. I know of one case where a cow died from this. The stomach, when opened, was covered with fine coe which looked like silk. When it is caused by fumes, cattle get lamed and reel about. Is it possible that the original of the word may come from the Norse *baal* or fire, and therefore means lamed from the fire, that the word should thus be 'Baal-lamed'. In the olden times the lead was smelted on the top of or brow of certain hills where there was a good draught; these are still called 'baal' hills, 'baal' banks, 'bell' banks, and so on. Under such conditions it was quite easy for cattle to become poisoned both from the fumes and the more deadly dust of the fires. Certain pieces of ground were avoided by the farmers, as their cattle were sure to suffer.

BELLISSES. Blacksmith's bellows.

BING. A weigh of dressed lead ore, blue metal as a rule, as white or grey metal carries a higher percentage of lead. It scaled 8 cwt.

BINGSTEEAD. Bin or storage place for dressed ore, ready for 'weighing off'.

BINKSTONE or BINKSTUN. Same as knockstone. Compare Norwegian *banke*, to knock, beat.

BIRDS-EYES. Vein matter carrying galena of the size of peas or birds' eyes. The word applied to the ore only, and was a standard of measure, like 'Brangly', when the specks were larger.

BLACK AIR or BLACK DAMP. Poisonous or unbreathable air. It is called black air, as no candles will burn in it, and consequently places where such air occurs are always plunged in darkness. In Yorke Level, Merryfield, for a length of 50 yards or so, no candle would burn. The galloway used for waggoning always stopped on his own accord when he was through the black air zone to allow the candle he carried in a lantern under his chin to be lit. (Joss Pounder told me this.) I have been told by old miners that this kind of air oozes out of the shale and grit rocks. I have never heard that black air occurs in limestone rock.

BLACK JACK. Zinc blende, sometimes also just called 'Jack'.

BLANCH. 'Blanched wey metal—glistening with streaks of ore. Not a blanch o' metal'—no sign of ore.

BLOBB. Lumps of ore from the size of a doubled fist.

BLUE JOCK. Fluor spar, in this case of a blue colour. A vein on the south-east side of Greenhow Hill was called 'Blue Jock Vein'.

BOOMMEL BEE ARS. When steel was tempered to show several colours, the temper was called 'boommel bee ars', and was considered the best temper for cold chisels and the like, being tough and hard at the same time.

BOOSE or BOWSE. Vein matter which has been worked out or wrought and which carries ore is called 'bowse.' It is separated out below, and when brought to the surface is emptied into the teems.

BRANGLY. Vein matter carrying galena in sizes bigger than peas is said to be 'brangly.' See birds-eyes. 'T' vein war nice an' brangly.'

BRASHY. Old wood attacked by fungus in a mine may look sound, but is 'brashy', or rotten.

BUCKER or BOOCKER. This is a kind of hammer with a broad and flat face, wherewith the ore or the bowse is crushed small into a reasonable size on the knock-stone. The foregoing operation is called to bucker or 'boocker.'

BUDDLE or BOODDLE. A flat trough of smooth boards or faced with cement on which the smithom is placed while a small stream of water washes the fine particles of sand and clay away down the slightly inclined surface of the buddle. The smithom is gently stirred and turned over all the time with a shovel.

BUDDLE WATER. The quantity of water used for the preceding process represented to the old miners as well as the present-day miners a measure of water by means of which they used to compare the volume of streams or trickles of underground waters. Thus a man will say: 'Mony a grate watter war roonnin in' or 'Mabbeay fower or five booddle watters brast oot wal shot went.' The graduation is: Grate watter, booddle watter, pisser, dropper, and 'Watter was suin' oot' or bleeding.

BUNNING or BOONNIN'. Platform in a shaft or in a rise or stope, resting on cross timbers or stemples let into the rock.

CANNEL (Candle). The old men used tallow candles, the best quality of which had a green thread in the wick. During the war, tallow candles were very difficult to get, and at times the tallow was quite yellow and brown, and smelt unpleasantly. The men told me it made them sick, and there was no doubt there was a rather sickly smell in the workings from these candles.

CALLISED. This word is generally used about building stones which have gone hard by exposure. It is, however, also used about all kinds of stone which the old men used to believe hardened through the influence of the atmosphere.

CAWK or COKE. Barytes or sulphate of barium, also called heavy spar.

CHATS. Bowse when broken up on the knock-stone ready for the hotchin tubs.

CLACK. The valves of pumps are called clacks.

CLARTEY. Clayey, dirty, sticky dirt.

CLIMMIN. Climbing.

CLIMMIN SHAFT. Climbing or way-gate shaft. Timbered and provided with bunnings.

COWL RAKE. An implement of iron provided with a long or a short handle. The iron portion was crescent-shaped with a socket at right angles to its plane, into which the wooden handle fitted. The long-handled ones were used for grating, while the short ones were used on the knockstone.

CREWK or CROOK. Hook used for drawing the kibbles on to the ground when they arrived at the top of the shaft. Kibble crewk.

CUNLITH or CUNDITH. Stone culvert. 'Cunlith' is not used as often as 'Cundith'; in fact, I believe the former not to be Greenhow at all, though Kit uses it. Probably the same as 'Conduit'.

DEG. To sprinkle with water, to leak. 'T' toob degs'.

DEM or DAM. A mine reservoir is called a 'dem' or 'dam'. It may be a reservoir to supply the boilers, engine dem, or to maintain a constant supply of water for dressing, or a catch-pit for waste, called a 'Cow Dem'.

DODGER. Pin fastening the door of a wagon or which prevents the wagon from tipping up by itself if a tip wagon.

DOG or DOG SPIKE. Square, thick nail with a one-sided head.

DOWK. A mixture of sand and clay which will run when wet is called 'dowk'. Occurs mostly in lough holes. On cutting some old workings, a man reporting this said: 'Thar war nowt bud dowk an' deeads, regular oade man.'

DROPPERS. In certain places water keeps dropping from the roof, either coming from some small and often invisible crack in the rock or the place may be the lowest point of the roof and water from several such minute cracks, or it may be condensation water which collects on the surface of the rock. Such spots are well known and avoided by the men. If they have to work under a dropper, they place boards up to catch the dropper. If the stream is rather powerful it is called a pisser. In wet seasons a dropper may become a pisser.

DUB or DOOB. (1) A deep place in a beck is called a dub or 'doob'; (2) a rain-water tub is also called a dub or 'doob'.

FAIRY PIPES. The small-headed clay pipes used a hundred years ago and more.

FELKS. Felloes of a wheel.

FLISH, FLISH OFF. Flake of stone knocked off an edge. Flaking a piece of stone off.

FLUID SPAR. Fluor spar, also by the old miners called 'Blue Jock'. Blue Jock is Derbyshire name for fluor spar, and has probably come in with Derbyshire miners in the past.

FODDER or FOTHER. One-twentieth of a ton of lead. Also used in 1794; about the same quantity of lead ore.

GALLOPER. Small vein striking off from the main vein when these lose them-selves or it may be a connection between two portions of the same main vein. It is not a cross thing or a north vein.

GIN. A gin was an apparatus used for hoisting ore, bowse, etc, out of a shaft by means of a horse. It consisted of a large wooden drum mounted on a vertical axle, one end of which was supported by a foot bearing and the other end (the top) was prevented from falling over by means of cross beams and stays. The drum was mounted high enough to enable a horse to be harnessed to a horizontal lever arm.

GLISSY. Shiny. 'Teem's very glissy' = The team gleams or glistens. Not considered a good and promising parcel of bowse.

GLUT. When stones and timber, or either, bind in a shaft, they are said to 'glut'. Old abandoned shafts are purposely glutted. When a shaft runs, it takes a long time to settle before the glutted materials settle down.

GOR. Sticky, dirty clay. 'Old man', as a rule, is very dirty, and I have heard it used when we cut an old man's sump-foot.

GRAIN. (1) This is a very old word meaning branch. I don't think there will be more than two men up on Greenhow now who will have heard this word used, Kit Storey and Will Longthorn. Will once said to me about two levels branching away from each other, holding his whip-stock and lash away from each other: 'T' levils grain like this.' Bin Hannam said: 'War Bleea Beck grains.' At Greenhow the word occurs in the place-name 'Thiefsty grains' — it means where the beck Thief-sty Gill branches out. (2) A wooden fork formed by a branch used for turning over the sheaves when threshing on the threshing-floor by hand was called a grain. This was told me by an old farmer, and shows that the word was used not only in mining parlance.

GRITS. Millstone grits. These are separated from the mountain limestone, in which at Greenhow the lead is found, by the shales called 'Blackness'. To the north of Greenhow, at Merryfield, and up Ashfoldside Gill, all the lead was got in the grits; they never got down to limestone beds.

GROOVE. Local term for a mine: Green Grooves, Staney Grooves.

GRUND or GROOND. Ground, mining area; virgin ground was called 'Hale groond'. Less worked, 'Haler groond'.

GROOND (To). To grind. Groondin mill = grinding mill.

HALE. Whole, unworked or virgin ground. (See Groond.)

HALE WHITTLE. A piece of pointed iron which is heated and then used for enlarging holes in wood. The small pokers in use generally where they burn peat are called hale whittles, or just whittles. Not a word in common use now, as more coal is burned than peat today, and a longer poker is then of more use.

HATCHET. A miner's axe is always called a hatchet, never an axe. It has a flat face where the edge is, curving back from the edge towards the shaft-hole. The hatchet has an edge on one side only, on the inside of the curved face.

HAZARDS. Last year's peats.

HINGBENCH. The uprights or 'stow-blades' of a jack-roll are mortised into the 'sole trees' to keep the latter apart. The sole trees are bolted to two pieces of timber, which are called the 'hingbench'.

HITCH. Throw or fault. 'T' vein 'as 'itched.'

HOLE. To 'hole' or 'hole through' is to cut into one working from another. To 'hole the old man' is to cut older workings; if not expected, this is not only an unpleasant experience, but one with which there is considerable danger connected, as the old workings may be waterlogged, and the water, carrying dirt and slurry with it, may cut off and drown men working in places branching off from the course of the water and slurry from the old man, which will sometimes pack a level roof-high.

HOPPER. A hopper is a big funnel situated in a rise from an under-level. The bowse is tipped into the hopper, and runs down into a wagon or bin at the bottom.

HOTCHIN TUB. When the bowse has been crushed sufficiently fine on the knock-stone, it is tipped on the floor alongside the hotching tubs or jiggs. This consists of a square deep box full of water, into which a square sieve dips. The sieve is suspended by means of adjustable hangers from a long pole, called a 'stang', which is an unequal-armed lever, the shorter arm supporting the sieve. The sieve is partly filled with broken bowse, chats, and then lowered into the water. The hotcher will now grip the end of the long 'stang', and by a combined quick movement of the wrist and a jerky motion with his ankles, so that he alternately throws his weight on the soles of his clogs, a peculiar jerking movement is produced as the sieve dips into the water.

JACK-ROLL. Windlass with wooden roll and either iron or wooden crank handles. The two sides, which are called 'stosses' or 'stowblades', are mortised into the two sole trees at the bottom, and at the top are connected with a piece of timber called the 'spin'le'.

JUDDS or JOODS. Strengthening pieces of timber. I have never heard this word used in the singular; they will say: 'T' judding ga t' way'. They also say to 'jood' or 'jooddin't.'

JUMPER. Short, heavy drill.

KANTED. Chamfered. 'Reet oade man's drills war kanted, han' kanted, thoo knoas'. These drills were made from square iron rods, case-hardened or 'blistered'.

KIBBLE. Large or small iron or wooden bucket used for drawing ore or deads out of a shaft. Top and bottom were both narrower than the middle, to prevent it catching the sides and spilling the contents.

KILE (To). To wedge; also used as a noun: A kile = a wedge.

KISHLY Hard, dry vein matter, poor in ore. 'A kishly vein.'

KNAP. A short, sharp blow.

KNOBBLE (To). To make a head on a spike or bar by hammering.

KNOCKINS. Lumps of ore, either loose or embedded in the vein material. Their size was at least as big as a man's fist: 'Knockins as big as me cloggs'. Knockins has to be broken up — knocked to pieces.

KNOCK-STONE. The stone bench on which the lead ore is buckered or broken small for the hotching tubs. (See also Binkstun.)

LAUNDER. A chute, generally of wood, to convey water.

LOUGH -'OLE. These are holes formed in the limestone by water. They may either be filled with stone and gravel or with clay. As a rule, they are not looked upon with any pleasure, as they are considered to indicate barrenness in the vein.

MATCHES. These were used to set the fuses alight, and were made of paper soaked in saltpetre solution, thus forming touch-paper, or they were made by greasing paper, which latter were safer to use as the others burned somewhat unevenly and were unreliable. Henry Newbould tells me they were made either by folding or screwing a strip of paper so as to form a spill, which was fixed to the rock by means of a lump of clay projecting out and below the straw fuse.

MIDDLINS. The central portion of a vein which in the limestone carries the ore at Greenhow.

MINER'S KNOCK. Signal given by knocking on the rock with a stone or a hammer. As a rule, it was two or three short knocks with two long intervals following. Thus (•—•) or (•—•—•).

NATURE. Strength; 'All nature hez gone'.

NIPPED. When a vein closes up, it is said to become 'nipped' Sometimes it may be a hard nip, when the vein can completely disappear.

NOG A short spike without a head. As a rule, they are square.

NOGGINS. Lumps of ore, generally larger than knockins, which can be broken by buckering on the knockstone. A noggin is as much as a man can lift at times.

OLD MAN. The meaning of this expression originally refers to a previous miner, but it has been transferred to mean his workings or anything he has left behind. Thus if one cuts an old working it is called cutting 'the old man' or 'Oade Man'; it may also refer to material which has filled up the old workings, thus: 'It war nowt bud oade man, dowk an' deads'. Implements lost or left by the old man are also called 'old man' or 'old man's tools'. The earliest miner who has worked a place is referred to as 'T' oade man o' all'.

PASHY. Soft, rotten; about wood.

PEAT-ASS. Black and red coloured clay sometimes found in the heart of a vein. Old miners thought it to be peat mould washed down and converted into ashes by the internal heat of the earth. It looks remarkably like peat ashes. I had some analysed; it contained zinc, manganese, lead and silver oxides (from Lonsdale Vein).

PENNY-RIB. Thin vein no thicker than a penny, carrying ore, is called a 'penny-rib'.

PINCHED OUT. A vein that has nipped clean out is said to have 'pinched out'; same as hard nip.

POWDER HORN. Powder was carried in a cow-horn, the wide end of which was closed with a wooden bottom, which was nailed on or fixed with copper nails or wire; the other end had a small hole bored in it which was closed with a wooden plug. Powder would keep for quite a long time if the plug was covered with clay.

PUNCH. Short pointed steel used for forcing of projections of the rock. After a shot was fired, a skilled man could often remove considerable quantities by this means.

RAFLACKS. Rubbish, refuse.

RICKET. This is the groove into which the driving-end of a stemple fits.

RUCKLE. Loose heap of stones. 'T'ole ruckle commed doon'.

RYDER. Ryder is calcite coloured brown, grey, or quite white. It crystallises in sharp-pointed pyramids, and is, therefore, when in that form, called 'Dog-tooth Ryder'.

SAAG. Saw. They say, however, 'sawing', not 'saaging'.

SAMM. Collect together. 'Samm oop tools' = Gather together the tools.

SHAGGLING. Loose. Compare 'Straggling along' = rambling, aimless and unsteady walk.

SHOCKLES or SHOGGLES. Stalagmites and stalactites.

SHILVE. To flake off stratified rock, like flag stones or shales.

SHIRLEY. Brittle. Used by Orlando Marshall and also by Calvert in his case about brittle spar. Calvert is an Arkengarthdale man; Orlando is Greenhow born and bred.

SNODD. Smooth, even; 'T' vein side war ez snodd ez glass.' Comfortable = 'It's a snoddish pleeace ta wurk in.'

SILE, SILIN. Streaming. 'T' watter war silin in', when coming in from overhead in pissers.

SIPE, SIPIN. When water comes in in small quantities, but steadily.

SLAM. Thin slurry and mud.

SLAPE. Slippery. 'Slape vein side'=slicken side.

SLECK TROUGH. Used by blacksmiths for cooling their work or tools and for tempering.

SLEW. Move sideways.

SLIFTER. A vein which has been or is worked from the day in a hill-side, so that it stands open to the day, vertically like a gash. is called a 'slifter'.

SLIGG. Sludge, running clay and mud.

SMITHOM. The part of the ore that goes through the sieves when hotching, and which collects in the hotching tub, referred to as 'the nest-egg', is called 'smithom'.

SNACK. Miners' dinner.

SNACK-TIME. Miners' dinner-hour.

SNAP. Another word for dinner.

SNAP-TIME. Another term for dinner-hour.

SNOO. Turn end for end horizontally, not upside down.

SNOUTIN'. Sharpening or pointing a piece of wood.

SNURP. Nip up, pinch out, when a vein closes up. 'Unless t'vein snurps.'

SOON or SEUN SHIFT An early morning shift; a special shift when work which had to be done in between times was done.

SPAKE. Spoke of a barrow.

SPELL. Thin piece of wood used to make up, when fitting or stopping.

STANG. The long pole which enables a hotcher to jerk the sieve of a hotching tub.

STANK. A small dam preventing water from flowing freely.

STEE. Ladder.

STEE-HOLE. Where a footpath crosses a wall, steps are provided, and the top stones are left out, this is a 'stee-hole'.

STEMMING. To stem a hole, or to tamp it, was the operation of ramming sand, a little clayey, into the hole to prevent the powder simply blowing out without effect.

STEMPLES. Round or square timber between two rock walls either in a shaft, a level, or in a stope.

STIDDY. Anvil. Compare old Norse as well as modern dialect Norse: *stede* = anvil.

STIRKEN. Anything which hardens by drying up or cooling. Thus: 'T' sligg hed stirkened or 'Cannle-greease stirkened'.

STOPE. Worked-out portion of a vein.

STOWER. Step of a ladder, or stee, is called a 'stower'. A small stick a foot or so long is also called a stower.

SUIN. Oozing. 'When we cut Pity Meay, watter war suin oot'.

SWAPE. The wooden connection between the gudgeon and the handle or 'peg' of a jack-roll was the swape, but, when speaking about a jack-roll handle, generally it was referred to as the swape.

SWASHY. One would call a likely vein, a vein which is sure to carry ore and form a bear, a swashy vein, a nice kind vein, not hard to work and carrying ore in places

TAK-NOTE. Take-note. Agreement with the mineral owner for the right to search and win ore.

TEEM. Receptacle for broken ore or bowse is called a 'teem'. The material is teemed into it. They are of circular shape, narrower at the bottom, which slopes forward. One side (the front side) is open, narrow at the bottom, and widening out upwards. Across the teem is a wooden launder provided with holes in its side; these holes can be plugged at will. The water runs over the bowse and washes the clay away, which escapes through a grid at the bottom of the opening at the front of the teem, level with the top of the wooden table on which the grater, or teems-man stands.

TENGS. Blacksmith's tongs.

TEW. Blast-nozzle of a blacksmith's hearth.

TOMMY. A short vertical piece of timber acting as a strut is called a 'tommy'. In soft ground, the bottoms were made flat, but in rock it might be made with an egg-end, the other end being square and fitted into a ricket like a stemple. 'Tommy' is also used for the miners' dinner or snack.

TROANES. A steel-yard like butchers use. It was larger than an ordinary steel-yard, and was suspended from a tripod, a kibble of known weight being hung on to the hook and filled with ore.

TROON'LE. Wheel of a barrow.

VAMP. Spongy, holding water. 'Vampy clay-hoale', about a hollow containing wet clay; also referred to as 'vamp-hoale'.

WEMMEL. To turn a thing over, upside-down.

WICK. When a vein or a bed shows specks of galena, it is said to be 'wick'.

WIMMEL. Augur, brace.

WITCH STONES. I have frequently found stones with natural holes in them placed in conspicuous positions in old workings re-opened by me. I did not at first realise their object, and like the present generation looked upon them as curios, until an old miner told me they were 'lucky stones'. In the past, these stones were placed in conspicuous places to scare away witches and evil beings. The evil spirits would often try and follow the spirits of dead miners down below, and, in particular, if tbe man had been killed by an accident. Anniversaries were particularly favourable times for the spirits to gain power over other miners, especially relations of those killed, who refrained from entering the workings and never did a night-shift at such times.

(1923)

KING ALFRED
AND THE CAKES

Ev ya ivver eard tell a that teeal aboot King Alfred an' t' ceeakes ?

It war a lang tahme back — when t' King wer fighting t' Daanes soomwheear doon i' t' sooth.

'E rammelled off intit coounthry — an' put on cleeas te mak issen lewk like yan o' t' coonthry fooakes, d'ye see.

Yah daay — scraffling alang — 'e cam tiv a lahtle wooden 'oose — an lifted t' sneck an gooad in.

E seed at ther wer a greeat rooaring fire — and at t' ooad wooman wer beeaking keeakes.

'Cum thi ways in', sha said — 'ah's fair clashed ta deead, an ain't tahme te dawdle wi thee — fer ahve joost getten t' keeakes it yune, an ah es anutter joadther te neead, sea tha can joost lewk efther em, an whativer tha dis, mahnd tha dissent bon em — fer ahve joost sliped oot t' worral ole — ant yune's varry nigh rid yat: an be sartin te ton em beath sahds tit' uther — else thou'll kep it.'

Bur 'is mahnd wer moithered like an e fergat all aboot t' keeakes — an tha began ti bon, an t' ooad wooman smelt t' reek — an cam back i' sike a fullock an all.

'Thou greeat doddthery bletherheead', sha saays — 'thou's letten em bon — isn't tha fair shammed o thisen — mebbe tha thowt tha warnt woth watching — but ah'll lay thou'll goup em oop — an trigg thi wamen fast eneeaf — fer ah'll awaud it thoos a belly-gut.'

An wi that sha up wiv er neeaves an fetched im sike a jowler ower t' lug ual it meead all fair ring ageean.

An afoor e ad tahme te saay owt, twea men drissed as officers cam in — they'd bin laatin im, d'ye see — an tha seeamed varry pleeased te see im an all — an neeamed im as Sire.

By gum, ya sud a seen t' ooad wooman — she nivver wer sea adreed i' er wick — sha war faair stagnated — an sha niddered an diddered fra top ta boddom — an sha war trying te mak it menseful tiv im — when e saays:

'Whia noo! ah seear ah addled all ah got, an ah ope et ya'll ev betther luck t' next beeaking daay.'

An wi that they all gat ageeat ageean.

An t' ooad wooman saays tiv ersen, sha says:

'Whia! Fahne feathers mebbe maks fahne bods — bud a man's nobbut a man — onnywaays.'

G Hardwicke (NR)

(1924)

yune, oven; *reek*, smoke; *neeave*, fist; *i' er wick*, in her life; *laatin*, seeking; *stagnated*, taken aback

---

COCK-LEET

It's nobbut cock-leet, Sweetheart! Hasta coom by Yorla Moor?
Whya, lad! tha mun be famished! I' ma muther's cheeany crock
Are spice-loaves an' fat-rascals! Dosta hear ma faither's snore ?
An' half-past four's soundin' fra Yorla tower clock!

Whisha noo! gie ower cuddlin' an' doan't be sae rough!
I' se t' cows ta milk, t' butter ta kurn an' tak' ta Dunnel Brig—
Yet I' se fain ta gan a-sweetheartin' by bonnie Altor Cleugh,
Forgittin' a' bud thee an' me, an' t' birks ev Wyersall Rigg.

Wheer t' moortops are a-ringin' wi' t' canty lilt o' t' lark,
Wheer foxes hide in t' brekkons an' t' grass is rare ta tread;
Aye, lad, I'll coom a-sweetheartin' wi' thee at t' edge o' dark,
Bud theer's wark ta do at cock-leet an' ma foaks are still a-bed!

Dorothy Una Ratcliffe (NR)

(1924)

birks, birch trees

SHEEP AND SHEEP-SCORING
J R Witty

The object of this paper is twofold, firstly to note the dialect expressions used concerning sheep, and secondly to record the various ways of counting or scoring sheep by the shepherds of the Yorkshire moorlands.

Sheep occupy so much thought in Yorkshire that they deserve some recognition. Whilst alive they are the concern of the farmer, the shepherd, the shearer and the stock-dealer. Dead, not only do they affect the butcher and the dining-table but as the *Encyclopaedia Britannica* of 1810 puts it: 'Staplers, scourers, pickers, scriblers, dyers, carders, combers, spinners, spoolers, warpers, queelers, weavers, fullers, tuckers, burlers, pressers, packers and clothiers depend upon the sheep just as much as do the fell-mongers, glue-makers, parchment makers, candlemakers, soap-makers, button-makers, and hornturners.'

Sheep is only a generic term. The males are tupps or rams. Those rams that have been cut are wethers or wedders. A hornless ram — a dodded tupp — is the best when it has a brant forehead, high between the eyebrows and the 'nose grissles'. Female sheep are ewes or yows. A lamb becomes a ewe after the second clipping; at first it is a gimmer lamb, then a gimmer hogg until its first shearing— the wool is termed hogget wool. It is now a gimmer shearling and only after the second shearing does it become a ewe. A barren ewe is called eild or yeld or gelde. Marshall in *Rural Economy of Yorkshire* names the impotent males, fat lambs, hoggards, shearling wedders and two shear wedders.

A lamb falls to the ground, ie, begins to eat grass instead of being suckled, when about five weeks old, for then they have had their fulth of milk. If lambs fall to grass too soon they prove to be short runtish sheep, which the shepherds call dumplings or grass bellied sheep. A lamb that has been fed at first on cows' milk and then put to a ewe will shoot and scowre until the cows' milk be voided, for until then, it will not throden or thrive. Lambs that lie skulking — with their heads close to the ground — must be searched because probably they have company, that is they are afflicted with maddes or mauks, ie maggots. Lambs, whose excrement berks together their tails and hinder parts are pinded, and the clags have to be clipped off. Lambs are marked with a tar mark by means of a botte on the buttock or the liske. Those that are weaned early are foreard lambs, the latest ones are backards. If a ewe is kittle on her yower or unkind to her lamb she is made to dance in a pair of hopples till she will stand to let her lamb suck. If a lamb dies, it is flea-ed, that is it is skinned, and the pelt is sewn on the back of another so that the ewe will take to it.

A good ewe has a broad buttock, showing tufty and thick wool down to the hough, her stapple is snod. A dodded sheep is better than a horned sheep because, being to blame, ie, troubled with sheep-lice, it will not tear or loosen its wool. A poor ewe is a waster and is chiefly noticeable because of its candle tail.

Sheep whose mouths always appear green and wet are troubled with chewing of gorre because their food works out of the wykes of their mouths after mastication instead of into the system. They often like a feed of battle-grass in place of the small sparry dry grass of the Wolds.

About Martlemas when sheep are first fothered, the flock is removed nearer home and is fed up to sell against Beverley Fair, ie, Cross days, for betwixt Midsummer and Lammas everybody will have fat sheep to sell. Old broken mouthed ewes and wormy skinned or kempe haired sheep go off best about All-Hallow Fair.

Well happed sheep are best for a hard faugh (fallow), but sheep want plenty of room in a fold, for fear of the older ones treading and smarring of the weakest lambs.

To make sheepfold-bars use willow which has been felled when it begins to bud and is mouse eared. Put the sticks in water to keep them reeky and moist, peel them and put them in a house lest the sun check and rive them, then split them with iron wedges into quarter-cliff. A bar consists of two heads four feet high joined by four or five spells about eight feet long and strengthened in the middle by a dagger and two slanting swords, the whole being fastened by cotterills or wooden pins. These bars are fastened to stakes by means of fold-hanks or hankings — a loose kind of string of two pletts. Hoggs do not take kindly to fothering, they go snuffling and snooking from heap to heap and take a day or two to fall sharply to their hard meat. In hard weather they will eat aught even windle-straw (streea). A shepherd rakes out hay with a hay-crook, evens it off and ties it into girlings.

Sheep are washed in a dyke not afore nine o'clock because the mornings are airish. If you use somebody else's sheep dyke you may have to pay gate-law. A sheep-dip may be made near a hecke or bridge by coupe-linings and the lecks (leaks) dammed with fawdes of straw. Loose wool is pulled off and thrust into a poake tied to a bar-spell. After weshing the sheep should lay anights on some clean leys or swarth ground, so that they do not mucky their wool.

They are clipped when the weather be set at a certain, the wool well risen from the skin, and the fleece walked together at the top with no bitts or locks in it. Shill out any sheep that begins to rag and lose its wool before the rest is fit to clip, and pull its wool. Scattered locks are put into a leape.

When showing sheep, amongst other things cut off the shaggy hairy wool which stands strickling up and make them seem more snod by forcing of them and cutting off all kempe-hairs.

Sheep suffer from many disorders, eg, the rubbers, the megrims—a disease of the head, sheep blindness, when a scum grows over the stive of the eye. The 'stoddy' is a disease something like water on the brain; 'brocken-mouths' when they lose their teeth; gid is short for giddiness; jogg, a swelling under the throat, lameness is foot-rot; moor-evil or wood-evil is sometimes called knuckle-evil or youghth or crook, when the neck or the leg grows crooked; the plaise is the liver-fluke; ticks are called sheep-lice; mads or mawks are sheep-maggots; starlings which perch on sheep and search for these are called shepsters; the 'goggles' are rickets or the staggers.

When using ointment for skin and wool troubles, the shepherds use a sheep-cratch or creel, ie, a bier, and the salver parts or sheds the wool to make a cleft for the ointment.

Moorland sheep are called jocks or rannocks, and Teesside sheep, mud-sheep. The common call to bring sheep to you is 'Chiddy-yow'. The right or place of pasturage, where they are baited, is a sheep-rake. A sheep that is laid on its back is akwerd or akwert, and in the North Riding rigged or rig-welted. The tangled masses of wool are cots, and the clippings of matted wool cut from the hind quarters are doddings.

If a sheep tends to stray, it is tied by the fore and hind legs and said to be side-line — side-lang.

Such are a few of the expressions used in our county having referenee to sheep.

The counting or scoring of sheep is a most interesting study. I cannot attempt to fathom the peculiarities but simply give the various renderings which I have collected.

These numerals were called to my mind by hearing some children chanting counting-out rhymes. I have collected these from several sources. You will probably recollect some of them — naturally some are badly mutilated and modernised, but all are interesting.

1.   One-ery, two-ery, ziccary, zeven,
Hollow-bone, crack-a-bone, ten or eleven,
Spin, spon, it must be done
Twiddledum twaddledum, twenty-one.

2.   Eena, deena, dine-a, dust,
Cat'lla, ween-a, wine-a, wust, etc.

3.   Ena, mena, mina, mo,
Catch a nigger by his toe,
If he hollas, let him go,
Ena, mena, mina, mo.
(A very common version)

4.   Eeeny, meeny, miny, mo,
       Cata-liny, sine-y, so,
       Kay o way, Kitty can lan,
       Thou shalt be my soldier man,
       O U T spells very fair,
       Rottom, bottom, dish clout. Out goes she.
                  (Hull District)

5.   Eena, mena, mina, mo,
       Kettla, weela, wila, wo,
       Spit, spot, it must be done,
       Twidalum, Twilum, Twenty-one.
                  (Notts border)

6.   Eeny, meeny, miny, mo,
       I ax you wheer mun this man go?
       Sum gans eeast and sum gans west
       And sum gang ower high crake nest.
                  (Wolds)

7.   Eena, meena, mina, mo,
       Ink, pink, pen and ink, etc.
                  (Farsley)

8.   Ena, mena, mink mank clink,
       Clank, clink, clank ooza,
       Vooza, vakla, dish via,
       Via Vo.
                  (Pudsey)

9.   Hurly, burly, pim bo lock,
       Fower squaares in a clock,
       Sit and sing, and turn the spring,
       Tee tie, tip it out, long spout,
       Where does this man go to?
                  (Colne Valley)

10.   Erla, berla, pimba, lock,
       Fiva mile, six o'clock,
       Letta, balloon, acarl acoon,
       O U T and out goes she.
                  (Huddersfield)

Now these apparent trivialities are not absolute rubbish, but of distinct value, since they are some of the present-day survivals of the old scoring numerals used in Yorkshire at least fifteen centuries ago.

Even in Celtic times sheep played an important part in the economic development of the county. They have left their mark on the place-names, eg Skipton, Shipton, Shipley, and Shepstowe, whilst shepherds have generally been associated with pure dialect as can be well seen in the Play Cycles of Wakefield and York. In the North of England sheep are always counted by the score, which is simply the number of the shepherd's fingers and toes, and the runs of five that are observable in the counts are probably due to this same method of numbering. Best of Elmswell in 1641 says 'Sheep are six score to the hundredth' (*Surtees Soc Trans*).

The Celts have been a pastoral people from prehistoric times, and such work naturally tends to conservatism and dislike of change. The work is solitary, and so liable to produce a lack of initiative, since in such an occupation there can be no great progress in mentality. Respect for old customs, reverence for old age and obedience to patriarchal experience would strengthen their innate dislike of new methods, and this must be one reason why these old Celtic-scoring numerals persist to this day in certain parts of the moorland.

That such enumerations are still current is remarkable. It is certainly indicative of an undisturbed, unchanged pastoral occupation. The geographical areas are naturally suited to such work and being non-arable, invaders would hardly consider them worth while as zones of settlement or if such invaders did so, perhaps they allowed the shepherds to remain, possibly to make certain of their own food supplies. Perhaps too they entertained the same feelings to the shepherds as did the Egyptians to the sons of Jacob, 'for every shepherd is an abomination to the Egyptians' (Gen xlvi, 34), and so left them to their work. Be that as it may, the shepherds did persist, and in these counting words of the fells and moors we have some survivors of a pre-Anglian language.

These numerals appear to be in use only in Yorkshire and a part of Cumberland on the Pennine Hills, north of the Aire Gap. This is an area of bare limestone country, which, despite its charm, is somewhat monotonously desolate, and which practically coincides with the greater part of that tongue of land known by the Brythonic names of Elmete, Loidis and Craven, which area was the last stronghold of the Celts in Yorkshire and where they were hidden from the English for a hundred years after the rest of the country east of the Pennines had passed into the hands of the invader.

Although the Anglian attacks on the Yorkshire coast began soon after the withdrawal of the Roman Army in 410, it was not until near the end of the sixth century that they reached the lower course of the Swale, and when Aelthelfrith crushed an attempt of the Northern Celts to drive him from Yorkshire in 603, Elmet still remained aloof and survived although he had probably made its king Cerdic do homage and pay him tribute. In 620 Edwin, son of Ælla, brought the valley of the Aire under his sway, and he it was who annexed the little Celtic state and expelled its king. But a great change had come over the character of the Anglian conquest during this period. At first the invaders exterminated the Celts, sweeping them away and taking their homesteads, making a complete clearance because the Anglian bent was entirely towards a country life. But as the tide of invasion swept westward, the necessity for the wholesale slaughter grew ever less and less as the Saxon obtained land for his settlements, and in 620 the war had changed into one for dominion only, and the native Celt was allowed in increasing numbers to retain his farm on owning the authority of the English and paying the tribute imposed. This I think is the chief reason for the survival of these scraps of Cymric.

For the next two hundred and fifty years until the death of Ælla the Unkingly in 867, slain by the Danes, the Anglian kings were constantly at war, either with their own people or with the states to the North or the South, or with the Danes on the East Coast, and all this strife would help the out of the way western state of Elmet to preserve its Celtic ideas throughout the Angian period, for it was rarely on the direct line of any assault.

The Danish and Norse invasion certainly reached this district but the invaders intermarried with the natives and adopted their customs. The Celtic-speaking shepherds probably survived as serfs but they retained their own method of enumeration, and the alliterative attractiveness and convenience prevented it from dying. Dr Rowe inclines to the belief that this attractiveness and musical alliteration had a great deal to do with the spread of the numerals. Upper Teesdale and Upper Swaledale, he says (*YAJ*, Vol 19), must have learned the count rather late, for they were uninhabited after the Wasting of the North by the Normans.

What then are these surviving numerals ? I give them according to the districts:

1.   *Near Knaresborough:*
   Yah, tiah, tethera, methera, pip;
   Teezar, leezar, catterah, horna, dick;
   Yah-dick, tiah-dick, tethera-dick, methera-dick, bumper;
   Yah de bumper, tiah de bumper, tether de bumper, mether de bumper,
   jigger.   (authority — John Wrightson, *Agric Gazette*, 1889)

2.   *Upper Nidderdale:*
   Yain, tain, eddero, peddero, pitts,
   Tayter, layter, overro, coverro, dix,
   Yain-dix tain-dix, edderodix, pedderodix, bumfitt,
   Yain-o-bumfit, tain-o-bumfit, eddero-bumfit, peddero-bumfit, jiggit.
              (authority — *ut supra*)

3.   *Nidderdale:*
   Thorpe's list is as No 2, but he puts 'later' for 'layter' and an alternative 'giggit' for 'jiggit'.

4. *Swaledale:*
Yahn, tayhn, tether, mether, mimp(h),
Hith-her, lith-her, anver, danver, dic,
Yahn dic, tayhn-dic, tetherdic, metherdic, mimphit (or mumphit),
Yahn a mimphit, tayhn a mimphit, tether a mimphit,
Mether-a-mimphit; jigit.
(authority — J R Dakyns)

5. *Craven and NW Moorlands:*
Arn, tarn, tethera, fethera, pubs,
Aayther, layather, quoather, quaather, dugs,
Arnadugs, tarnadugs, tetheradugs, fetheradugs, buon;
Arnabuon, tarnabuon, tetherabuon, fetherabuon,
gun-a-gun.　　(Taken down by Rev W Sykes at Rathmell in 1892)

6. *Wensleydale:*
Yan, tean, tither, mither, pip,
Teaser, leaser, catra, horna, dick;
Yan-dick, tean-dick, tither-dick, mither-dick, bumper,
Yan-a-bum, tean-a-bum, tither bum, mither bum, jigger.
(J Thomas, Hest Bank)

7. *Middleton-in-Teesdale*:
Yan, tean, tether, mether, pip,
Iezar, azar, catrah, horna, dick,
Yan-a-dick, tean-a-dick, tethera dick, methera dick, bumfit,
Yan-a-bum, tean-a-bum, tethera bum, methera-bum, jiggit.
(Wrightson and Wheater)

8. *West Yorkshire* (not specified, probably northern edge):
Ena, tena, tethra, pethra, pimps,
Sarfra, larfra, offra, doffra, dix.
(Arnold's *West Riding of Yorkshire*)

9. *North Riding* (not specified):
Ena, tena, tethra, pethra, pimps,
Sarfra, larfra, ofra, dofra, dix,
Ena dix, tena dix, tethra dix, pethra dix, bumfit,
Ena bumpit, tena bumpit, tethra bumpit, pethra bumpit, sigit.
(R Blakeborough, *Yorkshire Wit and Character*)

10. *West Yorkshire* (East slope of Pennines):
Ein, tein, tethra, methera, pimp;
Awfus, dawfus, deefus, dumfus, dik.
(Moorman, *Tales of the Ridings,* p34)

31

To understand their lingual origin it is best to compare them with other numerals.

Anglo-Saxon:
An, {twegen, twa}, threo, feower, fif,
Six, seofon, eahta, nigon, tien,
Endlefan, twelf, threotyne, etc, twentig.

Old Saxon:
En, {tuena, tua}, thria, fiwar, fif,
Sehs, sibun, ahto, nigun, tehan,
Ellevan, tuelif ... tuentig.

Old Frisian:
En, {tweer, twa}, thre, fiwer, fif,
Sex, sigun, achta, nigun, tian,
Andlova, twilif ... twintich.

Old Norse:
Einn, tveir, thrir, fiorir, fimm,
Sex, siau, atta, niu, tiu,
Ellifu, tolf, threttan ... tveir tigir (Icel)
tuttugu.

These will, I think, suffice to show that the shepherd's numerals are neither Anglian, Saxon, Frisian nor Norse. On the other hand, the Celtic numerals give us:

Erse or Irish:
Aon, da, tri, cethir, cuig,
Se, seacht, ocht, naoi, deich.

Gælic:
Aon, do, tri, ceithir, coig
Se, seachd, ocht, naoi, deich.

whilst the *Welsh* are:

Un, dau or dwy, tri or tair, pedwar or pedair, pump or pimp,
chwech, saith, wyth, naw or nau, deg or dic.
Un ar ddeg, deu ddeg, tri ar ddeg, pedwar ar ddeg, pymtheg,
Un ar bymtheg, etc ... ugain.

These three, particularly the latter, show at once distinct evidence of the counting numerals, so we can safely state that they are not Anglian but Celtic survivals.

(1927)

Editors' note: See also an alternative view of the origins of sheep-scoring in the article by M V Barry in Transactions *1967, pp21-31.*

T' SPERRINS

They've putten in t' sperrins, they're bahn ta be wed,
And sho'll be a reight bonny bride.
Sho's dimpled and rosy, wi' cheeks near as red
As t' mooin ower t' chimleys ahtside.

They've courted for years, and I' m reight glad and fain
They'v made up their minds ta tee t' knot.
When two young uns love it's a seet better gain
Ta wed and mak sewer o' their lot.

There'll be ringing o' bells, and singing and stuff,
And t' clatter o' knives, spooins an' forks;
There'll be supping o' ale, and takking o' snuff,
And pulling and popping o' corks.

There'll be kissing and cuddling, and shakking o' hands,
There'll happen be two or three tears;
And, maybe, enah, there'll be music fra t' bands,
All nations o' laughing and cheers

There'll be t' wahrming o't' hahse, wi' spice-cake and cheese
And t' teeing o' t' hoss-shoe o' t' door;
And happen i' time, sho'll bahnce on her knees
A barn nivver thowt on afore.

If ye'll nobbut agree ta be pairtners, ye two,
Baht fratching and nenging, I mean,
Ye'll hev nowt bud real happiness all yer life through,
And ye'll live all yer young days agean.

W J Halliday (WR)

(1931)

sperrins, banns of marriage

DEPPER, AWD MARE

Hev I ony awd 'osses, young fellow frev 'Ull?
Thoo's willin' tae buy 'em? Gie value i' full?
Why yis, I ha'e yan, i' this paddock doon here,
Cohup, then! Coom on, then! Coom, Depper awd meer!

No, she dizn't coom gallopin', bud then, you see,
A mare's a bit wankle-like, tonned twenty-three.
Thoo'll mebbe not be quite sae frisky thissen
When thoo's seen thi great grandsons grow up to be men!

Weel, what will I tak for her? Why noo, she's fat,
An' they tell me you give a bit extry for that,
Bud ah might as well tell tha, thoo'll not buy that meer
If thoo stands there an' bids me fra noo tae next year!

She was t' fost foal I 'ad when I com' upo'd place
An' fost she's been allus, i' shaft, pole or thrace.
 She's ploughed, drilled an' harrowed, rolled, scruffled an' led,
An' mothered Beaut, Boxer, Prince, Cobby an' Ned.

If threshin' machine gat stuck fast on its way
Young 'osses wad plunge, rahve an' tew hauf o'd day
Bud afoor it gat shifted, it allus was 'Here,
Away thoo gans, Thoddy, an' fetch us t' awd meer!'

When stacks was o' fire, afoor motor-car days,
She galloped tae Driffield when t'spot was ablaze,
Ower field, ditch an' hedgerow for t' gainest way doon,
Saved buildings, an' hoos an' three pikes, I'll be boon!

When t' missis took badly, when t' babby was born,
'Twas a life an' death jonny for t' doctor that morn,
An' though she'd been workin' at t' plough all day lang
T' meer galloped as tho' she knew summat was wrang.

Wi' never a whip, nor a jerk on her rein
She went like a whirlwind an' flew back again
Wi' t' doctor an' nuss, just i' time tae save life —
Aye, Depper, I owe thoo baith dowter an' wife.

On friends 'at's sae faithful we doan't turn wer backs,
Nor send 'em for slaughter tae'd foreigner's axe,
Nor let 'em be worked tae their death across t' sea,
Wheer nivver a Yorkshire voice shouts 'Wahve' nor 'Gee!'

34

No, noo 'at she's neither young, bonny nor soond,
She awns t' lahtle paddock, it's pensioner's groond,
An' stall i' yon stable, hay, beddin' an' corn,
Ah reckon she's addled a spot of her awn!

An' when the day comes 'at we do ha' tae pairt,
She'll gan in a way 'at'll not brek her hairt,
An' t' land 'at she's worked on an' loved twenty year
At last'll lig leet on my faithful awd meer!

F Austin Hyde (ER)   *(1928)*

wankle-like, weak, wobbly; *thoddy*, (third) farm labourer; *gainest*, shortest

---

WI' GENTLE, MODEST WAYS

Ther's sum folks varry swanky
'At owt to ha' moor sense,
Ther's uthers miles aboon 'em
'At mak's noa sich pretence.
Ther's sum gat rich soa quickly
They cannot carry corn,
An' uthers wi ther' riches,
Are natural as born.

Ther's sum 'at struts an' stammers
Becos they've getten on,
They'll mayhap miss t' morrer,
An' life an' wealth bi gone.
Best men i' all creation
Are modest i' ther ways,
An' t' humblest are most thankful
An' full o' honest praise.

Let's all bi plain an' homely,
Untouched wi' swank or side,
Noan clivvur ner conceited,
An' not puffed up wi' pride.
To uthers we can venture
To give a word o' praise,
But we wersen are stronger
Wi' gentle, modest ways.

Ben Turner (WR)   *(1931)*

GLOSSARY OF SHEFFIELD CUTLERING TERMS
B R Dyson

For many of the words in this glossary my warmest thanks are due to Mr Thos R Ellin, past Master Cutler of Sheffield, and member of the council of the Yorkshire Dialect Society. Thanks are also due to my teacher, Dr J D Jones, of Sheffield University, who suggested this subject to me.

AGON or Hack-iron. An inverted chisel, fixed cutting edge up on an anvil, used for cutting off the 'mood' or piece of metal to be made into a blade.

ARSEBOOARD. Sometimes spelt horseboard; a board slung from behind the grinder by a chain, and extending forwards between his legs to the wheel. Extra pressure is obtained on an object to be ground by holding it on to the wheel with the arseboard, on which the grinder sits, converting it into a powerful lever.

ASSIDUE. Thin Dutch metal or gold foil, used to adorn the horn handles of cheap pocket knives.

BAND. String, or by transference, a power belt. Cf Dutch *band*, string; German *Band*, tape.

BARMSKIN. A leather apron used by cutlers.

BECKHORN or BECK IRON. A punch fitted point up to the anvil, like the agon, to punch holes in a forging.

BELLUS. A smith's bellows.

BITIN' ON. A snack eaten about eleven in the morning, during a short interval from work. Generally used to be bread and cheese, or oatcake, and beer.

BLANK. The rough stamping in sheet metal of a spoon or fork before grinding.

BOSH A circular tub of water, used for quenching, or tempering heated blades.

BOWSTERS or BOLSTERS. The metal end of the scale, or frame of a pocket-knife, carrying the pin on which the blades turn. The bowster is generally not covered by the horn of the handle, but left bare, and highly polished.

BREAKIN' DOWN. The first rough grinding of a blade, to remove scale or oxide from the 'mood'. The metal is merely held over the grindstone, without exerting pressure. Generally left to the unskilled 'prentice.

BUFFIN. Highly polishing a blade etc, with a wheel of wood or rags, and powder polish.

BUFFALO. The ox horn used for the handles of pocket knives.

BULL WEEK. The week or fortnight immediately before Christmas, when cutlers 'bulled at t' wark', or made an extra effort, to earn extra for the holiday. May be connected with bull baiting usual at such feasts.

BULLET BOLSTER. A rounded bolster usually fitted to a candle-end knife.

BOWDER or BOLDER. Put on to the glazer to fine down the emery, and cause it to give a high polish.

BURRITED HEADS. Rivet heads protruding from the knife handle, and finished ornamentally like a little cap. Possible connection with Italian *biretta*, a cap.

BUTTONIN TIME. Same as bitin' on time, qv.

CANDLE END. A plain round handle for a pocket knife; a knife having such a handle.

CANNEL. To bevel or chamfer.

CANNELED EDGE. The chamfered edge of tool or knife.

CHOIL. The little nick at the pivot end of the cutting edge of a knife; made by the agon, to facilitate grinding the edge.

COE'S RAKE. A coal rake.

COLLAR. An entanglement of driving belt and shafting.

CORBO. A common, thick-handled knife of poor finish.

CUTLER'S PEIS. When peas were sold as cheap as 4d a peck, the cutler could afford to buy them, not before. At this price they were known as cutler's peis.

CUT SWAGE. A swage, or nick, along the back edge of a knife blade. A bevel swage tapers away to nothing at either end.

DAYTALEMAN. A journeyman cutler.

DOLLY. A wheel made up of a number of sheets of cloth or calico, revolving on the glazer's spindle, and used for polishing.

DRINKINGS. The afternoon equivalent of bitin' on.

DRUM. A large flat pulley carrying a driving belt or band.

ELSIN. A shoemaker's awl, cf Dutch *els*, an awl.

EQUAL END. A two-ended pocket knife with both ends equal, ie not tapering from one end to the other.

FACTOR. The owner of a factory, who sublets workshops to little mesters, and buys and markets their products.

FANNY. A 'dust masheen'; the fan which draws away the injurious dust from a grinding wheel.

FASCHE. A rough, turned edge, resulting from filing several sheets of metal together; a turned knife edge caused through sharpening to too fine an angle. Also used as a verb.

FEIGHE. To clean out sludge or mud from anything A grinder 'feighes t' trow under his wheel ivvera neet'. Cf German *fegen*, to clean.

FETHER-EDGED. Having one edge thicker than the other, as a razor.

FLASH. A spark of red-hot metal from a hammered forging.

FLATBACK. A cheap, poorly-made pocket knife. The components are assembled in the rough before grinding and finishing, while in a good knife each is finished independently. The name comes from the flat back of the knife, horns, scales, and spring being ground together in one operation.

FLOAT or FLOIGHT. A coarse file with straight teeth. Sometimes called a rape, or rasp.

FOOTALE. A new prentice in a cutler's shop was traditionally bound to stand footale, or beer, round to all the old hands before being admitted to his footing among them.

FRAME. The cutler's frame is a structure of wood and iron on which the glazing and polishing of the knife is done. It carries two poppets, upright cast-iron structures with oblong holes in them, in which are fixed nogs, or blocks of wood, held in place by a hand-screw. These nogs contain holes for the gudgeon ends of the glazers, etc.

GAFFER. A foreman or supervisor in almost any establishment; even applied to schoolmasters.

GAVELOCK. A lever, or crowbar.

GLAZE. To polish cutlery, generally with a rough wheel made of wood, with the edge of the grain outwards, or with a dolly, or cloth wheel.

GLAZING PETCH. A piece of leather worn on the finger to protect it when glazing by the old method of friction by hand, before the introduction of the dolly.

GLAZER'S SPINDLE. A power-driven spindle carrying various wheels for glazing.

GOFF. An old-fashioned trip hammer worked by water power. As a verb, to use the above.

GOYT, GOIT. A sluice or race of a water-wheel; the overflow from a mill dam.

GOOSENECK. A stout wire holder for a blacksmith's chisel.

GRINDER'S ASTHMA. Consumption, caused by breathing the fine stone and metal dust from grinding.

GRINDLE COWK. A grindstone worn too small for use. Nearly all the stepping stones near Sheffield are made of these.

HACKHAMMER. A wooden mallet used for true-ing up grindstones after each day's work by knocking off protuberances due to unequal wearing down.

HEFT. Handle of a tool or knife.

HEFT POIP. A temporary handle used by grinders to hold the tang of a knife or razor blade during grinding.

HOE. The rake used for gathering up wheelswarf and scale after grinding.

HORSIN. The board seat astride which the grinder sits to his wheel. May have originated from 'horse', though a horse in Sheffield is generally called 'poppo'.

HORSEBOARD. See arseboard.

HULL. A grinding shop.

JACKALEG or JOCKTILEG. A kind of spring knife, supposed to be named after one Jacques o' Liège, one of the cutlers who came to Sheffield from the Netherlands in the sixteenth century.

JIMPING. A milled, ornamental edge to the handle of a pocket knife.

KITT. A tub of water for replenishing the grinder's trough.

KNOBSTICK. A non-union workman.

LAP. To finish, wrap up, an article; also to give a highly polished finish to a knife blade by using a lead buff and emery.

LATTEN. Thin sheet brass. Chaucer, 'latoun' (*Prologue*).

LIKING. The probationary period of apprenticeship.

LITTLE MESTER. A master cutler who rents rooms in a factory, and completes all processes of manufacture, buying his own material, and selling his products to the factor, who has no control over him save through the wheel rent he charges.

LAMB-FOOT BLADE. A peculiarly named blade, called after some slight resemblance to a lamb's foot. It tapers off to a narrow point.

LOZING or LOISING. The coming of age ceremony of a cutler's prentice, heralded by a peal of 'bells' rung on suspended ingots, and celebrated with much drinking and singing of the traditional song, 'Houd yer licker aboon yer chin ...'

MOOD. The rough blank or forging of a blade or spring before grinding. Used as a verb also.

MOTTLED PIG. A type of pig iron.

NAIL NICK. The little nick by which a pocket knife blade is opened. A 'short nail nick' is in the design of a new moon, about the middle of the blade; a 'long nail nick' is a straight nick up the tang of the knife.

NATTY MONEY. The contribution to a trades union.

NEB HEFTED KNIFE. A blade with a point in the middle of its back, like a neb, or nose. Sometimes seen on old carving knives.

NICKERPECKER. A file cutter.

O'ER HOUDIN' or OVERHOLDING. See breaking-in. The blade was just held over the grindstone, without any pressure, to remove scale.

OUTWORKER. A small independent cutler, performing one or two operations in his own home, then returning the article for finishing by others.

PANE. The end of a hammer.

PARSER. A crude cutler's drill, worked from a breastplate by sawing with a bow, the string of which rotates the parser heft.

PARSER 'EFT. The bobbin carrying the drill of a parser. Such a tool is extraordinarily powerful, and will often touch metal which 'baulks' a modern drill. Origin, probably French *perceur*. A two-legged parser was a parser with two legs which sprung apart; used, with a plate. for drilling out the ornamental shields on the hafts of pocket knives.

PIKE. The beck, or pointed end of the anvil.

PINS. The rivets used for assembling knives.

PINNIN' ON HOILS. The holes drilled in the handle of a knife for fastening together the scales and horn grips.

PISTOL HAFT. The haft of a common pocket knife somewhat resembling a pistol butt in shape. These knives usually had a spear point blade.

POINTS. See pins.

PRESSED SCALES. Horn scales pressed into the required shape.

PETCH. The precursor of the dolly; a number of thicknesses of cloth used to rub shaved bone handles to a polish.

QUENCH. To temper a heated blade in water or oil.

RADDLE HOIL. A yellow nodule or flaw in a grindstone, showing the grinder the stone is dead, and liable to burst or 'fly' if set in motion.

RAPE. A rasp, or rough file. Used as a verb also.

RAT TAILED BOLSTER. A bolster (qv) with a hollow in it, so called because it was shaped with a rat tailed, or round file.

RATTENING. Wilful damaging of machinery by strikers. A favourite method of disposing of a blackleg grinder was to drive in the pegs which secured his grindstone to the spindle, slightly cracking the stone, which would show no flaw till set in motion, when it would burst.

RAKEN SLECK. Small, or slack coal used to rake, or damp down, a furnace to make it burn slowly.

RESURRECTION POY. A pie made of potatoes and 'scrag ends o' owd meit'; an unsavoury dish to which the cutlers were often reduced towards 't' shank end o' t' week'.

REVERSE KNIFE. Like a pistol haft knife with the handle reversed; usually carried a sheep foot blade.

REVITS. The same as pins. Rivets.

ROCKSTAFF. The handle of a great bellows of the old type; it was generally fitted with a cow's horn at the end to provide a comfortable grip.

ROSSIL. Resin, used as a flux in soldering.

ROTTENSTON. Used, mixed with oil, for file buffing.

ROUGH BUFFIN'. The first buffing of a blade.

SAND RAT. A moulder.

SCALE. (1) The coating of impure iron oxide on a forging. (2) The metal sides, or frame, of a pocket-knife, carrying the blades.

SCUMMER. A fire shovel.

SHAVED BONE. Bone knife handles, shaved to a smooth finish with an old razor with a fasched or turned edge.

SHIM. A thin washer.

SHADOW. A pocket- or pen-knife without any bolster.

SHOG. To oscillate; extended to personal use, to waddle.

SIDE. A cutler's side is a portion of a bench in a common workshop, rented by poor cutlers or setters-in, on which to assemble knives.

SKELLER. Of metal; to bend or warp with heat.

SLEEVE BOARD. A two-ended knife, broader at one end than the other.

SLITSPRING. The spring down the back of a pocket knife, in the slit between the scales.

SMITHUM. Slack coal.

SMITHY SLECK. Scales of iron oxide beaten from a forging. Cf German *Eisen schlacke*, the dross of iron.

SNAPS. A sort of horizontal vice with a long flat projection on the lower jaw, in which the cutler screws stag or horn scales to level them off.

SOW METAL. The worst type of pig iron.

SOURING. Drawing pay for work not yet done.

SPRING KNIFE. A double-bladed pocket knife, with a spring down the back to retain the blades firmly.

STAG. The horn of which pocket knife handles are made.

STAGE or STAGING. A small wooden platform behind the vice to hold tools.

STAIL, STELE. The long handle of a broom, hoe, hammer, etc.

STIDDY. A small iron anvil, with tapered square shank, driven into a hole in the bench, and used for rivetting on. A cutler's stidda has generally a flat beck at the back, a round hole in the left-hand side, and a slot in the middle through which to put the wire when nailing-in, or putting the knife together. It is often supplied with burritting holes, for finishing off rivet heads. OE *stede*, an anvil.

STITHY. An anvil. Old Norse *stethi*, anvil.

SUB. To borrow money in advance of pay day.

SUNK-JOINTED KNIFE. A knife where all the backs of the blades are sunk in the joint, unlike the common-joint, where the backs of the blades stick up above the scales.

SWAGE. A long ornamental nick down the back of a knife, generally a table knife.

SWARF. The yellow sludge of water and stone dust from wet grinding.

TANG. The metal spike by which the blade of a knife is fitted into the handle.

TANGS. Tongs. Cf Dutch *tangs*, same meaning.

TINE KNIFE. A knife with a haft of stag's horn.

TINES. Prongs, or points, of any instrument, eg, a fork.

TILT. A forge.

TILT HAMMER. A great trip hammer, worked by water.

TOMMIED-ON BOWSTERS. Bolsters, or ends, of the scales, made separately, and pinned on to the scale later, unlike the old knives, in which scale and bolster were forged in one piece.

TROW. Trough, such as that in which wet grinding wheels run.

TRUCK. Cinders, slag, etc.

TUE IRON or TURIN. The metal nozzle protecting the pipe of the bellows from the heat of the furnace.

TUMBLETREE. The massive beam or fulcrum on which the rockstaff of an old-fashioned bellows oscillated.

TWYER. The pipe carrying forced draught to a furnace. French *tuyère*.

UPGLAZING. Buffing a knife on a wooden wheel with the edge of the grain turned outwards. This removes all scratches, and leaves a fine, black finish.

WAAG (obsolete). A lever. Old English *woege*, a balance, weighing scales; cf Dutch *waag*, a balance.

WASTERS. Throw-outs; imperfect articles. Applied by transference to an idle, good-for-nothing fellow.

WERLIGIG POLISHIN. Polishing by a dolly, or other rotating wheel.

WHEEL. A grindstone. Applied by transference to the shop containing it.

WHEELRENT. Rent paid by the little mester for hire of a work-room in a factory.

WHITTENING. 'Whitening'; giving a fine finish to table knives by first grinding on sandstone, then on a soft, blue Brindliffe stone.

YALLER BELLY. A grinder, so called from his plentiful daubing with the yellow swarf from the wheel.

YARMOUTH BEEF or TWO-EYED BEEFSTEAK. A red herring, the only beef the poverty-stricken cutler could often afford.

(1932)

THE LIFE OF JOSEPH WRIGHT
by Elizabeth Mary Wright
Reviewed by W J Halliday

Joseph Wright was the founder of the Yorkshire Dialect Society. It began as a small committee which was formed in Bradford in October 1894, in response to an appeal by Professor Wright to collect Yorkshire material for the *English Dialect Dictionary*. Contributions, consisting in all of about 35,000 words and phrases from some ninety persons, were sent to the editor, and on the eve of the dissolution of the committee in February 1897, it was decided to carry on the work of dialect research. This was the genesis of our society, which has carried on without break up to the present day, a period of thirty-five years.

This biography, therefore, of the great Yorkshireman and scholar is of peculiar personal interest to our members, and I should like, at the outset, to urge all who can to procure a copy. As a biography, it is full of charm and deep humanity, and its subject is one that lies near to the heart of every lover of Yorkshire, of its rich dialect, and of its greatest and most lovable son.

The details of Joseph Wright's life read like romance. But it is romance which is built on a solid foundation of character and indomitable will. Joseph Wright never waited for opportunities to turn up: he made them. 'Luck', somebody once said, 'is what you make for yourself.' Joseph Wright made his own luck. This is the secret of his success. Most of us have long been familiar with the details of his life, but they will bear repetition if only to serve as encouragement to us all in battling with the cross-currents of life.

He was born in a small, one-roomed house in Thackley in 1855. His father was miserably poor, and for a short time the family was compelled to live in Clayton Workhouse. But if a shiftless father nearly wrecked the home, a wonderful and courageous mother never failed to repair the tottering fortunes. We have in this biography a remarkable picture of a remarkable woman. Joseph Wright's mother was of heroic mould, and the great scholar never tired of tracing his greatness to her, and of testifying publicly to the strong, spiritual bond that linked mother and son. From her he derived his dogged perseverance: from her he derived his staunch integrity of soul and mind. Naturally refined and dignified, she was a model of shrewd, practical common-sense. She was guide, philosopher, and friend to everybody, and Joseph Wright never made a momentous decision without first consulting her. She learnt to read at the age of forty-five in order to be in touch

Joseph Wright.

with her brilliant son. Joseph Wright was of course the darling of her heart, and her pride in the achievement of 'Ahr Joa' was boundless and ineffable.

With such a mother, Joseph Wright was learning in his younger days lessons more valuable than formal education could ever have taught him. In fact, during boyhood, his formal education was nil. At the age of six, he drove a donkey cart, carrying quarrymen's tools from 7am to 5pm. At seven he was a doffer in the spinning department at Salts Mills, working half-time for the princely wage of 1s 6d a week. He never had a full day's schooling in his life. He attended a special school for half-timers, the only one he ever went to, but he says himself that he learnt very little there except in arithmetic At the age of thirteen he changed from doffer to woolsorter, and contributed to the domestic life by doing all the house-work whilst his mother was out charring. The first desire for knowledge came during the Franco-Prussian War, when he was fifteen. Along with many of his work-mates, he was compelled to rely for news on the reading of the newspaper by some enlightened foreman at the works.

He taught himself reading and writing, mainly with the help of the Bible and the *Pilgrim's Progress*. He attended a night-school for a short time, but made most progress with the help of *Cassell's Popular Educator*, which he bought in fortnightly parts. Early on he was attracted to languages, and with a little outside help, started French and German. He tackled Latin alone. He studied mathematics, too, but the first certificate he ever got was for shorthand, at the age of nineteen. For a short time at this period he conducted classes in a night-school.

At the age of twenty, having saved £40, and the mill being closed temporarily, Joseph Wright set out for a term's study in Germany. He stayed four weeks at Cologne, and then went on to Heidelberg. Here he remained eleven weeks, studying mainly mathematics. On his return he started as a schoolmaster at Springfield School. He received £40 a year, and board and lodging from Monday to Friday. Whilst here, he decided to prepare for London Matriculation. He attended classes at the Yorkshire College, Leeds, and it is characteristic of his grit and tenacity that he always walked home — a distance of ten miles — because the railway fare, 9d, was too expensive. In 1878 he passed the London Matriculation examination. After three or four years' experience as a schoolmaster, he returned to Heidelberg in 1882.

This is, perhaps, the real climacteric of his career. He began philology under Professor Osthoff, and here discovered his true forte. His progress was rapid. Three years later he took the degree of Doctor of Philosophy, his thesis being 'The qualitative and quantitative changes of the Indo-Germanic vowel system in Greek'. He continued his philological studies under Bartsch, Leskien, Zancke and others, and published his first book in 1888, a translation of Brugmann's *Comparative Grammar of the Indo-Germanic Languages*.

His reputation as a philological scholar was now being surely established, and after his return to England and one or two minor appointments, he became Deputy Professor of Comparative Philology in the University of Oxford under Max Müller.

Mrs Wright gives us a charming picture of his life at Oxford. As a teacher, Professor Wright was as inspired, enthusiastic and successful as he was as a student. He always said that his own study, for the most part independent of outside help, gave him a peculiar insight into students' difficulties. But his students loved him, not for his skill, but for his complete understanding, his humour and his large-hearted generosity. Mrs Wright was one of his pupils, and tells with charming freedom the story of how the master fell in love with the pupil, and how the wooing progressed to a happy end in spite of occasional doubts and discomfitures. Joseph Wright wooed with all the ardour of a great and magnanimous soul, and the love letters that passed between them are almost sacred in their intimacy. We are thankful to Mrs. Wright for preserving them for us, for they bring us right to the heart of a great, noble, simple and sublime character.

At Oxford, stimulated by the suggestions of Professor Skeat, and fortified by his profound love for his native dialect, he projected what was to prove the crowning glory of a glorious career, the *English Dialect Dictionary*. The work, the magnitude of which only one or two competent scholars fully understood, was planned in the first instance by the English Dialect Society of which Skeat was the chief pillar. A committee had been appointed, and had begun the collection of material. But the question arose: Who is competent to undertake the editorship of such a colossal work? Two qualifications were indispensable in such a man — profound philological knowledge and love of dialect. To these must be added tenacity of purpose and a will that nothing could daunt. Joseph Wright was the only man who had these qualifications. He accepted the work, conscious of what it involved. He refused the Chair of English at Toronto which was offered him at the time. Here was a life of comparative ease to be had for the asking, but Wright took the harder way.

The difficulties seemed insuperable. The mass of dialect material to be sifted was colossal. At the very outset, Professor Wright took over a million slips, weighing very nearly one ton. The slips for the letter 'S' alone weighed nearly two hundredweight. Before the work was completed two million slips were examined and classified. The dictionaries and glossaries used in the preparation of the *Dictionary* cost £600. This takes no account of the thousands of other dialect works required and bought. No publisher would undertake responsibility: success seemed too problematical.

Joseph Wright was compelled to publish by subscription, and at his own pecuniary risk. Alone he undertook the task of getting subscribers and the necessary voluntary workers. In five months he sent out 50,000 prospectuses and wrote 3,000 letters. Besides all this, he addressed meetings in various parts of the country. Not a penny did he spend on ordinary advertising, and yet, with the most rigid economy — and Joseph Wright never wasted a clean half-sheet of notepaper — the undertaking required £1,400 a year, and on its completion was estimated to have cost £25,000.

Two years after the *Dictionary* was begun, Professor Wright, through the good offices of Mr Balfour, received a Civil List pension of £200 a year. The Oxford University Press lent the editor a room, and in this workshop, Professor Wright and his staff carried out their task. The staff consisted of one senior assistant — Miss Partridge — and two juniors. Miss Partridge contributes to the biography a fascinating account of the day's work. She dwells particularly on the stimulating activity of the editor himself, his contagious enthusiasm, his wonderful knowledge, his well-disciplined mind, his love of the Yorkshire dialect, and his sweet reasonableness and freedom from irritability even in the tightest corner. There were over 1,000 correspondents collecting material, and more than 6,000 queries were sent out annually from the workshop. Is it any wonder that this monumental work was to Professor Wright his proudest achievement? It was a labour of love, conceived and carried out under the inspiration of his love for his wife. It is always 'your Dictionary' in his letters to her. 'It is a work', he wrote to her, 'that is a most sacred task to me. Had it not been for you, nothing in the world could have induced me to undertake what seemed an impossibility to everybody else. But deep genuine love can overcome impossibilities ... It would be premature to enlighten the world at present, but some day it will all be made known what a man's deep love for a woman can inspire him to do.'

Part I of the *Dictionary* was published on the 1st July 1896, and the final part in February 1905. It met with the reception due to such a remarkable work. In England, in Germany and in America, it was hailed as the greatest contribution to dialect study the world had seen. Honours were showered on the incomparable and learned editor. Honorary degrees were bestowed by all the important universities on Professor Wright. He had succeeded Müller in 1901 as Professor of Comparative Philology, and now he was elected a Fellow of the British Academy. The learned world at once recognised the significance of the work. Professor Wright rounded off the *Dictionary* by the publication of a *Dialect Grammar*, a work which is, as he himself said, more important philologically than the larger work. With his customary generosity, Wright wrote to Skeat in 1905: 'The present and all future generations will owe a deep debt of gratitude to you as being the father and real originator of a big Dialect Dictionary.' But if the idea was Skeat's, the power and the glory belong for ever to Joseph Wright.

But even if there had been no *Dialect Dictionary*, Joseph Wright would go down to posterity as a great philologist by reason of his contributions to the study of Old English, Middle English, Gothic, Middle High German, and Greek. Of his own beloved Windhill Dialect he wrote a model Grammar, evolving a technique that all serious dialect students are bound to copy. He was a tireless worker. Sleep he almost ignored. Breakfast he accounted a superfluous meal as it wasted the fresh hours of the morning. And yet the great charm of this biography is the picture it gives us of a homely Yorkshireman, full of physical and mental vigour and light-heartedness, full of homely love for Yorkshire teacakes, Yorkshire 'speyks' and Yorkshire humour, and full of that large humanity that is the hall-mark of great souls.

His home life has an inexpressible charm, and Mrs. Wright is at her best when writing of the simple domestic happenings in this circle of pure happiness and joy. Professor Wright radiated contentment and serenity. Companionable, a gifted conversationalist, charitably disposed towards the frailties of others, he impressed on all who met him his sanctity of soul. The tragic loss of their two children was, in Swift's words, 'wounds near the hearts' of their parents. It is a moving story, and the reader shares the grief that lay too deep for tears.

Of their holidays on the Yorkshire moors, of their tea-parties, of their two kittens named 'Ablaut' and 'Umlaut', of their deep mutual love, of their truly Christian charity in the hour of others' needs, I cannot write here. But it is all told by Mrs. Wright with a winsome simplicity and absence of self-consciousness, rare in biography, ancient or modern. Professor Wright had the heart of a child, and the will and mental stature of a giant. His Yorkshire sense of humour was irrepressible.

When he was a student at Heidelberg, he was walking home late one night, and feeling hungry, knocked at the door of an inn. Just for fun and on the spur of the moment, Professor Wright addressed the innkeeper in his own dialect. 'Hes ta owt ta eit i' t' oyle?' and was astounded to receive as answer, 'Fer sewer, ah ev.' 'Wot es ta?' went on Wright. 'Owt ta likes', came back the reply. By a rare coincidence, Joseph Wright had stumbled on a man who had been ostler at a public house in Wakefield Row, Bradford, and knew the Yorkshire dialect, though unable to speak standard English.

Professor Wright never forgot his roots in Windhill. Was not his Oxford home called 'Thackley'? Success and fame never spoilt him. Yorkshire he loved, and next to Yorkshire, work. 'Can't you tell you are in Yorkshire now?', he said to his wife as they stepped out of the train at Hawes. Littondale, Horton-in-Ribblesdale, Austwick, Settle, Bolton Abbey, Burnsall, Ilkley — these are haunts that are for ever ours because in these places Joseph Wright lived and loved, and shed the pure white light of his unique personality over moor and stream, over crag and torrent, and over the hearths of his lowly fellow-countrymen.

When Professor Wright died in 1930, the world lost its most distinguished philologist, and Yorkshire her most famous son. Our debt to Mrs. Wright for preserving his memory is incalculable. She has written in pure love a biography that is in many ways unique. It has a quiet charm and a heart-to-heart appeal that bring us into close personal touch with the great man. She lays bare with the innocence of childhood the secret places of her heart, and takes us into the bosom of the family. It is the story of a great and lovable man who was helped to the fulfilment of his high destiny by the love of a good and lovable woman.

(1932)

AU'D GEORGE: A METHODY PIONEER

Au'd George war yan o' them strang-heeaded, rough an' riddy sooart o' men at wi used ti knaw up i' t'deeals when wi war lads, bud which seeam ti be dyin' oot fast. He hed neea eddication mich an' Ah sud doot if he ivver went ti skeeal aboon a twelvemonth. When he did gan t' skeealmaisther used ti tell him he owt ti fetch a few hens wiv 'im ti gether t' cooarn up 'at he scattered o' t' fleear under his desk.

George could mannish ti read, awivver, he used ti mak t' best use of his Bible and *Pilgrim's Progress*. He was sadly bothered becos ther' war neea chappil onywheear gainhand, an' he wadn't rist till he'd gett'n t'minister ti arrange ti ho'd sarvices iv his lahle tweea-roomed cottage.

Efther t' services 'ed been gahin' a bit Au'd George landed yam yah neeght wiv a harmonium on a handcart.

'Noo, what's ta browt?', ax'd t' au'd lady.

'Ah've browt sum music', replied George, an' telt young George, his twelve year au'd son, ti git ageeat larnin' reeght awaay.

'Thoo mun he' yah tune off bi Sunday, an' it mun bi a common measure. Ah sud like tha ti larn "Lyngham", t' au'd man said, bud thoff t' lad had a ga he meead nowt o' 't, an' to'n'd t' peeages o' t' hymn-beeak ower ti 'Arlington.'

He meead better oot wi' this tune, an' gat fo'st bar off i' neea tahm, an' affooar t'neeght war oot 'ed gett'n thruff t' fo'st lahn. Bi Setterdae neeght lahle George could git thruff t' tune an' he war aboot as excited as t' au'd man be Sunday neeght.

Au'd George met t' looacal preeacher at deear, an affooar he'd gett'n his coat off an his umbrella i t' cooarner George telt him he could he' as monny hymns as he wanted, bud the'd nobbut yah tune. T 'preeacher leeak'd hard at George, but said nowt as he knew 'at it war neea good argyin', an' sidled awaay inti a cooarncr ti chaange his hymns. Innoo he war riddy wi fower common measures.

The' gat thruff t' sarvice varry canny an' bi t' end t' lad began ti fancy hissel as an organist. Efther t' prayer-meeting was ower, an' all t' fooak hed gone yam, Au'd George telt t' young 'un he'd deean varry well bud mun he' another tune off bi t' followin' Sunday, an' 'at it mun bi a sho't measure this time.

'Ah think we'll he' "Cranbrook" ', said t' au'd man.

'Nay, faether, that's a hard 'un', said t' young man, 'bud Ah'll he' a ga at "St Michael" ', an' reeght eneeaf he hed it off bi t' next Sunday, an' when t' preeacher com' t' au'd man telt him the'd nobbut tweea tunes thoff he could he' as monny hymns as he liked. Preeacher hardlings knew what ti mak' on't, but thowt it best ti say nowt, an' cheease tweea common and tweea sho't measures.

The' gat on all-reeght an' ivverybody war set up wi' t'progress the' meead. T' lad went on larnin' a tune a week an' t'singing mended as the' went on.

Au'd George hes been deead a lang while an' young George is noo an au'd man. The' ha' a chappil near wheer George's cottage still stands, bud Ah deean't suppooas 'at ther's oft mich thowt o' them au'd days. Young George when he gan's ti t' chappil noo may hear sum o' t' au'd tunes bud Ah doot if the' soond as sweet as the' did i' t' early daays.

A Stanley Umpleby (ER)

(1933)

gan, go; *gainhand,* nearby; *inoo,* in a short while

The YDS at the Yorkshire Show, 1936; A S Umpleby, middle of back row.

THE DIALECT OF STAITHES
A Stanley Umpleby

ACKRUMS. Acorn.

AFTERTHOFT. Seat between scudboard and lowsethoft of coble.

ALLUNS. The Little Auk (alle alle). 'The'r leyke Alluns efther't.'

AMELL. Betwixt, between, in the midst. (Atkinson, 1858.) Morris (1892) states: 'The form "mellum" is or was till lately, used at Staithes, where the fishermen are said to divide the fish "mellum yan anuther".' Danish, *mellem* (between). The only sense in which it is used nowadays is when the fishermen sight Roseberry in a certain position, when they say, 'T' Cap amell t' moor' (I can see the Cap (Roseberry) in the middle of the moor).

AMIDSHIPS. Space between midshipthoft and lowsethoft in fishing coble.

ANONSKER. Eager, very desirous; set upon a thing (Atkinson). This word is only used very rarely nowadays. A child was coming down the street eating an apple, and another said: 'Aa, Edie, thoo's sett'n ma anonsker for 't.'

APPRON. Apron.

ARSEBAND. Band attached to rear of fishermen's skep.

ASS. Ashes.

ASSAND. In case. (Ah'll tak' this 'ere assand as Ah want it.)

ATWEEA. In two. (Ah could 'a'e bitten a naal atweea Ah war that mad.)

BACK BEEAN. (Back bone.) Main hazel of a skep.

BACKSTAN. A sheet of iron, sometimes a stone having an iron hoop to enable it to be hung over the fire, used to bake cakes upon. (Backstan-ceeak.) (Blakeborough.)

BACKUST. Bakehouse.

BADGER. Starfish.

BALK, BAULK or BAWK. Fishermen's line before hooks are affixed. Called line-balk when hooks have been attached. Baited line when hooks are baited. 'Ceeav'd line' when old bait has been removed.

BARKING. Tanning fishing gear and nets.

BARLSTEEAD. Ring that fits on oars.

BARMSKIN APPRON. Oilskin apron used by fishermen.

BEAT. Prepare. (The've gone ti beeat a line.)

BEEAT. Boot. (Ther's a hooal i' mi beeat.)

BEEAT-STOCKIN'. Stockings used with the sea-boots.

BEND. Fasten. (Bend that bowl on!)

BIRK. Birch.

BLAID-'OONDS. Bloodhounds. Runswick men say of Staithes men when they go after coal: 'The'r leyke blaid-'oonds efther 't.'

BLEEAD. Blood. (Blaid at Runswick.)

BLEG. Sea-hen. (Au'd wife at Whitby.)

BLETHER. Bladder. (He's i' t' au'd Allum 'oos blawin' bletherbowls.)

BLINND. Blind. (Ah could sheet blinnd e'e, ie without looking.)

BOOAT. Boat. (Give us 'o'd o' t' booat-'eeak.)

BOOAGY. Coble fire.

BOORN. Born.

BOTTERY. Elderberry.

BOUNS. ('Which line 'es t' meeast bouns?', ie Which line makes the biggest heap?) That line's bounsy.

BOWL START. Bowl to mark commencement of sheeting.

BOWLIN. Type of knot. Running bowlin, etc.

BRAT. Turbot.

BREEADIN'. Making a crab-pot. (Matt and Tich is ower yonder breeadin'.)

BREEARS. Briars.

BREET. Bright.

BREEAD WINND. North-north-west.(Ah thowt t'glass wad a gone up — ther's a breead winnd.)

BRIDLE. String attached to crab-pot to steady it.

BROON LEEAMERS. Ripe hazel nuts. (The' tumm'le oot leyke broon leeamers.)

CANDYBOUT. Feast of sweets provided when communally worked clip-rug is completed.

CARLIN. Seat nearest head of coble.

CEEAV'D LINE. Line from which old bait has been removed.

CHAAM'ER. Bedroom.

CHAVVLIN'. Chewing. (Wa maunt 'a'e them au'd rattens chavvlin' this gear.)

CHECKERS. Periwinkles. (Thoo's browt checkers like mice een.)

CHIMLAS. Chimneys.

CLAGGUM. General term for toffee.

CLAUVE. Placing of line hooks between two short hazels to prevent snuds or sneeads being barked; tanned.

CLEP. Stick with a hook on the end for hauling fish aboard. This is named a 'garthangle' at Filey. (Clep a ling bi t' tail, a cod, butt, an' brat bi t' eead, an' a conger eel bi t' naaval. Y'u deean't allus clep 'em wheer y'u wad leyke ti clep em, bud wheer y'u can git 'o'd.)

CORRIN. Current. (E wad gan onnywheer for 'auf a corrin.)

CORRK BUNCHES. Corks used as guides to pots.

COULPRESS. Continued breaking of sea. (It's breeakin' coulpress ower t' arbour mooth.)

CRAB-STICKS. Sticks to measure size of crabs.

CRIBS. Small compartments at side of coble.

CUDDY-HANDED. Left-handed.

DAN. Buoy.

DAN-LEET. Buoy light.

DEEAD. Death. ('E scarred 'im ti deead.)

DEED. Work. (Ther's thrang deed.)

DOG-CHOUPS. Fruit of dog-rose. Also 'dog-jumpers'.

DOGGERS. Green crabs.

DOG-'EEADS. Dog-heads. Repairs to fishing line that are not spliced.

DOLDRUMS. Lack of wind. Windjammer held up for wind is said to be in the 'doldrums.'

DOT BO'DS. Dotteril.

DOLLS. Sticks to hold sail to enable the fisherman's hands to be liberated.

DRAUGS. Sea anchors. (T'draugs slit reet atweea as wa war cumin' ower a gert sea.)

DUBBLER. Enamel bowl.

DUCK. Lamp flare.

DUCK WEEAKIN'. Wick for 'duck'.

EEAVUN. Oven. ('Yoon' generally in Cleveland)

EEARIN'. Sails of coble. (Lee and weather 'eearin'.)

ELL. Pour. (Ell us a cup o' teea oot.)

FASSEN. Fasten.

FEEAK. Miss. Also steal. When the fisherman is fastening the snuds (with hook) to baulk (twenty-two score and ten hooks to a new line), he measures the distance between each hook thus: heeak, heeak, feeak, ie, miss one; ie, tweea an' a feeak: 'Ther's nut moony 'es a heeak an 'a feeak.'

FEEATIN-PIECE. Piece of wood fixed between lowsethoft and midshipthoft in sailing cobles 'ti git foot-'o'd'.

FELTIES. Fieldfares.

FETTLED. Prepared. (Bi wi git fettled wa'll 'a'e bin taadin' an 'oor.)

FEWLES O' MUCK. Bad weather.

FLANG. Flung. ('E flang 'issel doon i' siken a temper.)

FLAYED. Afraid.

FLEEAD. Flood. ('E teeak t' fleead taade ti Yarmouth — iv a bucket.) (Flaid at Runswick.)

FLEET. Fifty-two crab pots. (Wa've lost tweea fleet o' pots this summer up ti noo.)

FLEETED. Grumbled, complained. (Walloper fleeted when Ann bowt all that wrangham [small fish].)

FLITHERS. Limpets. Flither gatherers used to all dress alike and travel as far as Saltburn and Robin Hoods Bay, in the early days afoot and later by train, returning on the rocks gathering flithers on the way.

FODTHER. Further. (T' 'errin's 'es gone fodther oot.)

FOND. Silly. (Thoo's as fond as leeace.)

FOREFEET. Front of keel of coble.

FOREROOM. Space between midshipthoft and forethoft.

FORETHOFT. Seat between carlin and midshipthoft.

FOR TI WHY ? Why ?

FOY. A boat requiring assistance.

GANTREES. Board flush with forethoft and carlin in which mast is fixed.

GAR ENDS. Boundary wall of village. End of passages overlooking sea and beck. (Ah see'd 'im o' T' Barber Gar Ends.)

GAUVIN'. Gapin. (Wheer's thoo gannin' gauvin' aboot?)

GAWSARKS. Exclamation! (Oh, gawsarks! wheeas this cumin'? T' staation gaffer for 'is mussel bill Ah's think.)

GILDET. Hair snare for catching birds. (Y'u caan 't cop a sparra' iv a gildet.)

GILNEY. Hole at coble head through which gilrope passes.

GILROPE. (See Gilney.)

GOB. Mouth.

GOG. Short, stoutish piece of stick for killing fish and removing hook. (Gog a cod bi t' snoot, a ling o' t' back o' t' neck, and a thoornbeck atwixt t' een.)

GO'NETS. Gurnets.

GOWLD. Gold. (Ah wadn't gan up theer for a gowld coo.)

GRADES. Grappling gear for recovering lost lines. (Y'u ma' graade all t' daay an' nut tak o'd.)

GUDGEON. Hole in casting at stern so that hook can be inserted to haul coble.

HAELED. Hauled.

HAELIN' ROOM. Space between lowsethoft and afterthoft.

HAIRY HATS. Round sealskin caps worn by fishermen up to five or six years ago.

HAU'F-PIECE. Standard length of fishing line (thirty fathoms). Thirteen half-pieces to the line.

HEEAK. Hook.

HOOAL. Hole.

HOOLIBALOOS. Blowers.

HOORN. Horn.

HOWSERS. Scoops.

HOWSUMIVVER. However.

HUMMOCK. Buoy for nets.

INTIV. Into. (As seean as t' butt com' Ah war intiv 'it.)

INWIRE. Wooden rail round inside of coble. (Thi mittens is i' t' inwire.)

JEEAT. Jet.

JIB ALLIOTTS. Rope attached to mast to hoist jib.

KANSH. Ridge of rock, sand or other obstacle in a waterway. (Sha's gitten ov a kansh, ie coble had run ashore on a ridge in the harbour.)

KELK. Codfish spawn.

KELKIN'. The knot fastening the snud to the fishing line. (Hing it i' t' kelkin'.)

KESSEN. Cast.

KIDGED. Twisted round the snud.

KILLATION. A fishwife's made word: 'It's killation'.

KNAPS. A local name for a part of the rocks.

KNOTT. A bad sea. (Sha teeak a nasty knott there.)

LANCH. Launch.

LANCHIN' WOODS. Woods used to launch coble. They are well greased 'wi' talla eightpence a poond at Jausiph's'!

LANTHRON. Lantern.

LATCHETS. Tabs inside sea-boots for them to be pulled on, and hung up to dry.

LAX. Cloud. (Sha's [t' sun] gannin' doon intiv a lax.)

LAZY COD. An ill-fed cod. ('E's neean lazy, 'e's warked 'issel ti deead.)

LEEAF. Rope that passes through parril.

LEEAF-HEEAK. Hook for the leaf.

LEEAR. Liar. (Thoo's as big a leear as Tom Pepper.)

LEEAT. Small coal-fish.

LEEAK. Christian name Luke. 'Leeak' White (Luke White).

LEET'NINS. Corked line affixed to tows for potting and fishing.

LEKS. Leaks. (Sha leks leyke a baskit.)

LEYKE. Like. (It leeaks leyke a lobster wi' yah claw.)

LIP TA'EN. Lip Taken, ie a fish hooked by the lip.

LISTINS. Ridge at joinings of planks round the coble.

LITHA. Look you.

LOBSTER STICK. To measure size of lobsters.

LONNIN'. Lane. (Ah see'd 'im up Jooa an' Andra lonnin'.)

LOOSE. Louse (parasitic insect). (Ah could crack a loose o' mi shackles!)

LOUND. Quiet, calm. (It's varra lound ti-neet.)

LOWSETHOFT. Coble seat between midshipthoft and afterthoft. This is removable, ie 'lowse' (loose).

MAFT. Suffocated. (Ah's fair mafted.)

MALLIMAWKS. Guillemots.

MALLY. Molly.

MA'SSY. Mercy. (Lawk o' ma'ssy.)

MEEANS. Moons.

MEEAT. Mate. (Meeat of a ship an' nut t' meeat 'at y'u eeat.)

MENSE. Finish. (Th'u wad nobbut ax us for a mense.)

MIDSHIPTHOFT. Coble seat between forethoft and lowsethoft.

MIRAK'LOUS. Remarkable. (Wa sumtaames git a mirak'lous fish.)

NANTLIN'. Wandering. (T' au'd wind's nantlin' aboot finndin' a 'ooal ti blaw in.)

NEEA. No. (Wa want neea white pots ... It 'es nea good in 't.)

NEEAKS. 'Is neeaks is weel doon', ie coble heavily laden; low down in the water.

NEB-BAND. Band at neb (head) of skep.

NOGGLETS. Local name for part of the rocks.

NOWTHERMOST. Most northerly.

OILSLOPS. Oilskins.

O'KKUD. Awkward.

OOR. Our. (Oor awn wyke.)

ORGIN. Young codling.

OVVER HEEAKS, OWER-'EEAKS. Large hooks, ie cod hooks as distinct from haddock hooks (forty used to line).

OVVIL. Boat requiring assistance. (See also 'Foy.')

OWERLIE. Placing baited hooks on neb of skep.

PAP LINES. Lines baited with rock anemones (sookers).

PARRIL. That sail hangs upon.

PEELIERS. Tiny young crabs with immature shell that can be peeled off. Used for bait.

PETRIL. Petrol.

PETS. Seagulls.

PISTIL. Pistol. (Y'u could 'a'e ta'en Steeas wiv a penny pistil.)

POOA'T. Port

PO'SS. Purse.

POT-TOWS. Used with crab pots.

POT STRINGS. do.

POTABOILIN'S. Off the end of Cowbar Steel.

POTTY HOOAL AN' TREEACLE. Backstan ceeak an' treeacle.

POTS. Crab pots. They contain: 4 bows, 4 side sticks, 1 top stick, 2 end sticks, 2 deear sticks, 2 bait bands, 1 slip band, 2 deear bands, 2 spoots or smoots.

POWL NETT. Pole net: the first net shot.

QUEER-UN. 'It's a queer-un if maane 'es ti bi mair 'an 'ers.' 'It war a queer-un when the' brak' a rudder-band iv a gale o' wind.'

RAM. Coble keel.

RATTENS. Rats.

RAXED MI SHACKLES. Sprained my wrist.

RECK'NINS. Weekly share out of fishermen. (Ther's neea reck'nins ti-neet [after a blank week]).

REEKIN'. Smoking.

REWLES. Rules. (The' 'a'e ti 'a'e rewles, thoo knaws, Billy.)

RIDDY RICKNORS. Ready reckoners; snuds with hooks affixed. (If wa ax'd for a heeak an' a sneead the' wadn't knaw what wa wanted, but if wa ax for a riddy-ricknor the' knaw what wa want.)

ROUSBY. Roxby. (Ah deean't knaw what wa s'ud deea widoot Rousby Trees [as a landmark]).

ROWLER. Roller. An apron or duster rolled up to protect the head when carrying coal, wood, etc. The Staithes women can carry great weights upon their heads. (See remarks re 'Flithers'.)

ROWTH IRONS. Irons on oars.

SAU'T. Salt.

SCUDBOOA'D. Small seat just inside stern of coble.

SCARBERS. Liver of ling.

SCAWLS. Clinkers.

SCRAUTIN'. Scratching.

SEEAT. Soot.

SEEAP. Soap.

SETTIN' A LINE. Fixing sneeads to baulk; preparing a line.

SETTIN' BOOA'D. Forty inches long: fisherman and his wife's initials cut in it, thus:

W V
A
William and Alice Verrill

SHACKLES. Wrists.

SHEEAPSTEEANES. Sheepstones (rocks near Staithes).

SHEEAN. Shoes.

SHEEARED. Small fish caught on hook and partly eaten off by bigger fish.

SHEEAT BLOCKS. Blocks used in sheeting.

SHEEATED. Shot. Act of casting lines or pots. (The've gitten sheeated.) Pots are shot nine fathoms apart.

SHIFTIN' MUSSELS UP. Changing the water that mussels are kept in.

SHOLL UP. Move up.

SHOOAT. Catch. (Oh, wa've a middlin' shooat.)

SHUTS. Darts. (It war makkin' sike gert shuts.)

SILVERWHIPS. Wild or sea cabbage (*Brassica oleracia*), which grows in great abundance at Staithes in the cliffs.

SKANE. Taking mussels out of shells.

SKEEAT. Skate (fish).

SKEEL. Wooden tub: formerly used for carrying water when each household had its own 'skeel' painted inside and out and bearing initials of the owner. They were carried on the heads of the womenfolk.

SKELLET. Saucepan.

SKEMS. Pigeons.

SKINNIGRYFF. Skinningrove.

SLARVE. Slice. (Give us a slarve o' breead.)

SLAVVERLAHNIN'. Baiting with flithers (limpets).

SMEEAD. Smooth.

SMEEARS. Fish spawn.

SNUDS, SNEEADS. (Formerly of horse-hair.) Short lengths of line with hook attached which are affixed to the fishing line proper (baulk).

SOFTIES. Tiny crabs before shell appears.

SOFT. General term for fishing grounds with sandy bottom. (Hummersty Soft, Bullfit Soft etc.)

SOOKERS. Sea anemones.

SPEEAN. Spoon.

SPEETS AN' RACKS. Used for roasting fish in front of fire.

SPERRIT. Spirit.

SPOTHS. Short supports at end of each coble seat. (Named 'knees' at Whitby.)

SPRAG. Codlings.

SQUIDS. Small herrings.

STARN. Stern.

STECKED. Fastened, closed. (Noo git thi gob stecked.)

STROP. Short rope tied to pot-tow.

STRING-KNOTT. Knotts to indicate which part of the line is in hand, eg 'string knott', 'half-piece string knot', etc.

'S'COS'LIT'O'TH'U. Literally 'God's curse light upon you.' An old Staithes woman was going to the polling booth, and one of the party touts asked her number. 'Scoslitothu!' she replied. 'Ah's seventy-three next!'

SWILL. Wicker basket used by flither pickers.

SWINGS. Forrud ropes of coble.

TAADE TI SAAY. Sure to say.

TAADIN'. Tiding. Resting at sea: waiting period between shooting lines and hauling them in.

TACK TAAKLE. Gear for tacking.

TAP LEETS. Coble lantern.

TEEA. Tea.

TEEAS. River Tees.

TELL ON'T. Remember.

THRANG. Busy.

THOWLL PINS. Uprights on coble side for oars to fit on.

THOORNS. Thorns (starfish).

TIMMERS. Timbers. Floor timbers of coble.

TOM EARS. Large dog fish.

UNDER-RUNNING. Hauling pots for examination and afterwards returning them to sea without hauling them aboard. Up-ower, In-ower, Doon-ower, Oot-ower.

VARMINT. Vermin.

WAHDNI BREECHES. Wide-knee breeches. Fishermen's trousers.

WAPS. Rough flannel with thumb-hole for maintaining grip of lines. These are named 'dag-cleeats' at Filey.

WEEAKIN'. Wick.

WEATHER. Good weather. (Wa'll gan if it's weather.)

WHEEALIN'. (Whaling.) Iron affixed to strengthen part where thowls are placed on the side of the coble.

WHIPPIN'. Affixing hooks to snuds.

WHITHER. The small bent part at end of a fishing hook.

WORRUMS. Worms.

WRECK, wrack. Seaweed.

WOW-TIN. Fishermen's lunch tin.

WOWTIN-CEEAK. Food that is not eaten at sea and returned in wow-tin.

WOARS. Oars.

WRANGHAM. Odd lots of miscellaneous under-sized fish.

YALLABOYS. Sovereigns.

YALLS. Yauls, yawls.

YAT-STOUPS. Gate-posts.

ADDENDA

ARDEN LOUP. Part of the rocks near Staithes.

BLAST, GURNET BLAST. Gurnet's bladder.

BO'DDIN. Burden, bundle.

BOO. Bow.

CEEASTRIN. Cistern.

CRAB CART. Empty shell of crab.

CUVVINS. Periwinkles.

DOCTOR' BOTTLE. Term for all medicine. ('A'e y'u browt oor John a doctor' bottle?)

HIGHLAWS. Name for shoes formerly worn by fishermen.

HOD NAB. Point on cliff near Staithes used as landmark.

LAGGERS. Name given to men who assist with launching of cobles.

MIFFY. Lobster without large claws.

MOPS. Small codlings.

MOY. Mouth.

NANNYCOCKS. Undersized lobsters. ('Pawks' and 'linties' at Whitby.)

RATCH. Exaggerate. (That Ridcar man wadn't ratch when 'e war talkin' aboot fishin'.)

REEASTED. Roasted. (Backust dinners is allus reeasted at t' top.)

SMOCK JACKETS. Fishermen's jerseys.

STRUNT. Cutting snuds off fishing line.

SWAAPE. Swape (oar).

TAUM. Piece of stick with twine and hook used by boys for catching pennock, etc.

TAUMED. Fallen off to sleep.

THEET. Watertight. (Them beeats is as theet as a bottle.) (Used also at Flamborough.)

TRATT. Fishing line used by youths and old men. They bait a line and anchor it to the rocks at low water and at the succeeding low water reclaim it.

TRIPPED. ('A'e sha tripped, ie Has the anchor become liberated ?)

WEEAK. Wake. 'White' water left behind moving ship. (Sha's makkin' a despert weeak.)

WARSIT. Hill. (Humersty Warsit, Huntcliffe Warsit, etc.)

WATTHER BO'N. Phosphorescence of herrings. (T' watther bo'ns on.)

(1935)

FOLKLORE OF THE PLOUGH STOTS
F W Dowson

We in North Yorkshire are in great part of Norse ancestry, and it was to the Norseman that we owed the introduction of sword dancing. This sword dancing is still practised in Yorkshire, Durham and Northumberland.

Our own county men use the long swords, some thirty or thirty-two inches in length, whilst the men of Durham and Northumberland use shorter swords, known as rappers (?rapiers).

Now the sword dancing in England has always been restricted, generally speaking, to a district northward and eastward from the Trent, and bounded generally on the west by the Pennines. This area includes parts of Nottinghamshire, Derbyshire, North Lincolnshire, and the three counties above-mentioned. Sword dancing, and similar performances in connection with the Plough Stots, has been in vogue within these northern shires almost from time immemorial until a generation or two ago.

Before dealing further with the Plough Stots, let me say that the sword dance is symbolic of a ritual and sacrifice which goes back to a time before history was written. These sword dances have been traced throughout Northern, South-eastern and Western Europe, and are still practised in various forms in eastern, and certain western countries, but chiefly in isolated districts. In Denmark, Norway and Sweden they seem to have died out, in the Middle Ages or even before. From certain personal enquiries in Scandinavian countries, and from Norwegian men of letters I have gleaned scraps of useful information regarding the boisterous sword dance formerly practised in the Northern lands, whilst I have assurance from Professor Knut Essol, of Oslo University, that research work may possibly reveal more concerning the old sword dances of Northern Europe. In Sweden I believe there has been a marked revival of old traditional customs, etc, in recent years.

We in England owe a greater debt to the late Mr Cecil Sharp, founder of the English Folk Dance and Song Society, than can well be imagined. It was he who first rescued and collected morris dance tunes and figures in the West of England, afterwards turning his attention to folk plays and sword dancing here in the Northern counties.

Mr Sharp visited Goathland in connection with the Plough Stots dances, and the old play, and collected a few traditional tunes, but his visit was of necessity too hasty. His keen enquiries however as to the old play, and the whereabouts of the manuscripts, etc, kept him busy and hopeful of tracing them, to the end of his life.

Indirectly, too, it led to the re-founding of the present team of Plough Stots by the writer. Their revival, however, was not a matter of a few weeks, or even months, but actually almost two years!

Incidentally, it may be mentioned that the manuscript of the Goathland play, which also contained directions for the sword dance figures, etc, was destroyed on a bonfire in the village almost forty years ago. The woman who had stored these things after her father's death, had thought that such would never be required again.

Returning to sword dancing, it seems to be an undoubted fact that the round dance, as now practised, is a survival of the dance of triumph around a victim, a sacred tree, or a sacrificial altar.

A reminder of this is still seen when the king of the dancers raises his 'lock' or 'rose' as a sign of triumph, and also at the time when 'Isaac', the 'awd man', or sometimes 'Betty', the 'awd woman', steps into the ring, and manages to be 'killed' when the swords are locked around his, or her neck.

To show the Norse origin of our dancing, I quote from the old description of sword dancing by Olaus Magnus, and you will notice at once many points of resemblance. He says:

First with their swords sheathed and erect in their hands, they dance in a triple round, then with their swords erect as before, afterwards extending them from hand to hand they lay hold of each other's hilt and point while they are wheeling more moderately round, and, changing their order, they throw themselves into the figure of a hexagon, which they call a 'rose', but presently raising and drawing back their swords, they undo that figure to form with them a four-sided rose, that may rebound over the head of each. At last they dance rapidly backwards, and loudly rattling the sides of their swords together, conclude the sport.

To return to the Plough Stots company — let it be remembered that here is a combination of two distinct elements, the Plough Stots themselves with their song, little play and attendant merrymakers, and the sword dancers. These latter form perhaps nowadays the chief, and certainly a very attractive part of the pageant.

I have spoken of the great antiquity of sword dancing, which has persisted down the ages to our own time, and which has undoubtedly been practised in our Yorkshire dales and certain villages for many centuries. There are records, too, of Plough Monday performances in most of the Midland and Eastern counties of England, and these took place at times even in London itself, so that the Plough Stots, too, may lay claim to great antiquity.

'Stot' means a bullock, and bullocks and oxen were formerly used for draught purposes in our English counties, in some places almost down to our own days. The name 'Stot' was transferred to the young men who dragged a plough on their rounds each year. I have no definite date as to the last appearance of the plough amongst our own Plough Stots, although I have heard eyewitness accounts of the fun created by the teamster, who carried a bladder, with peas inside, attached to his whiplash. At intervals he belaboured his team of stots, to the great amusement of the onlookers. The Egton plough was in use in the early years of last century, and my grandfather was one of the team which ploughed a furrow in coming down Egton 'Cliff'.

The teams were known by other names in various parts of the country. For example, in the Pickering and Scarborough districts they were called 'Fond Pleeaves' — 'fond' meaning silly, daft, or foolish. In the East Riding, Driffield area, they were known as 'Ploo Jags' (Jacks). This name is found, too, in the Selby district and in North Lincolnshire; but in Derbyshire they were simply 'bullock lads'. The Northumbrian teams which toured the villages were known as 'Fool Plough' teams.

All these companies set out in the winter season, ie round about Christmas and the New Year, as a rule, though the variations ranged from Martinmas (23rd November, old style) to Easter time in the case of the North Riding and West Yorkshire plays. Incidentally, the Driffield 'Jags' went out in their district in November, a similar date to that of Lockton, to be mentioned later.

'Plough Monday' is the first Monday after Epiphany or Twelfth Day, and this has always been the commencing day of the Goathland Plough Stots. As a rule, the company gave the first performance in its own village, following up with a tour of the surrounding countryside, and especially to villages which had no team of their own. Visits to nearby market towns were arranged for the busy days, with the object of adding considerably to the funds. Goathland Plough Stots on one occasion had a fortnight's tour of the Pickering–Scarborough area.

Somewhat akin to the Plough Stots of our districts were other forms of acting and amusement, a few of which are still practised in certain villages, and many of which have vanished only within living memory. There are still bands of mummers in certain Cleveland villages, I believe, as there are in Gloucestershire. In one village of that county the practice is said to have been kept up from time immemorial, and is still carried out annually.

Nearer home, there was the Lockton 'Tar Barrel', held in November, and combining features of the Guy Fawkes type, but really a very much older pageant. The actions and dialogues are of the usual witty type, interspersed with robust fooling. There are local people and others who witnessed this performance not many years ago, and I am fortunate in possessing a fairly good account of the characters and dialogues, etc, by one of the participants of some forty years ago.

There is, too, the 'Pace Egg', or 'Peace Egg' or Paschal play, as still performed in certain Pennine villages of the West Riding, at Eastertide. Lastly in this connection, I mention the old Ampleforth Play, also formerly acted in Easter week. This play was rescued by the late Mr Cecil Sharp, and reconstructed in its entirety. Since then it has been played as in the old style, and I was fortunately able to see and study this in London a few years ago. Similar to the Ampleforth Play was the Old folk Play at Goathland, the differences being chiefly those of local allusions and incidents, and perhaps minor additions, such as a 'cushion dance'. This play, which Mr Sharp failed to trace, was acted at the Lord Nelson Inn, Beckhole, and at the Crossed Pipes Inn, Goathland, some ninety years ago. Certain fragmentary descriptions of this play were made known to me by witnesses and performers, a few years ago, and the account will be found in part 27, vol 4, of the YDS's *Transactions*.

Lastly, I must refer to a remarkable play, with its sword dancers and fiddler, in the far away isle of Papa Stour, Shetland. A comparison with our Goathland and Ampleforth plays is both instructive and interesting. There are also features common to the 'Pace Egg' play in this remote corner of the British Isles. It seems a strong confirmation of the Norse origins of our modern sword dancing, for the Shetlands were in the possession of Norway for some hundreds of years. Notice, too, that in all these plays, a *fiddler* is the accompanist. This dance was seen, and described by Sir Walter Scott in *The Pirate*, after his visit to the Shetland Isles in 1814. Another description was by Dr Samuel Hibbert in his *Description of the Shetland Isles*, published in 1822.

Returning to the Plough Stots, there is a tradition that on the first Monday following 'Twelfth Day', the plough was first put into the ground after the Deluge. For centuries the week following Plough Monday was looked upon as the agricultural labourers' holiday, which they began by attending service at their parish church, and afterwards continued by perambulating the district, dressed in fantastic attire, and dragging a plough after them whilst asking alms for the fun they created by their antics

I quote here from the author of *Manners, Customs and Observations*. Leopold Wagner says:

> On Plough Monday the ploughmen and rustic labourers were supposed to return to their labours in the field, but they did not actually do so until the following day. They attended the parish church, and there offered lighted candles before the high altar, by way of calling down a blessing on the labours of the year.

The Reformation did not succeed in abolishing the ploughman's festival, just as the Roman Catholic Church had not succeeded in abolishing the sword dancing of the older pagan days. What the Church could not eradicate, it sanctified and turned to nobler and higher uses, whenever and wherever it could do so. Here, in our secluded Yorkshire dales and coastal villages, the old customs and practices have survived to our own day.

Flamborough and Staithes had their teams of sword dancers, amongst others — indeed, the former is in a manner still existent. Kirby Malzeard dance figures, like those of Sleights and Goathland, are still often used in displays. Let us now consider the characters, their customs and actions. These vary from district to district as might be expected, but there are many evidences traceable to a common origin.

In the plays, which were mediaeval in origin and character, we have such figures

66

as 'St George', and other Champions of Christendom, also 'Beelzebub', 'Devil Doubt', 'Big Head', 'Doctor', 'Sergeant', 'Foxey', etc, etc.

In our Goathland Plough Stots the characters were:

(1)   The 'King' and 'Queen', or 'Gentleman' and 'Lady', who always led and controlled the company, in a more or less dignified way.

(2)   The set of 'Toms', or collectors, quaintly or even grotesquely attired, and, of course, disguised.

(3)   The company of sword dancers in sets of six, and headed too by their 'King'.

(4)   The fiddler, and, at times, a clown or 'merryman' accompanying him.

(5)   Following, came the Plough Stots, dragging their plough, themselves dressed in smocks or substitute shirts outside their dresses. The team was in charge of a teamster with his 'gad' (goad) or whip, to the lash of which was affixed a bladder containing rattling peas. The driver plied his whip vigorously upon the heads and bodies of his team, thus contributing a fund of merriment for old and young alike.

(6)   Lastly in this procession, which might number anything from sixteen to forty or even fifty men, came the 'Awd Man' and 'Awd Woman', known as 'Isaac' and 'Betty'. These (men) asked for alms too, and always brought up the rear of the procession — a complete contrast to the 'Gentleman' and 'Lady' at the head.

'Isaac's' quaint rig-out, his odd stockings, old hat and tattered coat, crooked stick, wooden spectacles, etc, together with 'Betty's' old rags, her besom, etc, and their antics and patter, put the finishing touches to a processional show not soon to be forgotten. All the above characters were of course males.

I append one version of the opening song of the Goathland team, the Sleights version of which is very similar:

> Here's a host of us all,
> From Goathland go we,
> We are going a rambling
> The country for to see.
> The country for to see,
> Some pastime for to make;
> So freely you will give to us,
> So freely we will take.
> And now you see us all
> Dressed in our grand array.
> Think of us what you will,
> Music, strike up and play!

Whilst the dancers in their gay uniforms, blue tunics with white facings, and pink tunics with similar facings, all bedecked with rosettes, ribbons and streamers, were busy dancing their various figures to the fiddler's old tunes, the 'Toms' were busy, too, pestering all and sundry, to contribute, even to their 'last hawp'ny'. No one was safe from their attentions — they formerly entered houses, and even helped themselves, unbidden, to food and drink. Probably this was due to an excess of hunger, as well as of zeal, and it often earned a rather unpleasant name for the whole company. Woe betide the churlish or unwilling giver! It was then that old 'scores' could be paid off, and not infrequently the order was given to put in the plough, and uproot the stones, or turn a furrow on the lawn.

One of the 'Awd Man's' acts was to enter the dancers' ring, and give a step dance, solo, generally in the final figure. He managed to get his head and neck fixed in the lock, which, when the swords were withdrawn, appeared to make him collapse as if beheaded. This action is significant, and carries us far back to the old days of a sacrificed victim. The colours, blue and pink, were the old political colours of the Tory and Whig days, and the semi-military uniforms often bear traces of that period, too. The fiddler, dressed in a combination colour tunic, is in the old Norse tradition.

There were five original dance figures in the Goathland sword dances, and all of these have, very fortunately, been recovered, and are now in use again as they were generations ago.

Sleights' Plough Stots had four figures, practically similar to four of the Goathland ones, but the 'No Man's Jig', an extra, and very graceful figure, was more elaborated in the Goathland dance.

It was the custom to invite the womenfolk — wives, sisters, sweethearts — to the final 'Do', which was a supper and dance, and which was held at one or other of the local inns. This invitation to the 'Do' was a reward for the hard work involved in preparing the team for its journeyings. The expenses of the tailor and mantle-maker had to be met out of the takings on tour, and a sharing out took place as a rule at the weekend, but a balance was always reserved, and spent at the final supper and dance.

The old teams did not necessarily go out on tour every year. Sometimes a period of two, three, or even five years elapsed, but this was owing to difficulties in raising full teams. After a revival, however, the enthusiasm was often greater than ever. The dancers were of course taught by old members of the former companies, and the practice room was often a barn floor. As a rule the practices commenced about Martinmas, the 23rd November, as still kept in the old style.

On one historic occasion it is recorded that the Goathland Plough Stots were led over the moors into Whitby, headed by a horseman and a band of music, the company numbering fifty members or more. Imagine the task of feeding and controllng such a crowd of men! It was indeed the lack of a firm controlling hand that led to the breaking up of village teams.

I deplore the fact that teams formerly existing in such villages as Staithes, Egton, Fylingdales, Aislaby and Sleights have all died out, and no efforts have been made to re-establish any of them. It is not too late to do so even now, and the teams if reformed could be assured of hearty support. A remarkable feature following on the Goathland revival by myself in 1922-23, was the interesting press correspondence in many of our Northern newspapers. This was evidence that many people had lively remembrances of the old pageants and that numbers of old performers were still alive.

It may be fitting to give a paragraph or two from old descriptions in this district more than a century ago. Dr Young, in his *History of Whitby*, published 1817, writes:

On Plough Monday, the first Monday after Twelfth Day, and some days following, there is a procession of rustic youth, dragging a plough, who, as they officiate as oxen, are called plough stots.

They are dressed with their shirts on the outside of their jackets, with sashes of ribbons fixed across their breasts and backs, and knots, or roses of ribbons, fastened on their shirts and on their hats. Besides the plough draggers, there is a band of six, in the same dress, furnished with swords, who perform the sword dance, while one or more musicians play on the fiddle or flute.

The sword dance probably introduced by the Danes, displays considerable ingenuity, not without gracefulness. The dancers arrange themselves in a ring, with their swords elevated; and their motions and evolutions are at first slow and simple, but become gradually more rapid and complicated; towards the close each one catches the point of his neighbour's sword, and various movements take place in consequence, one of which consists in joining or plaiting the swords into the form of an elegant hexagon, or rose, in the centre of the ring; which rose is so firmly made that one of them holds it up above their heads without undoing it. The dance closes with taking it to pieces, each man laying hold of his own sword.

During the dance, two or three of the Company, called 'Toms' or 'Clowns', dressed up as harlequins, in the most fantastic modes, having their faces painted or masked, are making antic gestures and movements to amuse the spectators, whilst another set called 'Madgies' or 'Madgypegs', clumsily dressed in women's clothes, and also painted or masked, go about from door to door, rattling old canisters in which they receive money.

When they are well paid they raise a 'Huzza'; when they get nothing they shout, 'Hunger and starvation!' When the party do not exceed forty, they seldom encumber themselves with a plough. They parade from town to town for two or three days, and the money collected is then expended in a feast and dance, to which the girls who furnished the ribbons and decorations are invited. Sometimes the sword dance is performed differently; a kind of farce, in which songs are introduced, being acted along with the dance. The principal characters in the farce are, the king, the miller, the clown and the doctor.

Egton Bridge has long been the rendezvous for sword dancers in this vicinity.

(1936)

A DAY-TAL CHAP

Ah've addled mi' brass bi' t' sweeat o' mi broo,
Sen a lahtle bit lad aboot ten.
If Ah live whaal next Mart'mas, then eighty Ah's tonn'd,
An' still yabble ti fick for missen.

Neea skeealin' Ah gat i' theeas new fangl'd waays
Bud Ah hansell'd mi pleeaf ower seean —
Beeath o' Sundays an' war-days Ah plugg'd in at work
An' gat falder'd bi' t' tahm it was deean.

Mi havver-ceeaks teeaf, Ah cowl'd 'em frae t' ass,
Varry thenk-ful ti greease 'em wi' seeam.
O this mally-mawk breead 'at they moother i' t' mill,
For an awmus Ah weeant tell mi neeam!

A poddish-pot meeal it clags ti yer ribs,
Suet dumplins an' broth wi' yan's meeat
Ti theeas gran-bairns 'at's dainsh'd wi their peeaste an' their puffs,
Sike a jawther's nut menseful ti eeat!

Mi hodden-grey cooat still haps up mi rig,
What a kenspack Ah is ti be seear!
Bud a feg for ye dandies an' poother-puff weeans —
Ower gaumless ti maaze oot o' t' deear.

F W Dowson (NR)

(1938)

fick, struggle; *pleeaf,* plough; *poddish,* porridge; *jawther,* mess;
rig, back; *kenspack,* sight

JOHN HARTLEY
W J Halliday

John Hartley was born in Bedford Street, Halifax, on the 19th October 1839. His father was a tea merchant and his mother a Quakeress. After a short spell at a dame school kept by a Miss Gilpin, he passed to Park Place Academy, which was kept by John Farrer, a headmaster of the old school, who never believed in spoiling a pupil by sparing the rod. John Hartley was a clever, but mischievous lad.

In his early days, he showed signs of those gifts of leadership and that robust courage which were, in later years, to enable him to overcome the slings and arrows of outrageous fortune. He showed, too, that taste for 'dressing up' and theatrical display that played a great part in his subsequent development. And, above all, he early gave proof of that keen sense of humour that was later to find expression in his poems and sketches. One May Day he walked round the streets with a gaily-decorated donkey. He left school at twelve and began work as a pattern designer at James Ackroyd and Sons.

Some time in his early twenties he became a member of the Beacon Club, a kind of literary institute that held its meetings in the Corporation Arms. Here, one night, as his contribution to the evening's entertainment he wrote and recited *Bite Bigger*. As a first poem, it is an amazing achievement. Directly inspired by Edwin Waugh's *Come Whoam to thi Childer an me*, it has all the sincere simplicity and the dramatic sense that is found in the best of Waugh. It was enthusiastically received, was published as a broadside and sold by the hundred at one penny a copy.

This poem brought John Hartley into contact with the promoters and publishers of the *Halifax Original Illuminated Clock Almanack*. The result of this was that John Hartley took over its editorship and in October 1866 he published his first almanack — that is, the *Clock Almanack* for 1867.

I have heard, and also seen in print, that John Hartley's first *Clock Almanack* was for the year 1868. Copies of the 1867 almanack are rare. It is not in the British Museum or any of the libraries of Halifax, Leeds, Bradford or Wakefield.

The first Hartley *Clock Almanack* was issued in two forms, a popular edition in paper backs at 2d each, of which 5,000 copies were sold in a few weeks, and a stiff-backed edition at 1s. From the beginning it was a popular success. Some 80,000 copies were sold of the 1887 issue. Even today, so firmly has Hartley established its reputation, its sales almost reach this figure.

John Hartley

In the midst of this apparent happiness and tranquillity, a bolt fell from the blue. Some time — possibly in 1863 or 1864 — John Hartley had married. He lived one period at Dirk Carr Farm and three children were born. The circumstances of this early married life are obscure. All that is known is that John Hartley suddenly and secretly sailed for America in 1872. There was about John Hartley, all his life, a curious temperamental instability. One could never forecast his next move. Impulsive, generous in prosperity, calm and unbowed in adversity, he took the path where the mood of the moment led him. Improvident he always was, as many poets both before and since his day have been, but he was intensely loyal, both to people and to principles.

He landed first at Quebec, and if the account of a transatlantic voyage in those days which he gives in *Grimes' Trip to America* has any basis in his own experience, it was an appallingly uncomfortable journey. In Quebec, with his usual impetuosity, he hired a hall and advertised a recital. It was a tragic beginning. Bad weather — and perhaps the fact that his name was completely unknown — resulted in an audience of one and before this solitary person, he went through the whole of his programme. The venture left him nearly penniless, but undaunted. He moved on to Montreal where he became an odd-job man, a newspaper canvasser, a painter, a master painter, a theatrical producer and a theatre manager — all within the space of six months. From Montreal he passed into the United States, where he lived a precarious existence for a couple of years. In 1875 he returned to England.

On his return he took up his residence in London. He at once resumed the management of the *Clock Almanack* which had languished in his absence, and began a literary career. During this period many volumes came from his pen. Before he left for America he had published *Hartley's Yorkshire Budget*, a volume which contained the whole of the Rambling Remarks from the *Clock Almanacks* of 1867 to 1871 inclusive. This was followed by *Yorkshire Ditties* (first and second series),

Yorkshire Tales, Yorkshire Puddin in 1876, *Seets i' Lundun* in 1876, *Grimes' Trip to America* in 1877 and *Seets i' Paris* in 1878.

Some of John Hartley's best work is to be found in these books. For his day, he was a much-travelled man, and his keen observation, his lively sense of humour and his quick human sympathies, joined to a facility of expression and a love of his dialect, give the works a high place in dialect literature.

In February 1880, John Hartley moved to Bradford and became the licensee of the Druid Arms. He left the following year and took up residence in Leeds. His stay was short and in January 1882, with his second wife and the sons of his first, he set out again for America. The second Mrs. Hartley was Sophia Ann Wilson, only daughter of Mr Wilson, the hatter, who had founded the *Clock Almanack*. Miss Wilson was a singer of local repute and a teacher of music. She is the Mally of John Hartley's tales. John and Mally were a very happy couple, of similar tastes and outlook, and John Hartley's debt to his managing capable wife was a theme of which he never tired. Their conversation was witty and scintillating and exactly the sort that he set down so charmingly in his writings.

The Hartleys settled in Philadelphia, where John set up his own occupation as carpet and upholstery designer. He still retained his connection with the *Clock Almanack*, and continued to give readings. For many years he lived the life of a successful business man in Philadelphia. But good fortune never smiled on John Hartley very long and it appears his business ended abruptly. He returned to England in 1894.

From that date to the end of his life John Hartley remained in England. In 1895 he was living in Harehills Terrace, Leeds, and in the following year at Shadwell. Two years later John Hartley and his wife sold up their home and went to stay in Blackpool for a few months. They left behind their daughter, who had a post as teacher in the Roundhay Road Board School. After their stay in Blackpool they took up housekeeping again at 11 Seaview Avenue, Liscard, Cheshire.

Writing seems to have been his main source of livelihood at this time, and there are indications that life was sometimes a struggle. His wife was a tower of strength, not only managing the household with economy and care, but eking out the family income by giving music lessons. An attempt was made in 1909 to procure for him a Civil List pension but this was unsuccessful. But he was happy in his work and, during this latter period he had issued an edition of his poems, both in dialect and standard English under the title of *Yorkshire Lyrics*. It is a fitting memorial to a true Yorkshire singer.

He became a Freemason and was elected an honorary life fellow of the Yorkshire Literary Society in 1907. He visited old friends, and in 1900 paid a memorable visit to that other great Yorkshire dialect poet, Ben Preston, then eighty years old, at the latter's country cottage at Eldwick.

The closing years of his life were difficult times for John Hartley. His name was a household word wherever the Yorkshire dialect was spoken, and that means far beyond the confines of his native county. But he never lost his spirit, although he must have felt at times the burden of man's inhumanity to man.

In 1909, on the occasion of his seventieth birthday, a banquet in his honour was held at the Great Northern Hotel, Bradford, when he was presented with a purse of 100 guineas and a life-size portrait. In his reply he said:

An old Yorkshire phrase I am very fond of repeating when I am down on my luck is, 'I hev nowt and I can pay nowt, but I owe nowt.' It's all right as far as 'I hev nowt and can pay nowt', but you have placed a debt upon me which I can never repay: your kind words are more value to me than gold or precious stones.

This was not the last of the public tributes to John Hartley. Three years later another banquet was held at the Old Cock Hotel, Halifax, to celebrate his seventy-third birthday. In appearance, he is described by one who was present as still having a good supply of hair, bushy at the back; a straggling beard and moustache, gaunt cheeks flushed with excitement, and eyes patient and tired.

He was presented with a purse of £74 and an album inscribed with the names of all the guests and containing quotations which the presenter (Mrs. A B Wakefield, of Hipperholme) hoped 'would bring him consolation when he was reading to his Mally by his fireside in the peaceful and restful days of his life.' At the end of a touching reply John Hartley said, 'I will do what I can as long as I live to uphold Yorkshire and my native twang.'

But both John Hartley and his beloved Mally were suffering grievous ill-health in these later years. One who visited him at Liscard in 1913 said that he was a constant sufferer with neuritis in the legs and was unable to go far from home. Mentally he was as alert as ever. He discussed with his visitor contemporary writers and acknowledged the influence of Edwin Waugh. When asked which he considered his best effort — poetry or prose — he replied, 'I have tried to put my best into all my work.' He talked with intimate knowledge and affection of Sam Laycock, J H Eccles, Ben Preston, the Tweddells and other writers of Yorkshire dialect. He still preserved his keen sense of humour and often delighted his visitor with his witty and wise sallies.

On the 22nd January 22 1915, Mrs Hartley ('Mally') died. In September of the same year John Hartley married Mrs Annie Spencer, a native of Manchester. She had been a schoolmistress in Todmorden and Hebden Bridge, and later in Vancouver, BC, and she had published a volume of verses under the title of *Roses and Rue*.

But John Hartley did not long survive this marriage. Three months later, on the 19th December 1915, following an attack of pneumonia, he passed peacefully away. He was buried in the same grave as 'Mally' in Rake Lane Cemetery, Wallasey.

It has been stated — and the statement has been published — that John Hartley was buried in a common grave because there was no money for a private one. This alleged fact had been used as evidence of neglect and indifference on the part of Yorkshiremen. There is no truth in the statement. I have verified the facts at Wallasey.

John Hartley was the most prolific and the greatest of writers in Yorkshire dialect. Like many another artist in words, he was a man of complex character. He never attempted to hide his weaknesses, and it was this very candour of thought and honesty of mind which laid him open to the harsh judgment of the world. Restless, unstable and improvident he always was, but his loyalty to his home and to his friends, his great human sympathies, and his deep sincerity were attested by all who knew him, and shone through everything that he wrote. His devotion to his wife, 'Mally', was a thing of tender beauty. A favourite remark to her when cross-currents had disturbed the domestic calm was, 'Tha's allus finding fault abaht summat, but tha's a grand owd lass for all that.'

His daughter has given many instances of his happy home life and his instinctive generosity. On Sunday mornings — the only time when he did not have breakfast in bed — he prepared the breakfast for the family, and on one occasion, Mrs Hartley came downstairs and found him at the front door surrounded by a group of children. He was telling them to hold out their pinnies, and into these he was tossing the small cakes that Mrs Hartley had baked for the week.

His love of fun was irrepressible. A witty conversationalist, he delighted in the company of congenial friends, and would keep his audience amused for hours, with his fund of stories and his gift of repartee. With children and old folk he was seen at his best. Many and many a time, he gave recitals free at old folks' treats, and poverty or suffering found in him a staunch helper and a willing friend.

He never knew the meaning of fear, and any new and novel experience appealed at once to his adventurous spirit. Once when he was managing a theatre in Montreal, he had engaged a troupe of acrobats and trapeze artists. Looking round the theatre one day, and seeing the trapeze hooked to the gallery, he thought he would try one of the tricks of the artists, swing out and back and so reach the gallery again, just as he had seen the performers do. He unhooked the trapeze and let himself go. To his great dismay he failed to swing far enough back to reach the gallery, and there he remained, swinging in the air until rescued by some of the theatre staff.

The secret of John Hartley's success as a writer was his humanity. The people who read the *Clock Almanack* found there a deep understanding of their own problems and difficulties, a sympathy that was manly and deep, a humour that was kindly, a wit that was wise and a downright integrity of mind and spirit. Poor as a crow himself, John Hartley preached contentment. To the rich he preached charity:

> Aa! it's grand to ha plenty o' chink!
> But doan't let it harden yor heart:
> Yo 'at's blessed wi' abundance should think

An' try to do gooid wi' a part!
An' then, as yo're totterin' daan,
An' th' last grains o' sand are i' th' glass,
Yo may find 'at yo've purchased a craan
Wi' makkin' gooid use o' yer brass.

He had many poems which showed his love of children. *Bite Bigger, Another Babby, The Little Stranger* and many others expressed this feeling. He had many poems on nature — *To a Roadside Flower, To a Daisy, To th' Swallow* — but, like Pope, he believed that the proper study of mankind is man, and his nature poems invariably end on the human note.

But perhaps it is in his prose writings that he is found at his best, and it is more difficult to write genuine and impressive and sincere prose in dialect than it is to write verse. It was because he had such a close understanding of the people about whom he wrote, and because also the dialect was to him a living language that one finds in his prose a depth of feeling and sincerity that are not always present in his verse.

Broadly speaking, John Hartley's sense of pathos comes out in his poetry; his sense of humour in his prose. Some of his essays are worthy, in their verbal dexterity, their wit and their humour, to take rank with the essays of Lamb and Goldsmith. He had the happy knack of distilling a homely truth or a subtle thought in a quick, scintillating epigram, and it would be easy to compile an anthology of these gems Here are a few specimens:

A chap 'at's liberal wi advice is generly niggardly wi' his brass.

A workman 'at's ashamed of his smock is noa longer prahd of his trade.

A gooid way to stop a chap's maath is to keep yer awn shut.

Never despise a chap becoss he's net as sharp as yorsen: if he cannot grow tulips he can happen grow turnips.

His descriptive writing was marked by keen observation and a feeling for dramatic effect, and his description of the breaking up of the ice in the frozen St Lawrence river in *Grimes' Trip to America,* shows to what heights dialect prose can rise.

But it would be absurd to make extravagant claims for John Hartley as a writer. It would be absurd to compare him with Burns. Burns, by the force of his genius was able to impose a dialect on the world. Hartley had neither his width nor his range nor his lyric gifts. Nevertheless, John Hartley was a genuine singer of homely songs, and as long as Yorkshire dialect is read, so long will John Hartley be cherished and loved.

(1940)

UNCLE VICTOR'S EVACUEES

Yon staggarth yat's cum of it' creeak,
Seea that's anuther shoo'der-yat!
Ah see the've scattered t' bit o' theeak,
An' slitten that new sheet Ah gat;
The've weeasted t' tin o' waggin fat,
An' tippled ower tweea skeps o' bees;
The've gi'en t' flay-kreeake mi bran-new hat,
Ah's think it's them evacuees!

Wheea's pulled t' taal-feathers off t' au'd dreeake?
Ah see the're laid oot theer o' t' mat;
An' t' au'd cock leeaks a queer au'd leeak,
Ah laay the've hed ti mell o' that;
Ther's nowt Ah see but's hed a bat!
The've rovven bark off meeast o' t' trees;
The've ta'en t' eggs fre t' au'd 'dotte thoo sat,
 Ah's think it's them evacuees!

The've chasst all t' pullets off the'r peeak,
Pulled hawf o' t' reeaf off wheer the' scrat;
Meead mincemeeat o' t' kye bit o' ceeake,
Put t' cat i' t' trap Ah laid for t' rat:
Mi clawver pikes is trampled flat,
Just when ther's cum a bit o' breeze:
If Ah could nobbut catch 'em at' t!
Ah's think its them evacuees!

What ha'e the' deean tiv oor poor Natt?
Leeak here, he's cutten beeath his knees!
He's lost sum teeth! That's bleead he spat!!
Ah's think its them evacuees!

A Stanley Umpleby (ER)

(1940)

staggarth yat, stockyard gate; *flay-kreeake*, scarecrow; *kye*, cattle

AN OLD YORKSHIRE CHIMNEY SWEEP
H J L Bruff

The Ven Archdeacon Bartlett, when he read his paper 'Speech Survivals', at our annual meeting in York last autumn, did me the honour to refer to some notes and a word list of mine, made many years ago, on an alleged 'Chimney Sweep's' language, which we had discussed. The archdeacon did not think that my word list indicated a separate language, nor that the old chimney sweep's statement, that at one time sweeps had been gypsies had any real foundation. As others may be able to throw further light on the question, the following notes give the substance of my notes.

The old chimney sweep from whom I obtained the information was Mr Tipling, of Knaresborough. About 1905 or so, he came to sweep our chimneys; he was then about eighty years and remarkably vigorous for his age. He must, therefore, have begun to learn his trade somewhere between 1825 and 1835, as he told me that he began to go to work when he was six.

It was quite accidentally that we got to talk about sweep's language; I wanted to find out from him what labour conditions were like when he first went to work. What he told me about his early experiences was almost unbelievable and reminded me of Charles Kingsley's *Water Babies*. What, however, was even more incredible was that he had gone through the mill and learnt his trade from his father, who had been trained in the art by his father and grandfather. In those days they had no machines, as they call their brushes, but little boys were made to climb up inside the chimney flues, and in the mere passage they would bring the soot down. If they did not get along quick enough or got stuck, the master sweep would light a newspaper and hold it up the flue, and old Tipling said he always had to carry a bundle of old papers for this purpose. 'You see', he said, 'when one climbed up the flue one had to draw up the knees and then straighten out so one was wedged, and then get hold with one's hands and squeeze oneself up. If one slipped one might drop down to the bottom or get "glutted".' He remembered boys who had lost consciousness when stuck in 'a natchy lew' and choked with the smoke. It had not happened to him, but he said: 'It was an awful job to get the suffocating lad out, and that was the reason why the master sweep would never allow anybody to be present when he carried out a job.'

I asked him what he meant by a 'natchy lew', and he said it was 'Sweep's Language' meaning 'awkward flue'. He went on to tell me that sweeps originally had been gypsies and that sweeps and gypsies understood each other's language and always showed hospitality to each other. He had often had meals with them when he met them on the roads or came across them in the lanes. He said it was very handy to have a language amongst themselves, as one could then get useful information on the quiet. If, for instance, one did not know what to charge at a certain place one would ask 'What lower do they tip there?', meaning 'What do they pay in that house?' He told me the names of a lot of things, some of which I wrote down at the time, but when, a short while later, I went to see him to get some further terms, poor old Tipling was no more.

Mr Tipling, as well as his family, were all of them very dark, with black shiny hair and black eyes, and I think that there could be little doubt but that he had a good deal of Gypsy blood in him. He was a little, cheerful man, well liked by everybody and most thorough and reliable in his work.

Below are the words which he gave me, their corresponding English and Gypsy equivalent and also Archdeacon Bartlett's suggestions:

Sweep's Language	English	Gypsy, AB's Suggestions
Gadge	Man	Gojo, Gorgio (Romany)
Kenn	House	Cean (Gaelic), Ker, Ken (Cant)
Peck	Food	Popular Slang
Lush	Drink	Cant
Kelp	Hat	
Swush	Brush	Rhyming Slang
Lower	Pay	Lowa (Romany?)
Lew	Chimney Flue	Rhyming Slang
Prod	Horse	Gry (Romany)
Slurry	Corn	
Kid	Brush Machine	
Timmy	Rod	
Queer	Soot	Back Slang: 'Reek'
Room Kid	Master of House	
Room Mannish	Mistress of House	Manushi (Romany?)
Natchy	Awkward	
Meek	Half Penny	Medjig ? (Shelta)
Winn	Penny	
Thrum	Three Pence	
Flagg	Four Pence	
Sy	Six Pence	
Nine Winn	Nine Pence	
Hog	One Shilling	
EighteenWinn	One Shilling Six Pence	
Two Hog	Two Shillings	
Half a Bull	Two Shillings Six Pence	
Bull	Five Shillings	Popular Slang & Thieves' Cant

(1942)

LONDON PIECE

Ah nivver thowt it 'ud coome ti pass;
Oor Jackie's wedded a city lass!
Wi' poodther an' paint she clarts 'er phiz,
An' she talks lahke fawks on t' wiyerless diz:
Fower years 'e wer' coortin' Robi'son' niece,
Bood 'e's been an' getten a Loondon Piece.

She walks oop t' village on 'eels that 'igh
All t' lartle lads mocks 'er, mincin' by;
'Er sket's that tight she could nivver fraame
Ti climm ovver t' stahle; whyah, yer'd think 'er laame.
Till she clicks oop 'er petticawts, bowld as brass —
Yon shaameless Piece of a Loondon lass!

Annie Robi'son's awmly; aye,
Bood 'er ooncle's getten a bit put byah;
She's a 'oose-proud lass, is Robi'son' Annie —
She's quiyet an' menseful, kahnd an' canny;
An' she'll get 'is brass when 'e dees, will t' niece;
Jack's getten nowt wiv 'is Loondon Piece.

She can't baake breead an' she weean't scroob t' flooar,
Nor yet wash t' step on 'er awn froont dooar;
'Is Dad wer' allus a careful man,
Bood she's maade Jack buy on t' instalment plan;
'E'll rew', says t' Meeasther, 'Bood t' fond yoong ass
Mun fick it oot, wiv 'is Loondon lass.'

Ruth Hedger (NR)

(1947)

clarts 'er phiz, daubs her face

80

A VOCABULARY OF MARBLES

John Lloyd Bailes

The following list of words has been compiled from my own memory, from random search in Joseph Wright's *English Dialect Dictionary*, and from conversations with friends and colleagues. It is no more than a preliminary list. Many of these words will undoubtedly have a currency wider than that indicated here, and will occur in variant forms in different dialectal areas. It is worthy of note that many of these words, numbering in all 205, are restricted solely to the vocabulary of small boys when engaged in playing marbles, yet there is material of great philological interest in even this humble branch of our vocabulary.

While there exists a great variety of marble games, for the purposes of this study four main types of game will be considered, and will be referred to as 'the ring game', 'the hole game', 'the line game', and 'the game of hundreds'. In the first of these, the ring game, eg *boodie, brewery, pig-ring*, each player puts a given number of marbles inside a circle marked out on the ground with the heel or a pointed stick, the players retire to a starting position marked by a straight line, viz. the *bunt, stance,* or *tawline,* and cry in order 'Foggy! Seggy! Thirdy! Laggy!' This decides the order of play, the quickest with his tongue being first.

The order of play may be decided by a trial roll, viz a *purling* or *shirleying,* for the circle, the nearest to the ring being first. In turn each player then fires his *shooter,* usually his best marble, his *ally* or *taw,* and aims to knock a marble from the ring. If he succeeds, then the marble is his and he is entitled to a second shot. If, however, his own marble is left in the ring, ie is *fat* or *bizzing,* then he forfeits both a shot and his winnings. Each player firing in turn, the game is continued until the ring is cleared or *skinned.* Any infringement of the rules, for instance moving a taw nearer to the target than is lawful, ie *fubbing, fudging, trigging,* is punished and the culprit must have his knuckles shot at with a marble. This penalty is termed *beaks, knucks,* or *picket.* The penalty may often be avoided, however, by an immediate cry claiming immunity, eg by shouting *skinch* or *slips.* The second game, the hole game, *billy-hole, knuckpits* or *scophole,* consists of a progress from the base-line through a series of small holes in the ground.

The order of play is decided as in the ring game, and the progress from hole to hole is governed by a complicated system of rules varying from locality to locality. The third game, the line game, has a similar set of rules, but the target marbles are placed on a curved line, viz the *heel* or *score*, which is scored in the ground with a swing of the heel. The fourth game, the game of *hundreds, boss and span, holy bang,* or *langyspangy,* is normally played by two. Two marbles are held together and dropped from a certain height, so that when they hit the ground they are shot apart at 180 degrees. In turn the players now aim at one another's marble and score one hundred for a strike; the first to score one thousand wins a stake previously decided upon. In one form of the game, if a player's marble rolls so close to the other's marble that the distance can be spanned by the outspread hand, fifty is scored, for which reason the game is often called *boss* (ie strike) *and span,* or *knack and span.*

On the whole, the games receive their names from the marbles with which they are played. The marbles, in turn, fall into three categories, those which are named from the material from which they are made, eg *ally, clayer, marble, whinney,* those which are named from their appearance, eg *barrio, boss, peedee, ginger;* and those which are named from their function, eg *chuck, gull, knuck.* Apart from illogical combinations such as *glass-ally,* from *glass* and *alabaster,* there are several for which no origin is obvious, eg *stog, stonk, taw.* The reader will be able to perceive from the definition of the words listed below into which of these categories most of the words for marbles fall.

Several processes in the formation of marble words may be perceived. Many of the words have also diminutive forms in *-ie,* eg *stoggie, knuckies, blunchies,* in *-le,* eg *nickle, saggle, stoggle,* and *-ly,* eg *pottly, saggly.* There seems to be a tendency to substitute *g* for other consonants, eg *glag-ally, margle, ogle, stog,* and a vowel change to denote a slight change in meaning in *dogle, deegle.* Finally there is a kind of phonetic embroidery, eg *langyspangy, marrididdle, stonnacklerool.* It is possible to see traces of even closer relationships than I have indicated below, for instance, there may well be a connection between *bize* and *bizzing.* It is also noteworthy that most of the words for cheating by moving closer to the target than is allowed begin with *fu-, fo-,* eg *fob, fub, fudge, fulk, fullick, fullock, funks.*

In the list below, the abbreviations used are those used in the *New English Dictionary on Historical Principles* (OD) and Wright's *English Dialect Dictionary* (EDD). The orthography is that of the authority in which the word was found, or, where no authority is cited, is based on the orthography used by Wright.

The order of entry is as follows: i. The word; ii. The area in which it is found; iii. The definition; iv. The authority cited; v. Relevant comparisons; vi. The suggested etymology.

Note. A great many cries, eg *no moves, knockie twoses,* have been omitted from the list as being of little philological interest, but is it too rash to see in the credit given in marble games to a quick reply, a survival of the Scandinavian love of word contests and the favour given to a quick tongue, and a survival of the yet more primitive belief in the power of the spoken word ? Doubtless the traditions of juvenile games are very tenacious.

ALIBLASTER, sb, Gen dial. A large alabaster marble, EDD. A variant of *alabaster*, fr OFr *alabastre;* a spelling with intrusive *l* is common in the sixteenth to seventeenth centuries, and arises from confusion with *arblaster,* a crossbow-man; see OD sv and *arbalester.*

ALLY, sb1, Gen dial. An alabaster marble, a choice marble, EDD. An abbreviated form of *alabaster* (see above), first recorded 1720; see OD under *ally,* sb2.

ALLY, sb2, Gen dial. The game of marbles, EDD. Cf OD under *alley,* sense 4, a long narrow enclosure for playing bowls, skittles, etc; adopted from OFr *allée,* mod Fr *allée.*

ALLY-TAW, sb, Gen dial. An alabaster or glass marble, EDD. First recorded 1865, cf OD under *ally,* sb2 (see prec); the second element is of unknown origin, cf OD under *taw,* sb2; see also *taw* below. In the plural the word has a wide distribution in the sense of the game of marbles, cf EDD.

BACK-ALLEY, sb, Oxf. A stroke in which the marble rebounds from the wall before striking the target, EDD; formed of *back* (OE *bæc)* + *ally* (see above).

BACK-KNACKS, sb pl, Du. With the same sense as *back-alley* (above); formed *back* (see prec) + *knack,* knock, from ME *knak,* of echoic origin, cf OD sv.

BALSER, sb, Brks. The largest stone marble, about one inch in diameter, EDD. Cf *bull's-eye* (below).

BARRIO, sb, Sc. A glass marble decorated with bars of colour.

BEAKS, sb pl, Nhb. A punishment inflicted on the loser in a game of marbles by firing a marble at the knuckles, EDD.

BILL-SLIPS, phrase, Lancs. A cry claiming a replay when the marble slips from the fingers; alternatively *bills is* used, EDD

BILLY-HOLE, sb, Du. The hole game.

BLOOD-ALLEY, sb, Gen dial. A white *ally* (see above) streaked with red, EDD. Formed *blood* (OE *blod)* + *ally* (see above).

BLUNCH, v, Du. To move a marble by placing the side of the left foot next to it, striking the left foot with the right as in coming to attention. See OD under *blanch,* v2, sense 4, to turn away, used transitively. Of imitative origin.

BOLLY, sb, Yks. A steel ball-bearing used as a marble. Cf OD *boll,* sb, sense 4, a round knob (OE *bolla); boll,* sb2, a ball (OFr *boule).*

BOLLY, v, Du. To roll a marble off the palm of the hand (OFr *bouler).*

BOODIE, sb, Du. The ring in the ring game, also the game. Cf OD *brough* sb1, a halo around the moon; *brough* sb2, the ring which is the target in curling (ON *borg,* a round tower). Formed from confusion between *boorie* (see below) and *boodie,* Du dial, made of earthenware. Cf *penker-boody* (see below).

BIZE, sb, Yks. The base line in any game of marbles, EDD.

BIZZING, adj, Du. Of a marble, left in the ring or on the line after a stroke. Cf *bize* (see above).

BLOBBY-HOLE, sb, Du. The hole game. Formed *blob* (metathesis of *bubble*) + *hole*.

BOOL, sb, NCty. A marble, EDD. North dial form of *bowl* (OFr *boule*). The word is also found as *bools*, NCty, the game; *booler*, Inv, a large marble; *booley*, Corn, a very large marble.

BOORIE, sb, Nhb. The ring game, EDD. From ON *borg*, a round tower. Cf Prompt Parv *Burwhe*, cercle; see also *boodie* above. Also found in a metathesised form *brewery*.

BOSS, sb, Nhp. A large marble, EDD. From OFr *boce*, a protuberance.

BOSS, v, Ches, Notts, Leic. To strike one marble with another, EDD.

BOSS-AND-SPAN, sb, Gen dial. The game of hundreds. Formed *boss* (see prec) + *span*, to measure with the hand (OE *spannan*).

BRODGE, v, Lancs. To win all one's opponent's marbles, EDD.

BULK, v, Sc. To play at marbles, EDD. Contraction of *ballock*, a small ball, a marble, transferred to the act.

BULKIE, sb, Wig. The line game. EDD. Diminutive of *bulk* (see prec).

BULLOCKER, sb, Nhb. A very large marble, EDD. Formed from *ballock*.

BULL'S-EYE, sb, Yks. A white marble with circular rings of colour, EDD.

BUNGUMS, sb pl, Yks. The hole game, EDD. Formed from *bunghole*? Cf *bunhole* (see below).

BUNHOLE, sb, Yks. The hole game, EDD. Formed from bunghole.

BUNT, sb, Du. The baseline in all games. Cf OD *butt* sb, the boundary line in a game.

CAPEY-DYKEY, sb, Forfar? A game with marbles and caps, EDD. Formed *cap* (OE *cappa*) + *dyke* (ON *dik*, a ditch).

CAT-KNUCKLES, adj, Nhb. Applied to an awkward way of holding a marble, EDD.

CHUCK, sb, Dum, Yks, Lancs. A marble, EDD, OD. From ME *chock*, formed from ME *chocker*, to throw, from OFr *choquer*. Also found in Yks in the sense of the ring in the ring game.

CLAY, sb, Corn. A clay marble, EDD. Also in form *clayer*. From OE *clæg*.

COB, sb, Yks. A marble, also the game of marbles, EDD.

CODNEY, sb, Du. A home-made marble. Also in the form *cogney*. Cf Prompt Parv *Cod*, of mannys pryuyte, OE *codd*.

COMMONEY, sb, Gen dial. The commonest kind of marble, EDD, OD. First recorded 1837.

DEEGLES, sb pl, Ches. A name given to marbles which leave the area in which one game is played and become involved in a game being played nearby. These marbles are claimed as *deegles* to distinguish them from the *dogles* (see below) with which the games are being played. Apparently a deliberate change of the stem vowel of *dogles*.

DICKIE-EDGER, sb, Du. The marble on the end of the line in the line game. An arbitrary addition to *edge + er* of the name *Dickie*, but cf *dickie-(h)edger*, the hedge-sparrow.

DOG, v, Du. To win all one's opponent's marbles; also in the form *dogger*. Cf *doggered*, Cu, bankrupt.

DOGGIE, sb, Gen dial. An unglazed marble, EDD. A sense transferred from *doggar*, globular masses found in Yorks marble beds.

DOGS, sb pl, Du. The charitable return of a number of marbles to an opponent who has lost all his marbles in a game. It is not repeated a second time. Either a specialised sense of *doggie* (see prec), or a formation from *dog* (see above).

DRAKES, sb pl, Yks. The base line in any game, EDD. Cf OD *dreigh*, sbl, length, distance, extent. From OE *dragan*, to draw out, extend.

DREGS, sb pl, Yks. With the same sense as *drakes* (see prec).

FAT, adj, NCty. A marble is *fat* if, after a stroke, it is left in the ring or on the line, EDD, under *shot*, sense 5. From OFr *faute*, a fault.

FOG, interj, Gen dial. 'I'm first.' Found in many forms of which *foggie, foggie-fost, forrie* are the most common, EDD. Cf ME *foge*, due order *(Owl and the Nightingale*, ed Atkins), OE *gefog*, adjoining.

FOLLY-TAR, sb, Nhb. The game of hundreds, EDD. Formed *follow + taw* (see below).

FUB, v, Midl. To cheat by moving closer to the target, EDD. Formed from ME *fobbere*, from OFr *fobbe*, one who has been cheated, a fool.

FUDGE, v, Gen dial. With the same sense as *fub* EDD. Cf OD *fudge*, v, sense 1, b, to thrust in awkwardly.

FULK, v, SCty. With the same sense as *fub* (see above), EDD. First recorded 1784. Also found in the form *fullick*, in Du.

FUNKS, sb pl, Abd. A forward movement of the arm in firing a marble, EDD. Cf OD *funk*, v3, to kick.

GIDS, adj, Yks. Applied to marbles which are an equal distance from the target, EDD.

GINGER, sb, Cum. Red clay marble, EDD.

GLAGALLY, sb, Du. A glass marble. A distortion of *glass-ally*.

GLASSIE, sb, Gen dial. A glass marble, EDD. Diminutive of *glass*.

GULL, v, Suff. To strike a marble with another, EDD.

GULLSTONES, sb, Suff, Nrf. A game of marbles (the hole game?), EDD. Formed *gull* (ME *goul*, from OFr *goule*), a channel, + *stones*.

HEEL, sb, Du. The line in the line game, made with a swinging stroke of the *heel*.

HOB, v, Notts. To stop a marble with the foot, EDD. Cf EDD. *hob,* a boot.

HOLEY, sb, Du. The hole game. Diminutive of *hole.*

HOLY-BANG, sb, Gen dial. The game of hundreds. Formed *holy* (from prec) + *bang* of imitative origin. Note that in some forms of the game a hole is used.

HUNDREDS, sb pl, Gen dial. The game of hundreds, EDD. See introductory remarks for full description.

JARIE, sb, Sc. An earthenware marble, EDD. Diminutive of dialectal *jar,* earthenware.

KILLEMS-OUT, sb pl, Nrf. A marble game (the ring game ?), EDD.

KNACKERS, sb, NCty. The game of hundreds, EDD. Cf OD *knack,* v7, to strike together so as to produce a sharp, abrupt noise. From Dutch *knakken,* to knock.

KNACK-AND-SPAN, sb, War. The game of hundreds, EDD. Formed *knack* (see prec.) + *span,* to measure with the hand.

KNACKS, sb, Du. A method of commencing the game of hundreds in which two marbles are dropped together so that on striking the ground they fly apart. Cf OD *knack,* sb1, a sharp, sounding blow. From Dutch *knakke,* a knock.

KNOG, v, Lancs. A penalty incurred in a game in which a marble is fired at the knuckles, EDD. Cf Lancs. *knockus,* the knuckles.

KNUCK, sb, Yks. The hole game, EDD. Also found in the plural and in the combination *knuck-pits* in Cornwall, with the same sense. From ME *knoke,* the knuckle. A marble is fired by an increasing pressure between the knuckle of the thumb and the side of the forefinger.

KNUCKLE, sb, Yks. The hole game, EDD. From ME *knokyl,* diminutive of *knoke,* the knuckle.

KNUCKLE-DOWN, sb, NCty. A marble game, EDD. Cf OD sv. First recorded 1859. Formed *knuckle* (see prec) + *down.* Also found in Lancs in the form *knuckley.*

LACKY, interj, Yks. 'I' m last!' Found in several forms as below:
> *Lag,* Du.
> *Laggie,* Gen dial. A diminutive from prec.
> *Larrie,* Gen dial. A slurred pronunciation of prec found where *ferry* is used for 'I' m first! '
From ME *lag,* the last. Cf OD *lag,* sb1.

LAG, sb, Gen. A game of marbles, EDD. Cf OD sv. First recorded 1845 in form *lag-out.* Also found in form *laggie,* Cum., in the sense of the hole game, EDD

LIGGER, sb, Yks. The largest earthenware marble, EDD

LONG-TAWL, sb, Brks. The game of hundreds, EDD. Formed *long* + *taw,* with parasitic *l.*

MARBLE, sb, Gen. A small round earthenware, glass or clay ball used by children in certain games, EDD. First recorded 1694. From OFr *marbre*. Found in various forms as below:

Marable Shet, Yks, Der, Lancs. From prec with svarabhakti vowel, EDD

Marbae Perth. Diminutive of *marble*, EDD

Margle Du. Fr *marble* influenced by *muggle, muggie*,qv

Marl Midls. Fr *marble,* with loss of *b*, EDD

Marp Lancs. Fr *marble,* with unvoicing of *b* and loss of *l*, EDD

Marvel Gen dial. Fr *marble* with dissimilation, EDD

Muggle Du. Fr marble influenced by *muggie,* qv.

Muckle Abd. Possibly from *marble* influenced by Sc *Mickle Friday, Muckly Friday,* Good Friday, on which day marble contests are common.

MARRIDIDDLE, sb, Du. A home-made marble. A whimsical elaboration of *marble*, cf *stonnacklerool* (see below).

NAKE, sb, Du. A player 'has his nake' if he ends a game with the same number of marbles as he started with. Apparently not from ME *nok*, a share or part, which would give *niuk* in Du, but from a ME *nak*, with which cf OI *gnaga*, to gnaw, to cut out, Swed *nagg*, a notch; and note that the common method of counting was by cutting notches on a rod or stick.

NIEVE, sb, Abd. A surreptitious movement towards the target with intent to cheat, cf EDD under *funk.* From ON *hnef,* the fist.

NIGGIN, sb, Lancs. A marble, EDD. Cf Lancs. *nig,* a wooden ball.

OFF, sb, Dor. The base line in all games, EDD.

OFFMARK, sb, Lancs. The line game.

OLD-LASS, sb, Yks. The last hole in the hole game, EDD.

PAST, sb, Nhb. The base line in all games, EDD.

PEEDEE, sb, Nhb,Du. A very tiny marble, EDD. A sense transferred from *peedee*, a serving man, footboy, groom, cf OD, sv; in the nineteenth century on the River Tyne the boy on board a keel. From Latin *pede,* on foot.

PENKER, sb, NCty. A large stone or iron marble, EDD. Cf OD *pink,* v3, to make a tinkling noise; Dial *penkin,* a small piece of coal; Swed *pennka,* to strike softly. Also found in Nhb. as *panker.*

PENKER-BOODY, sb, Nhb, Du. The game of hundreds. Formed *penker* (see prec.) + *boodie,* earthenware.

PICKET, sb, Rxb. A penalty incurred in a game in which a marble is fired against the knuckles. Cf ME *picquet,* v, to punish by tying over a sharpened stake. From OFr *picque,* a point.

PIGGER, sb, Sc. An earthenware marble, EDD. Cf Sc. *pig,* adj, made of earthen ware. From ME *pigge,* of uncertain origin.

PIGRING, sb, Berks. The ring game, EDD. Formed *pig* (see prec) + *ring.*

PIPER, sb, Abd. A *pipeclay* marble.

PLUGGY, sb, Yks. A large pottery marble, EDD. Cf *plug,* Yks, a small lump (of clay).

POP-ALLY, sb, Gen dial. A frosted glass marble, EDD. Formed *pop,* an effervescent drink, + *ally* (see above). Bottles of 'pop' were stoppered with small glass balls which could be used as marbles when the bottles were broken.

POPPO, sb, Gen dial. With the same sense as *pop-ally.* An elaboration of *pop.*

POT-ALLY, sb, Gen dial. A large pottery marble, EDD. Formed *pot* + *ally* (see above).

POT-DONNICK, sb, Yks. With the same sense as *pot-ally.* Also found as *pot-dummock.*

POT-QUOIT, sb, Nhb. With the same sense as *pot-ally.* A specialised use of OD *quoit,* sb3, sense 3, any object which is thrown. From ME *coyt,* of uncertain origin.

POTTY, sb, Nhb. A large pottery marble. Diminutive of *pot.*

PURL, v, Du. To roll a marble off the palm of the hand towards the line to decide the order of play. Cf OD *pirl,* v, 2, to throw or toss with a spinning motion.

PURLEY, sb, Nhb. The line game, EDD. From prec.

RENTS, interj, Yks. A cry on seeing someone stealing marbles, EDD.

SAGGY, sb, Cum. The hole game, EDD.

SCOGGERED, adj, Du. Having lost all one's marbles. Distortion of *doggered* (see above)?

SCOPHOLE, sb, Cum. A game played in holes made close to a wall, EDD. Cf OD *scope,* sb2, sense 2, a mark for shooting or aiming at. From Italian *scopa.* Cf also dialectal *scop,* a potsherd.

SCORE, sb, Lin. The baseline, EDD.

SCORIE, sb, Renfrew. The line game, EDD. From prec.

SCRAB, v, Yks. To steal marbles, EDD. From Dutch, *schrabben,* to grab.

SEG, interj, Du. 'I'm second!' From dial *segn,* pronunciation of *second.*

SHIRLEY, v, NCty. To roll a marble off the palm of the hand towards the line to decide the order of play, EDD. Cf Ger dial *schurren,* to slide off.

SHONK, v, Yks. To lose all one's marbles in one game, EDD. Cf OD *shonk, v,* to shatter, and dial. *shonker,* Yks, to go bankrupt.

SHUNKERT, adj, Sc. Having lost all one's marbles, EDD. From prec.

SHORE, sb, Loth. The ring game, EDD, sv *shore,* sb1, sense 4.

SHUVVY-HOLE, sb, Berks. The hole game, EDD. Formed from diminutive of *shove,* to push, + *hole.*

SKIN-THE-LINE, v, Du. To remove all the marbles on the line at one try.

SKINNED, adj, War. Having no marbles left, EDD. Also in form *skint,* Du. (Past participle of *skin,* to denude).

SKINCH, interj., Du. A cry claiming immunity from a penalty for an offence just committed, EDD.

SKINCH, v, Yks. To move a marble closer to the ring with intent to cheat, EDD

SPANGY, v, Du. The game of hundreds, EDD. From OE *spannan,* to stretch, clasp. See introductory remarks for description of the game.

SPANK, v, Lancs. To fire a marble, EDD.

SPANNIMS, sb, EAng. The game of hundreds, EDD. Formed *span* (OE *spannan,* see prec) + *ems* (them(s)).

STANCE, sb, Sc. The base line, EDD. From OFr *estance.*

STEELY, sb, Gen dial. A steel ball-bearing used as a marble.

STODGER, sb, Yks. A common earthenware marble. Cf *stodge,* Yks., rough and coarse, strongly made.

STOG, sb, Yks. A stone marble, EDD. Either a corruption of *stone,* or from prec.

STONEY, sb, Gen dial. A stone marble, EDD. Diminutive of *stone.* Also in the compound *stoney-marvel, Cu;* formed *stoney* (see above) + *marvel (marble,* see above).

STONEDY, sb, Sc. A stone marble. A corruption of *stone* (see above).

STONK, sb, Lancs. A marble, the stake in a game, the game of marbles, EDD.

STONNACKLEROOL, sb, Ches. A stone marble, EDD. A whimsical elaboration of *stone* (see above).

STRAND, sb, Sc. The base line, EDD. A specialised sense of *strand,* a stretch of ground, cf OD sv From OE *strand* .

TARLIES, interj, Du. A cry claiming advantage of a marble's position which would otherwise result in a penalty. Formed *taw* (see below) + *lies.*

TAW, sb, Gen dial. A marble, usually the best in the player's possession, EDD. Also used in the sense of the game of marbles, and the base line. First recorded 1709. Etymology obscure, cf OD sv. Found generally in compounds *taw-ally,* formed *taw* + *ally* (see above); *taw-laking,* formed *taw* + *laking,* playing; *taw-line* formed *taw* + *line,* the baseline.

TRIGGING, adj, Du. Cheating by moving the marble closer to the target. Cf OD *trig.* v2, dial, to make a score on the ground for a player at bowls, quoits, etc. From ON *tryggr,* steady, reliable ?

WHINNEY, sb, Sc. Du. A white marble. From *whin,* a white stone. NB Jamieson suggests ON *hwyna,* to whir in flight.

(1948)

OATBREAD
F W Moody

One afternoon in October of this year (1949) I was drinking a cup of tea in the kitchen of a farm near Addingham (three miles north-west of Ilkley, in the West Riding of Yorkshire) when the farmer, who had been sitting by the fire puffing at his pipe, stood up and reached towards the beams of the ceiling. 'A this wi' a bit o' butter on', he said, and handed me a piece of oatbread.[1] I ate it, my head tilted back. For what I saw I cannot do better than quote what I read later in Frederic Montagu's *Gleanings in Craven*, written in 1838:

> Here, as throughout the whole district of Craven, in every house, from the rich man's to that of the labourer who contributes to his wealth, the stranger will be much struck with what at first sight has the appearance of pieces of dried wash leather,[2] placed upon a wooden frame pendant from the ceiling of the kitchen by four iron staples. This useful machine is called a 'fleeok',[3] and is generally made of ash or deal. It is rarely ever painted, and the bars are lozenge-shaped, the better to hold the 'oat-cake', for the reception of which it is made.[4] (p13)

This link with the experience of another traveller, 111 years previously, led me into an investigation of the history of oatbread-making in the Addingham area and an examination of its terminology.

Until the early years of the nineteenth century oats was the principal cereal grown in West Yorkshire. George Walker (from whose book, *The Costume of Yorkshire,* the illustration of the woman making oat-cakes is taken) wrote in 1814:

> With perhaps the exception of some parts of Lancashire, it [oatbread] is almost exclusively made in the West Riding of Yorkshire, and constitutes the principal food of the labouring classes in that district. (p27)

A History of the Typhus of Hepstonstall-Slack, 1843-4,[5] thus describes the conditions in the home of a hand-loom weaver:

> It may fairly be said oatmeal and potatoes are well nigh what they contrive to exist upon ... The dinner consists of small pieces of suet fried with the addition of water and salt; a quantity of boiled potatoes is now added ... This with a portion of oaten bread constitutes the dinner ... The tea and supper are united so as to form one meal, which is ordinary oatmeal porridge, old milk and oaten bread. (p57)

In and around Addingham it appears that the oatbread has for a long time been of the type I saw hanging from the 'fleeok' in the farmer's kitchen. An essential feature of its manufacture was, and still is, that the mixture is *thrown* on to a hot 'bakstone'.[6] The throwing gives the bread its necessary thinness — about a quarter of an inch when moist and an eighth of an inch when dried — and produces an oval cake about twenty inches long and five inches broad. The first description of the making of oatbread which I have been able to find is in Walker's *Costume* previously referred to:

> Some dry meal is sifted upon a flat board, and a ladleful of the mixture poured over it. The cake is formed and brought to a proper size and thickness by a circular horizontal movement of the board as here represented. It is then laid upon what is termed the Backstone, or hot hearth, to bake, which does not require many seconds of time, and afterwards placed upon a cloth to cool. An inverted chair, as seen in the Plate, frequently serves this purpose. The cakes are then hung upon a frame, called a Bread Creel,[7] suspended from the ceiling of almost every cottage in the district. (p27)

Walker's statement that the cakes were *laid* upon the bakstone, and his use of the word 'creel' without 'flake', suggest that his illustration was made at some distance from Addingham — probably near Halifax or Huddersfield, for these places are named further on in his text (p28).[8] Montagu exactly places his own description — at Bolton Abbey, three miles north of Addingham; and his description accords much more closely with later methods of oatbread-making in the Addingham area:

> These cakes are made of oat-meal and water or buttermilk ... The meal is generally mixed the night before in the kneading-tub ... The tub, which is kept expressly for the purpose, is rarely ever cleansed with water, but merely partially scraped out with a knife. The particles adhering to the sides ferment, and cause the next quantity of meal put into the tub to rise more speedily... On the morning of baking, the backstone (formerly a slate,[9] but now invariably a plate of iron let into a frame-work of bricks over a stove) is thoroughly cleansed — a fire is lighted and kept at a mean temperature — near to it a table is placed, and beside it on a chair is the kneading-tub with the ladle in it, and the meal ready for use ... A flat piece of wood, about seventeen inches square, with lines scored upon it cross-ways, called a backboard,[10] is sprinkled with some dry meal — the hand is then moved over the surface of the board in a circular direction, leaving an area of meal in the centre, upon which a ladleful from the kneading-tub is poured. The board being lifted off the table, is shaken with both hands, and the meal obeying the rotatory motion, spreads in a circular form — this is transferred to a piece of thin linen, or at times cartridge paper, called the 'turning-off', resting on a smooth board called a spittle,[11] very similar to the backboard in shape, having the addition of a handle and an edge of iron — the cake is then with a strong jerk thrown laterally upon the backstone and the linen is taken up — this

movement requires great dexterity, as the length of the cake proves the efficiency of the baker. After baking for a minute, the spittle is put in request in turning it — another minute completes the baking, and the cake is placed on one of the bars of the 'fleeok', its shape being oval and from half to three-quarters of a yard long. (p15)

I turn to oatbread-making as carried on now or within living memory.

Montagu's description adds special interest to an old bakstone at Barden Scale, which is two miles north of Bolton Abbey and therefore five miles north of Addingham. The bakstone is in the smaller of two kitchens in an old farmhouse. It has been out of use since 1921; that is, since the death, at the age of eighty-five, of an old gentleman who demanded oatbread for supper, and often for breakfast and tea. He remembered the days when white bread was seen only on Sundays. The present occupants remember oatbread being made, though some details are uncertain. The meal was kept in an ark[12] — and perhaps, very long ago, in a magnificent oak 'kist'[13] which is now in another part of the house. The dough[14] was mixed in an earthenware bowl on the night before baking. Buttermilk was used. When the dough stiffened, a 'witch's cross'[15] was drawn across it with a finger.

The rest of the operations were very much as in Montagu's time though the spittle, which is still preserved, appears to have been used only for throwing, not for turning; and the 'bakboard' was not known by this name but was called a riddling-board.[16] The finished product was called 'oatbread', 'riddlebread', or 'haverbread'. The bakstone rests upon two thick columns of local gritstone.[17] A bread-flake, exactly like the one described by Montagu but now used only for drying clothes, still hangs in the wide passage outside the kitchen.

Oatbread was last made in Addingham about twenty-five years ago, at a farm-house on Addingham Moor. It was made in an out-house which has since been destroyed, together with the equipment which was in it. The existence of the equipment can be traced back to about 1880, before which date it is lost in obscurity. The oatbread was made almost entirely for sale, not, as at Barden, for home consumption only. Two iron bakstones, side by side, were heated by two separate fires. Brickwork supported the bakstone and enclosed the fireplaces. One of the bakstones was kept at a higher temperature than the other. By the other side of the hotter bakstone was a fixed table which held a canvas belt between rollers. The oatmeal was taken from a wooden bin[18] and mixed by hand in a wooden knead-kit.[19] The mixing took place early in the morning; meal, yeast and water are the only ingredients remembered. The mixture, now called dough, was allowed to stand for an hour while the bakstones became hot. Their temperature was tested by sprinkling a pinch of meal[20] on them and noting how long it took to brown. A tin ladle,[21] holding about half a pint, was dipped into the kneadkit and a portion of the dough was 'teemed'[22] on to the riddling board, on which dry oatmeal had been sprinkled. The dough was 'reeled'[23] on the board (which was made of hard wood — oak or chestnut), then dropped on to the canvas belt. A handle connected with the rollers — the details are forgotten — was then pulled over smartly and the carriage holding the belt shot forward, along rails, throwing the dough into a long oval piece on the nearer bakstone. In less than a minute the bread was ready to be moved. The blade of a long knife[24] was slid underneath to loosen it. It was then picked up by the fingers, turned over, and placed on the second bakstone. From there it was moved to a table to cool and the pieces were eventually piled in dozens. A dozen sold for about sixpence.

The first bakstone required a 'face'. Brown sugar[25] was sprinkled on the *warm* bakstone and a piece of suet was rubbed over it. The bakstone was then polished with a cloth until it was smooth or 'snod'.[26] Every few minutes during baking the face was rubbed with a cloth on which was a little 'saim'.[27]

The oatbread was packed in a long box which was placed in a 'trap'[28] and covered with oilcloth. The baker had a round which took in the triangle Adding-ham–Steeton–Ilkley Moor, the area being in part determined by other bakers' rounds. Many of the farms visited were far from the road and the baker's son carried oatbread to them in a basket. At such places, which received no newspapers and few letters, he was regarded as an authority on the world's news and he was not allowed to hurry away. Very often he was asked to hang the oatbread on the flake; I suspect that this was a ruse for trapping him indoors. It was a busy and wearing life. 'Ye 'ad to be nimble',[29] said one who had seen much of it.

The oatbread which I myself saw at Addingham had been bought at Skipton on market day (six pieces for elevenpence-halfpenny). Until five years ago there were two old-established oatbread businesses in Skipton. One of the bakers died, and his equipment was destroyed or dispersed, in accordance with his own expressed wish. This baker was conservative in his methods — and incidentally very successful.

He used only one bakstone, which had no 'face'. He poured the dough from a ladle on to a circular piece of flannel which rested on the spittle. Then he threw the dough, together with the flannel, along the bakstone. The flannel fell on the bakstone at a distance from the dough, and was then replaced on the spittle ready to be thrown again with the next measure of dough. When the cakes were baked they were cooled for a few minutes on a 'creel'[30] or 'cratch'.[31] This was a wooden frame about the size and shape of a camp-bed, strung with string or 'band'.[32] The oatbread maker who is still active in Skipton took over the business from a much older man about two years ago. If anyone is tempted to think that oatbread baking is an unskilled occupation he should have a talk with the man who now runs the business. As this may seem to suggest that his products are below standard, I hasten to add that my farmer friend at Addingham buys some every week, and there is no better authority to be found anywhere. This baker uses a bakstone which is said to be a hundred years old. The iron plate was once finely ribbed but indications of this are to be seen now only at the corners. It is heated by gas jets, which have recently replaced the coal fire. The front, back, and sides are of cast

Making oatbread.

iron; on one side of the fire-place stand out the words: 'Joseph Wright, Patent, Shipley'; and on the other side: 'Evil to them that evil think'.

My account has centred on Addingham; Otley is rather outside my narrow picture, but my experience there is worth telling because it shows very clearly how dialect words die. I talked with a man between thirty and forty years old who had stopped making oatbread about eighteen months ago. He was the last man to make it in Otley. He had taken over the business from his father, who was now old and ill — too ill to be interviewed. The son was anxious to be helpful. He spoke of the steam-heated hot-plate, now used only for muffins and crumpets. He knew that oatbread used to be hung up near the ceiling. Words like 'bakstone', 'spittle' and 'bread flake' were either unknown or so vaguely remembered that they would not come to mind without prompting.

Yes, one by one the fires under the bakstones are going out for the last time, oatbread is something of a curiosity, and words which were once common currency are forgotten. But today there are still many whose memories are quickened at the sight or mention of oatbread. They tell you about the best way to eat it: moist or dry; with butter, cheese, jam, or wrapped round a cut from the joint; soaked in the rich gravy in the tin which stood under the leg of lamb as it twisted on a jack before a roaring fire; broken up in hot milk with salt and pepper to taste. Only the happy days are remembered. Oatbread was given away in country inns on Saturday nights, with cheese or soup. There used to be 'bits o' feasts'[33] in many farmhouses in the days when people made their own fun. A 'sheep-head'[34] broth with plenty of oatbread in it would provide the main dish, and afterwards there might be a bit of dancing in a 'chamber',[35] a concertina providing the music. Those days are gone; and Addingham is no longer the 'fearful spot for oatbread'[36] it used to be.

This little investigation has been of great interest to me; narrowly (if you wish to put it so), as a student of language; more broadly, as one of the many who like to know how people lived and how they live now. The terms employed have their own interest. 'Bakstone' needs no comment. 'Creel' and 'reel' appear in particular senses apparently peculiar to West Yorkshire. 'Bread' and 'cake' are differentiated in an unusual way. In many houses the frame on which clothes are hung to dry is called a 'bread-flake' even though it is no longer used for its original purpose. The word 'spittle' is seen undergoing a change of meaning; first used for turning the oatbread, the spittle is later used also for throwing the dough on to the bakstone and finally it is used for throwing only, its shape remaining the same but its function changing.

Finally, if there are still any who think that dialect investigation is a dull and soulless occupation, let me assure them that they are about as wrong as they can be. My inquiry, besides bringing to light much of dialectal interest that I have not been able to include in this article, has had its illuminating and often amusing moments. I have picked up many odds and ends of information, from particulars of a typhus epidemic a hundred years ago to the right and only way of holding a concertina. I have been mistaken for a government official, journalist, antique dealer, would-be purchaser of a bakery, and commercial traveller (twice — for bakers' equipment and for patent medicine). And everywhere I have met the kindness and good humour which flourish best in country places.

I gratefully acknowledge assistance from the people and sources already mentioned, and from the following books and articles: W B Crump, *The Little Hill Farm*, reprinted from *Transactions of the Halifax Antiquarian Society*, 1938, pp115-196; 'DM', 'The Oatcake Maker of Skipton' (*Dalesman*, July 1942); Ella Pontefract, 'Oatcake' (*Dalesman*, Sept 1943); J Walton, 'Yorkshire Fireside Survivals' (*Yorkshire Life*, July-Sept 1947). I also thank Mr J Ogden, curator of Keighley Museum, for his help in this as in other inquiries. The Keighley Museum has a good display of old oatbread-making equipment. And to Mr R Ellis of Skipton I owe special thanks for a perfect demonstration of how oatbread is made to-day.

(1949)

[1] [oət briəd] 'oatbread' (OE *ate* + OE *bread*). Other names are [oat keək] 'oatcake-, [havə briad] 'haverbread', [avə keək] 'havercake', [ridl briəd] 'riddlebread', and, jocularly, [snap an krakl] 'snap and crackle'. 'Cake' is probably from ON *kaka*, 'haver' is from ON *hafre*, and 'riddle' from OE *hriddel*.

I use the form 'oatbread' deliberately. Among older dialect speakers in the Addingham area 'oat' is far more common than 'haver', and 'bread' is more common than 'cake'. Older people preserve a distinction between [briəd] 'bread', and [keək] 'cake'. [briəd] with no qualifying word is oatbread, while [keək] with no qualifying word is wheat bread. See EDD, cake, sbl, 2.

[2] Cf William Carr's *Dialect of Craven* , 1828, Vol II, p300: 'he teuk 'em, as they laid at fleeak, for round bits o' leather'.

[3] [fliək] 'flake' (perhaps ON *flake*).

[4] It is put on the flake to dry.

[5] By R Howard. Published by W Garforth of Hebden Bridge (1844). Heptonstall is in the West Riding, fourteen miles south-south-west of Addingham.

[6] [bakstən] spelt variously 'bakstone', 'backstone', 'bakestone' (OE *bacan* + OE *stan*). Early bakstones were, of course, slabs of stone. See note 9.

[7] [kri:l] 'creel'. Etymology uncertain. This word is sometimes used at Addingham in place of [fliak] 'flake'. 'Creel' in this particular sense appears to be confined to W Yks. See EDD, *creel* sbt, 2, and note 30 of this article.

[8] Cf Alfred Easther's *Glossary of the Dialect of Almondbury and Huddersfield* (EDS, 1883): 'Leather-cake: It was formerly the custom to make some oatcakes not *thrown* as usual but simply *reeled*'.

[9] The type of stone used is generally referred to as 'mudstone'. The quarrying of bakstones was concentrated at Delph near Saddleworth, but there were other sources: it is noteworthy that within a quarter of a mile of Bolton Abbey there is a farm marked *Baxonstone Cliff* (1843) and *Bakestone Cliff* (1867). Mudstone alternates with gritstone in this area. See note 17.

[10] OE *bacan* + OE *bord*. I have never heard the word used in this sense. [ridlinbɔəd] 'riddling-board' is now used. See also note 16.

[11] [spitl] 'spittle', a spade or small spade. See OED, sb² (OE *spitel).*

[12] [a:k] 'ark': a chest, box (OE *arc).*

[13] [kist] 'kist', northern form of 'chest'. Cf ON *kista.*

[14] [dɔəf] 'dough' (OE *dah*) .

[15] Easther (see note *8)* tells of a baker who plunged his knife into dough which would not stiffen. The local witch appeared next day with her arm in a sling.

[16] ['ridlin bɔəd] 'riddling-board'. Cf 'riddle', a coarse sieve (OE *hriddel).* The motions of using a sieve and a riddling-board are very similar.

[17] ['gritstən] 'gritstone' (OE *greot* + OE *stan).* Cf note 9.

[18] [bin] 'bin' (OE *binn* or ON *bing-r).* See OED *bin* and *bing,* sbl.

[19] [neid kit] 'knead-kit', 'knade-kit', 'nakit' (OE *cnedan* + ?MDu *kitte).*

[20] [miəl + meil] 'meal' (OE *melo).* The form [meil] is heard most often in the combination [ɔətmeil] 'oatmeal'. The dialect thus differentiates between [meil] 'meal', 'grain', and [miəl] 'meal', customary occasion of taking food (OE *mæl),* which is never heard as [meil].

[21] [ladl] 'ladle' (OE *hlædel).*

[22] [ti:m] 'teem', 'pour out' (ON *taema).*

[23] [ri:l] 'reel', 'cause to roll'. See OED, vl, 8. Of uncertain origin. 'Reel', in connection with making oatbread, appears to be restricted to West Yorkshire. See EDD *reeling* and cf note 7.

[24] Designed to keep the hand away from the bakstone, the shaft of the blade being turned through two right-angles.

[25] [siugə] 'sugar' (OFr *sucre).*

[26] [snɔd] 'snod', 'smooth' (?ON *snoðinn).*

[27] [seəm] 'saim', 'lard' (OFr. *saim).*

[28] [trap] 'trap', two-wheeled horse carriage (OE *trappe).*

[29] [jad tə bi niml].

[30] [kri:l] 'creel'. Cf note 7. OED, under *creel,* sb3, gives 'A framework, varying in form according to its purpose'. Compare the description of this creel with the creel in the illustration.

[31] [kratʃ] 'cratch'. At Addingham a [kratʃ] is usually a strong low framework on which pigs are killed or sheep are sheared.

[32] [band] 'band', 'cord' (ON *band).*

[33] [bits ə fiəsts].

[34] [ʃi:p iəd].

[35] [tʃeimə] 'chamber'. See EDD, sb, 1, 'An upper room, either in a bouse or outbuilding'.

[36] [fiəfl spɔt fər ɔət briəd]. Here [fiəfl] means 'remarkable', 'noteworthy'.

THE FARM-CART
Annie E Langrick

Of the many and varied implements to be found on any farm, perhaps one of the most useful is the common farm-cart. Whether a farm is predominantly concerned with the rearing of cattle or the growing of crops, some form of transport is essential.

Each type of farm has particular kinds of wagons for specific purposes, for example the milk-float of the dairy farm, or the four-wheeled hay-wain to be seen in Gloucestershire and elsewhere. Nevertheless, for general purposes, the ordinary two-wheeled cart is to be found everywhere, and it shows considerable uniformity throughout the country. This, together with its ubiquity, makes it an ideal medium for the study of dialectal English.

Although an apparently simple object, it is composed of many individual parts each of which has its own technical name. These names are peculiar to the farming community and have thus been comparatively uninfluenced by the Standard Language. It is in such words that the genuine dialect is likely to be preserved longest.

Below is a list of the names of the parts of a cart that are used in Bubwith, a village in the East Riding of Yorkshire:

The Body

'*sole*'. One of the four longitudinal beams which are fastened beneath the body of the cart to strengthen it. (F *sole*.)

'*ligger*'. The beam across the front and back of the cart at the top of the body. (Not recorded in this sense, but probably based on OE *licgan.)*

'*sliver*'. The same meaning as 'ligger' above. (Not recorded in this particular sense, but possibly from OE *slīfan.)*

'*evering*'. The top ridge along each side of a cart. (OED records it as 'the rounds of a wagon', says it is obsolete, but gives no etymology.)

'*? hay-brede*'. The beam at the front and back of the cart at the bottom of the body. (Not recorded in this sense. The second element is perhaps from OE *Craedu*, 'breadth'.)

'*dog*'. The bumper of the cart on which it rests when the cart is 'tipped up' in order to empty it. (Perhaps from LOE *docga,* previous history unknown. This sense is not recorded in the OED.)

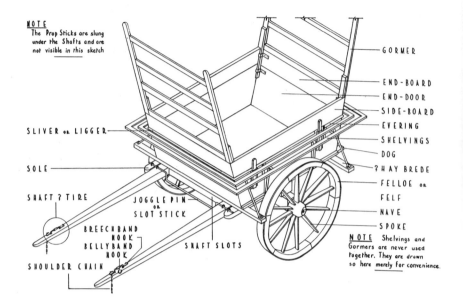

The parts of a farm-cart.

'end-door'. The detachable piece which forms the back of the body. (OE *ende*, 'end', + OE *duru*, 'door'.)

Extensions to the Body

These are used in order to increase the carrying capacity of the cart.

'side-boards'. Boards about eight inches wide which can be fixed to the front and sides of the cart (OE *sīde*, 'side', + OE *bord*, 'board'.)

'end-board'. A board, similar to a 'side board', which is fitted onto the back of a cart. (OE *ende*, 'end', + OE *bord*, 'board'.)

'shelvings'. Horizontal rails fixed on all sides of the cart. They are used especially for carrying hay or corn. (From 'shelf' sb, apparently adapted from (M)LG *schelf*, cognate with OE *scylfe*, of uncertain meaning.)

'gormers'. Upright rails fixed on the front and back of a cart. These are also used for carrying corn and hay. (Not recorded in the OED.)

The Shaft (OE *sceaft*)

'shaft-slots'. The transverse pieces of wood between the shafts, near the body of the cart. (OE *sceaft*, + OFr *esclot*, of obscure origin.)

'shaft-tire'. The three hooks on the shaft. (Not recorded in this sense.)

'joggle-pin'. The rod which is removed in order to 'tip up', ie empty the cart. (Origin uncertain, perhaps from 'jog' = 'jag', a projection.)

'*slot-stick*'. Same meaning as 'joggle-pin', though perhaps originally the latter referred to a pin and the former to a rod. (The first element is from OFr *esclot.*)

'*prop-stick*'. The two prop-sticks are fastened to the shafts of the cart, and used to support the shafts when the horse is removed and the cart is to remain in a horizontal position. (cp MDu and Mod Du *proppe* = 'vine support'.)

The Wheel

'*strake*'. Before the hoop, the iron rim round the wheel, came into use, the wheel was covered with numerous sections of iron, each one a 'strake'. (ME *strake*, apparently belonging to a Teutonic root **strak-.*)

'*felloe*'. Each section of a wooden wheel. (OE *felg*.)

'*to sole a wheel*'. To make the wood even and smooth, before the hooping process begins.

'*spoke*'. (OE *spaca.*)

'*tenor*'. The projecting part of the spoke which fits into the felloe. (Corrupt form of 'tenon', adapted from Fr *tenon.*)

'*tang*'. The same meaning as 'tenor'. (Adapted from ON *tange* = 'point, spit of land'.)

'*nave*'. (OE *nafa, nafu.*)

'*to stoke a nave*'. To make the holes in the nave into which the spokes fit. (Perhaps from OFr *estoquier.*)

'*linch-pin*'. The peg that used to pass through the 'arm' of the axle and kept the wheel in position. In the former the first element is from OE **lynis,* in the latter from 'lin' from ?OE **lyne.*)

'*collect and pin*'. This now performs the function of the old-fashioned 'linch-pin'. (OFr *collet.*)

'*bush*'. The metal lining of the axle-hole of the wheel. (Adapted from MDu *busse.*)

'*axle-tree*'. The axle. (ON *öxul-tre.*)

'*clout*'. A plate of iron on the axle to prevent wear. (OE *clut.*)

'*strap*'. The end of the axle that continues a little way into the 'bed piece' or centre part of the axle. (Not recorded in this specific sense.)

'*hurter*'. The strengthening piece on the shoulder of the axle. (From Fr *hurtoir,* from *hurter* 'to strike'.)

(1949)

DEATH AND ANNIE MARIA

Eh Nu'ss, it's tha! Eh Nu'ss, Ah's pleased tha's coom — Ah feel reight aht o' mysen, Ah dew that. It's mi rigg at maks me wankly-lahk, it warks that bad! Ah'd getten t gangerine i' mi fooit, tha knaws, an' they tewk mi leg off … bud they cann't tak me rigg off, can they, Nu'ss! Leastways nett this side o' t' grave!

Eh, Ah 'ed a reight bit o' fun wi' 'em all in t' Infermerry, Ah did that! Ah 'ed ter keep 'em cheerful, tha knaws. Theer wor all o' three doctors coom ter lewk at mi owd fooit — reight serious-lahk; so Ah ses tiv them: 'Nah then, lads', Ah ses, 'Ah'm noan bahn 'oam on mi two feet *this* tahm', Ah ses; 'so Ah'm tellin' yer', Ah ses. 'Ah'm fair sick an' stalled o' yon bad 'un', Ah ses, 'an so wud ye be ef it wor yorn. Ah reckon Ah'm noan ower grand i mysen', Ah ses, 'Bud ef it's reight bi ye, it'll bi reight bi me; an' ef it's wreng, Ah'll noan bi t' one ter natter, this side o' t' grave ner yet on t' other.'

So they tewk it off, an t' Sister ses! 'It's all over now, Dear.' 'Ah knaw, luv', Ah tellt her; 'Ah 'eard yer chuck mi owd fooit in t' bucket, so yer can't kid me on that rooad!' Eh, they did laff at me!

Next mornin' t' eead doctor-chap cooms rahnd t' wards wi' t' Sister. By! Bi' t' carry-on they mad fer 'im, 'e mwot ha' bin t' Lord Almighty Hissen.

'Nah then, Mrs. Binks', ee ses, 'An' how are we?'

'Ah's reight eniff', Ah ses, '*an* smilin' yet. Did yer reckon ter finnd me roarin' lahk a barn ?' Ah ses tiv 'im. 'Eff ye did, ye're mistakken — Ah'm noan that sooart!'

Laff! They fair brasst wi' laffin' at me … bud Ah kept theer spirits oop in theer, Ah did that!

'*How* old are you, Mrs. Binks ?', he ses.

'Eighty-three coom September, young man', Ah tellt him, 'An' Ah've seen more mucky days in mi tahm than all t' lot of yer standin' on yer 'eeads, an' Ah'm laffin' yet', Ah ses. Ah 'ed ter keep 'em gooin', doosta see? …

Eh Nu'ss, Ah dew feel badly … Hod mi hand ageean whol this lot's ower, willta? … Ah get reight muzzy efter these 'ere dews, Nu'ss; th'll nivver credit it, bud a bit back Ah thowt Ah seed Ahr lahtle lad i' t' door-oil theer — 'im at we lost wi' t' fever. It wor nobbut a bo'd on t' doorstun, an' it fliew up an' left t' dark shadder of its wings on t' wall, lahk it mowt ha' bin t' Angil o' Deeath fotchin' me.

Ah reckon Ah'll noan last ser lang, Nu'ss; Ah can feel mysen slippin'-lahk … Nay nah, Ah doant want ner doctor ner t' Passon nawther — Doctor wants 'is beauty sleep, po'r lad. 'E's ower threng fotchin fowk *inter* t' wo'ld, leave by shoovin 'ov 'em aht. An' Ah reckon t' Lord 'll appreciate mi sins an' mi short-comin's baht t' Passon's help. Ah'll nett 'eve bin *that* bad, takkin' all wi' all — Ah doan't call ter mind at Ah've played a mean trick on onnybody — not at Ah knaw on, lahk ...

Theer wor yon lad in t' fusst war — thra Canida he wor — 'E'd lost is wife back 'oam, 'ad t' lad, an' 'e 'adn't weer ter lay 'is eead bud on my breast. Passon 'ud call it a sin o' th' flesh ... bud it worn't ... nett that one ... Passon's nivver 'ad ter shift fer hissen baht 'oam an' fowks lahk t' Lord an the lad had onceover. Cansta see yon photigraph on t' dresser, Nuss? Ah cann't thoil ter see it reight missen some road — it's all dimmery-lahk — It's 'is lad, bud it 'ud dew fer 'im t' way 'e wor then. He's bin a grand son ter me, Nu'ss; nivver once chucked it i' mi teeth at 'e didn' knaw 'is dad ... best o' t' bunch, 'e wor ...

Hod mi 'eead a bit, Nu'ss, it's warkin' ageean ... Nay, Ah willent ligg mi dahn! Ef Ah can sit up ter welcome t' squire, Ah'll sit up fer t' Lord an' all! ... Ah wunner, couldsta thoil ter lewk ter mi owd cat, Nu'ss, tha er thi sister ? Missis Brahn, 'ere, reckons shoo can't abide its yowlin', bud it onnly yowls 'cos t' vary sahnd an' smell o' Missis Brahn puts it past itself. Ah'd ha lahked owd Moses ter've ganned at front o' me, bud t' Lord God is merciful, even wi' Tom cats, so Ah mun see an trust Him ...

Eh, an' theer's Martha, Nu'ss! Her an' me's bin thicker ner twins this sixty year, an' Ah'm fleered ter leave 'er with hersen. Ah can call ter mind onceover she wor i' terrible trouble, an' t' thowt o' tellin' her mother wor nigh killin' 'er. Ah wor weshin at Monda mornin' when Ah 'eeard 'er shahtin' o' me: 'Annie Maria! Annie Maria!' An' Ah ses: 'Hod on, Ah'm coomin', Lass!' An' wi' that Ah drops t' peggy an' sets off laupin' fer t' river more 'n a mile off. Did ivver yer hear t' lahks o' yon! An' when Ah wor getten theer, all flummoxed an' aht o' puff, Ah seed summat liggin' on t' benk, an' mi heart tu'ned ower i' mi breast. It wor Martha sowsed wi river watter, an' coomin aht ev a swound. Shoo lewks at me, despert-lahk, an' shoo ses: 'Annie Maria, Annie Maria! Whyfor cudn't tha let me be? Ah'd ha' doon it bud fer thee! Ah'd coom nigh on ter t' deepest bit when tha sed: 'Od on, Ah'm coomin', Lass! an' lugged me backards bi' t sku'tt' ... Did ivver yer hear t' likes o' yon!

Ah tewk 'er 'oam 'an 'er mother wor reight grand wi' 'er, an' Ah've sed nowt tiv 'er ner onnibody, then ner since . . us's bin thicker ner twins this sixty year ... Nay! Eff it inn't ma lad ageean, keekin' in thruff t' door-oil! Coom thi weays in, tha lathtle good-fer nowt ... an' ... let me ... wesh ... thi ... fea–

Gwen Wade (WR)

(1950)

rigg, back; *warks,* aches; *stalled,* weary (of); *roarin',* crying; *ower threng,* too busy; *Ah willent,* I won't; *thoil,* bear, manage; *fleered,* afraid

THE TERMINOLOGY OF THE BEER BARREL AT QUEENSBURY IN THE WEST RIDING
Pamela J Ambler

So far it seems that no investigation has been made into the dialect of coopering, and my own work on the subject has been limited to the terminology of the beer barrel. While I was studying the dialect of Queensbury for my BA thesis, my attention was drawn to coopering by one of my informants, Mr John Hardy, aged seventy, a native of Queensbury and a retired cooper. I then spent several hours in the cooper's shop at Heys Brewery in Bradford, watching Mr Albert Rayner and an apprentice cooper making and repairing beer barrels. Fortunately, Mr Hardy still retained all his coopering tools, which he has since given to the Abbey House Museum at Kirkstall, and I was thus able to study and draw them, as well as learn their local names from him.

To make a beer barrel; the cooper,[1] tubber[2] or tubthumper[3] takes about twenty staves[4] or lags[5] of, preferably, Russian Memel oak. First they are backed with the flat knife[6]; that is, the back of a stave is tapered towards each end; and then they are hollowed with the hollow knife.[7] Earlier, when barrels were made completely by hand, the backing and hollowing were done on a large frame, a mare,[8] but with the advent of machine-cut staves, this has largely passed out of use. After backing and hollowing the staves, the cooper joints them on a jointer,[9] a large plane about six foot long which remains on the floor while the wood is worked up and down on it. On the jointer the ends of the staves are made narrower than the middle, and the sides are shaped so that they will fit together tightly when the barrel is made.

When all the staves have been treated in this way, the barrel is reared up,[10] and begins to take on its familiar shape. The staves are placed pointing downwards into a hoop, called the dinger[11] by Mr Hardy, and the rearing-hoop or plate hoop[12] by Mr Rayner. Next are added the wooden truss hoops,[13] the belly hoop[14] or bulge hoop,[15] and the quarter hoop,[16] which are all driven on with the hammer[17] and driver.[18] The barrel is then turned upside down and placed over a cresset[19], a small fire in an iron frame, to warm the wood and make it pliable. Nothing must be burnt in the cresset but oak, since any other wood might 'taste' the beer, that is, might spoil its flavour. When the cask is thoroughly warmed, the other truss hoops are added, and each end is bevelled,[20] that is, it has a bezel[21] cut in with the adze.[22] Mr Rayner first topped each end with the topping plane,[23] a small curved plane about nine inches by three.

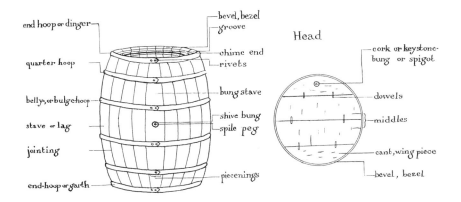

The terminology of the beer barrel.

The parts where the grooves[24] will be cut are now chivered with a chive,[25] formerly with a jigger,[26] and the grooves are put in with a croze,[27] a semircular wooden tool containing a small iron blade. The projecting part of a stave between the groove and the end is called the chime end.[28] The inside of the cask is then dressed out, that is, planed, with an inside swift[29] or inshave.[30]

To make the circular headal[31] or end, which will fit into the groove, the cooper first obtains the radius for it with a 'pair of compass'.[32] These are actually large dividers with which, by trial and error, he measures the inside of the groove by adjusting the dividers until they will fit round the groove six times, The cooper then uses this radius to scribe[33] the circumference of the head. This is made up of two middles and two cants[34] or wing pieces held together by dowels[35] and cut round with either the cooper's axe or the band-saw.[36] Nowadays this is done mostly by an electrically-driven bandsaw which Mr Rayner called a tape saw.[37] Both sides of the head are bevelled with the heading knife[38] and the back end is put into the barrel first. An iron end-hoop is substituted for the wooden truss hoop, after which are added the belly hoop and quarter hoop, so that the end is now held firmly in position.

Next the cooper must 'lie the barrel on its belly'[39] and bore the bung-hole, using a brace and bit, and enlarge it with the auger.[40] An iron bush is inserted into the bung-hole and rivetted in on the bushing-block. The tap-hole is bored in a cant in the head, and the cooper, putting his finger through the tap-hole, fastens the head into the groove of the barrel, steadying it with an S-shaped piece of piping, the knocker-up,[41] which is inserted through the bung-hole. The outside of the staves is cleaned with another plane, the downright,[42] and the other hoops or garths[43] added. The ends of the hoops are fastened with rivets,[44] driven in on the cooper's anvil, the beak iron,[45] and the places of joining, the piecenings,[46] must be in a line down the bung stave on the opposite side to the tap-hole.

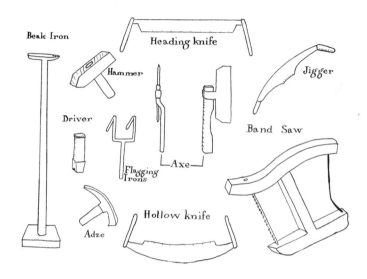

Cooper's tools.

The bung, known as the shive,[47] contains a small peg, the spile peg,[48] which is removable, so that when beer is to be drawn a porous peg may be substituted for it. The tap bung, formerly made of cork but now made of wood, which was called a keystone[49] by Mr Rayner and a spigot[50] by Mr Hardy, is then driven into the tap hole, and the barrel is complete and ready to be seasoned.

Other interesting terms found in coopering include pitch,[51] the diameter of a barrel at its widest part, and flagging irons, [52]a tool used in repair work. Rushes are used extensively in barrel making and repairing, and when staves are badly jointed, a piece of rush is put between them, and they are pulled back into position by the flagging irons.

It seems probable that coopering will yield valuable dialect material, which is not surprising since it is a very ancient craft that has apparently changed little from the days of Roman Britain until the recent introduction of machinery. It is to be hoped that the craft will not die out completely; certain processes have still to be done by hand and it is unlikely that metal casks will take the place of the traditional wooden barrels altogether.

In conclusion I must record my grateful thanks to Mr John Hardy and Mr Albert Rayner, who have given me so much help in the preparation of this paper, and also to Mr Blackledge, the university photographer, for his help with the two drawings which illustrate the article.

(1955)

[1] [kuːpə] 'cooper'. ME *couper*, of LG origin.
[2] [tʊbə] 'tubber'. From ME *tubbe*.
[3] [tʊbθɒmpə] 'tubthumper'.

4 [ste:vz] 'staves'. ME *staves*, OE *stafas*.

5 [lagz] 'lags'. ON *logge*.

6 [flat nɑ·'f] 'flat knife.' ON *flatr* + OE *cnif*.

7 [ɒlə nɑ·'f] 'hollow knife.' OE *holh* + OE *cnif*.

8 [mɛə] 'mare.' OE *mere*.

9 [dʒɔɪntə] 'jointer.' From OF *jointe*.

10 [ɹɪəd ɷp] 'reared up.' From ME *reren*, OR *ræran*.

11 [dɪnʒə] 'dinger.' Not recorded in OED or EDD; perhaps from ON *dengja*.

12 [ple:t u:p] 'plate hoop.' Not recorded in OED or EDD; OF *plate* + OE *hop*.

13 [tɹɷs u:ps] 'truss hoops.' F *trousse* + OE *hop*.

14 [bɛlɪ u:p] 'belly hoop.' OE *bel* + *OE hop*.

15 [bɷlʒ u:p] 'bulge hoop.' OF*boulge* + OE *hop*.

16 [kwa:təɹ u:p] 'quarter hoop.' OF *quarter* + *OE hop*.

17 [amə] 'hammer.' OE *hamor*.

18 [dɹɑ·'və] 'driver.' From OE *drifan*.

19 [kɹɪsɪt] 'cresset.' OF *cresset*.

20 [bɛvɪld] 'bevelled.' Seventeenth century *bevil* < OF* *bevel*.

21 [bazəl] 'bezel.' Seventeenth century *bezle* < OF* *besel*.

22 [adz] 'adze.' OE *adesa*.

23 [tɒpɪn ple:n] 'topping plane.' Not recorded in OED or EDD. OE *top* + F *plane*.

24 [gɹo:vz]+ [gɹɷəvz] 'grooves.' ME *grofe* < D *groef*.

25 [tʃɪv] 'chive.' Not recorded in OED or EDD.

26 ['dʒɪgə] 'jigger.' From seventeenth century *jig*. Of obscure origin.

27 [kɹo:z] 'croze.' OF *croz*.

28 [tʃɑ·'m ɛnd] 'chime end.' MDu *kimme* + OE *ende*.

29 [swɪft] 'swift.' From OE *swift* (adj).

30 [ɪnʃe:v] 'inshave.' OE *in* + OE *seafa*.

31 [iəd]+ [ɛd] 'head.' OE *heafod*.

32 [pɛ:ɹ ə kɷmpəs] 'pair of compass(es).'

33 [skɹɑ·'b] 'scribe.'

34 [kants] 'cants.' ME *cant* from OF *cant* or MLG kant.

35 [daɷɪlz] ME *dowle* from OF *douelle* or MLG *dovel*.

36 [band sɔ:] 'band saw.' ON *band* + OE **sa͜u,*

37 [te:p sɔ:] 'tape saw.' Not recorded in OED or EDD OB *tæppe* + OE •*sa͜u.*

38 [iədɪn nɑ·'f] 'heading knife.' From OE *heafod* + OE *cnif*.

39 [lɪg t'baɹɪl on ɪt belə']

40 [ɔ:gə] 'auger.' OE *nafugar*.

41 [nɒkəɹ ɷp] 'knocker-up.' Not recorded in OED or EDD. OE *cnocian*.

42 [daɷnɹɑ·'t] 'downright' Not recorded in OED or EDD.

43 [ga:θs] 'garths.' ON *gjorð*.

44 [rɛvɪts] 'rivets.' OF *rivet*.

45 [bɛk ɑ:n] 'beak iron' = 'bickern.' F *bigorne*.

46 [pi:snɪnz] 'piecenings.' Not recorded in OED or EDD.

47 [ʃɑ·'v] 'shive.' OE **scifa*.

48 [spɑ·'l pɛg] 'spile peg.' MLG *spile*.

49 [kɛɪstən] 'keystone.' Not recorded in OED or EDD. OE *cæz* + OE *stan*.

50 [spɪgət] 'spigot.' ME *spigot*, ME *spigote*, early Prov **espigot*.

51 [pɪtʃ] 'pitch.' Not recorded in OED or EDD.

52 [flagɪn ɑ:nz] 'flagging irons' ME *flagge, of* obscure origin, + OE *iren*.

DIALECT IN THE QUARRIES AT CROSLAND HILL NEAR HUDDERSFIELD, IN THE WEST RIDING

D R Sykes

Crosland Hill is a village just over two miles south-west of Huddersfield, lying on the Millstone Grit series of rock. It has a population of about 200, and its chief industry is the quarrying of stone. There are many quarries and stone-crushing plants in and around the village, and one of these quarries is claimed to be the largest in the North of England. The many mounds of quarry waste covering the area provide ample evidence that quarrying has been carried on here for centuries. The local manor house, Crosland Hall, was built of the local gritstone during the Tudor period.

Since, in this machine age, the tendency is to employ as much machinery as possible, thereby precluding the use of the traditional methods and tools, and consequently the local names for these implements, the task of recording the quarry dialect must be undertaken immediately. Moreover, there remain a small number of quarries which are worked by only a few men using the older methods and skills and speaking the good old vernacular. It is to these quarries and quarrymen that we must turn in order to find the oldest living dialect.

In the Crosland Hill dialect a quarry is known as a *delf-hole*[1], and there are many place-names in the area containing the word *delf*, and many places known solely as *Delves*. A curious point about the word in place-names is that it is invariably spelt 'delph', though why someone felt the need to connect the local dialect with Greek, I cannot imagine!

To begin our examination of the local quarrying words in detail, the face of the quarry gives us our first crop of terms. Looking at the face, fine layers are distinguishable. The top layer is known as *muck*[2], and at Crosland Hill this is never more than three to four inches deep. The next layer is known as *gravel*[3], which is a mixture of small pebble-like stones and soil. This layer is approximately a foot in depth, and lies immediately above the *grit*[4] or *rubble*.[5] In this layer the stones, though still loose, are considerably larger than those in the gravel. The fourth layer is known as the *bearing*.[6] Here the stone is seen to be in well-defined beds, though of poor quality since it is usually very gritty. Finally we come to the deepest layer that is worked — the *ashlar*,[7] or the *bottom lift*[8]. This layer can be from six to twenty feet thick, but it varies within a very small area. For instance the ashlar in one quarry may be qualitatively superior to that of another even though the two quarries are separated only by a road.

Now for the actual process of quarrying. First of all you start *bearing*[9] which means removing the muck and the gravel, which is waste. This work is done by a man called a *top-delver*,[10] *delver*[11] being the local name for a quarryman. When the muck and the gravel are removed, the grit becomes exposed. This has to be *loosened*[12] before it can be removed, since it is *fast*,[13] and this is done by *blowing*[14] it with gelignite. This is the only stage in the process where explosives are used. The grit is merely loosened, an operation that requires a high degree of skill, for the beds of ashlar below would be ruined if they were shattered by the gelignite. The loosened grit is *loaded*[15] into boxes, which are then hoisted away to the crushing machines on another part of the site. Prior to the introduction of stone-crushing machinery, the grit was regarded as waste and had to be *cussen*.[16] The many mounds so formed are known as *cussen muck*.[17] Very often the top-delver will find *backings*[18] in the exposed grit, these being flat pieces of stone used for dry-walling and requiring no *dressing*.[19] After the grit has been removed, the bearing is exposed, whereupon the stone will appear in *beds*[20] or *lifts*.[21] The stone is of no use to the mason, for besides being too coarse-grained the lifts are too shallow. This stone is designated *boarding*,[22] which probably means that it splits into 'boards', namely large thinnish layers of stone. A delver can easily remove the upper layers of the bearing with a *crowbar*[23] and a *maul*.[24] Further down, where the stone is less gritty and the lifts thicker, a *dog*[25] and *chain*[26] are used. In this operation the dog, which is a hook on the end of the crane rope, is wedged under the stone. Then the crane, in order to lift and free the stone, *sets up*,[27] that is winds in the rope, and so dislodges the stone. Once freed, the chain is attached to the stone, which is now *hoisted*[28] on to a flat surface on a higher level in the quarry. The name given to such a large piece of stone is a *tup-lump*,[29] because the *tup*[30] is required to break it into smaller pieces suitable for the crushers. In this process the tup, a large iron weight of about twenty-five hundredweights, is raised above the lumps and then allowed to fall on them, thus breaking the stone up into manageable pieces. If any stone is found to be too finegrained to *board*,[31] it is used for making *wallstones*.[32] It is known as *wallstone lumps*.[33]

With the bearing removed and the ashlar exposed, we are now in the province of the *bottom-delver*,[34] *hole-bottom man*[35] or *hole-bottomer*.[36] His job is to get the *posts*[37] or *blocks*[38] from the ashlar beds. A post is a large mass of ashlar weighing many hundredweights. To free a post from the beds, the delver has to have one side of it exposed, in order to have room to work. If, therefore, the quarry is new and the ashlar has just been uncovered, you have *to blow one to bits*.[39] This gives the delver a clear way into the posts and also loosens all that *lift*.[40] The post which it is proposed to lift is then marked out by drilling holes as deep as possible along the outline of the post. As the lift is usually thicker than the depth to which a drill can reach, the process known as *dogging-up*[41] begins. Here the dog is put under the block in the bed, and the crane sets up. While the crane is setting up, metal wedges are driven along the bed under the block. These wedges are driven in until the post *bounces up*,[42] that is, frees itself from the bed. A chain is passed round the post, which is then hoisted up to the *delf-hill*.[43] And so the bottom-delver continues *working-up*[44] posts until the lift runs out. Sometimes, instead of finding ashlar, the bottom delver will find *flatstone*[45] or *flags*.[46] This stone is in thin beds, which can be easily *riven by hand*[47] or split from one another. The implements used are a hammer and a *nicker*,[48] the latter being a chisel with a very wide, flat edge.

We can now leave the hole-bottom and make our way up to the *delf-hill*[49] by means of the *stays*[50] or *stees* or ladders, in order to see what happens to the post after it has left the beds. The posts are taken to the *delf-hill*,[51] which is a working place at the edge of the quarry where the stone is dressed. Here the posts are *fettled*[52] or *scrappled*,[53] that is, have their sides straightened so that they will stand up vertically for the sawing process. This work is done by the *delf-hiller*[54] using a *scrappling-pick*,[55] which has a small pick-head and a long shaft. The small pieces of stone knocked off the post are known as *scraps*,[56] and any large piece that has to be taken off is called a *dog's head*.[57] The delf-hill is also the place where the wallstone-dresser works. He works in a shed *dressing*,[58] or making, wallstones from the wallstone lumps. To get the lump in a suitable position for dressing, he lays it on a *banker*,[59] which is a stone bench supported by wallstone pillars. The lump is first nicked, and then broken on the bed, so that the wallstone has a good face, The dresser always wears an *apron*,[60] *clogs*,[61] and *yorks*,[62] ie pieces of string tied round the trousers just below the knees.

In the above an attempt has been made to describe the method of quarrying employed by the smallest firms at Crosland Hill. As is only to be expected, the larger firms use more machinery, and also employ masons and sawing machines on the spot. This is just another example of how modern methods are revolutionising one of the older industries. It will be readily understood that before cranes were available the methods of quarrying differed vastly even from those used to-day at the smaller quarries. In those days the quarries were driven in *at the skirt edge*[63] on the hill-side of a valley. Roads had also to be made into the quarry, so that horses and carts could be driven in to bring the posts out. Any quarryman who can remember this method of quarrying and the terms and implements used would be a valuable source of the older dialect terms, which are now almost lost. That is why the subject of quarrying in the old days should be investigated now while the oldest methods are still used or remembered.

(1953)

[1] [dɛlfɒil] 'delf-hole.' ME *delf*, OE *dælf*.
[2] [mɒk] 'muck.' Probably from ON *myki*.
[3] [ɡɹavil] 'gravel.' o.F *gravel(l)e*.
[4] [ɡɹɪːt] 'grit.' OE *greot*.
[5] [ɹɒbil] 'rubble.'
[6] [bɛəɹɪn] 'bearing' From *bear* v, < OE *beran*.
[7] [atʃilə] 'ashlar.' OF *aiseler*.

8 [bɒðm lɪft] 'bottom lift.' OE, *botm* + ON *lypta*.

9 [ða staːts beəɹɪn] 'you start bearing.'

10 [tɒp dɛlvə] 'top delver.'

11 [dɛlvə] 'delver.' From *delve* v, from OE *delfan*.

12 [lɔːzd] 'loosened.' ON *louss, lauss*.

13 [fast] 'fast.' OE *fæst*.

14 [bloːɪn] 'blowing.' From *blow* v, from OE *blawan*.

15 [luədɪd] 'loaded.' Ultimately < OE *lad*.

16 [kɒsn] 'tipped'. ON *kasta*.

17 [kɒsn mɶk] 'cussen muck.' ON *kasta* + ON myki.

18 [bakɪnz] 'backings.' Ultimately from OE *bac*.

19 [dɹɛsɪn] 'dressing.' OF *dresser*.

20 [bɛdz] 'beds.' OE *bedd*.

21 [lɪfts] 'lifts.' ON *lypta*.

22 [bɶədin] 'boarding.' < OE *bord*.

23 [kroːbaː] 'crowbar.' OE *crawe* + OF *barre*.

24 [mɔːl] 'maul.' OF *mail*.

25 [dɔg] 'dog.' OE *docga*.

26 [tʃeɪn] 'chain.' OF *chaine* .

27 [sɛts ɶp] 'sets up.'

28 [ɔɪstɪd] 'hoisted.' Origin obscure.

29 [tɒp lɶmp] 'tup lump.' Origin of *tup* unknown, ME *lump*.

30 [tɒp] 'tup.' Etymology doubtful.

31 [buəd] 'board.' OE *bord*.

32 [wɒlstnz] 'wallstones.' OE *wall* + OE *stan*.

33 [wɒlstn lɶmps] 'wallstone lumps.'

34 [bɒðm dɛlvə] 'bottom-delver.'

35 [ɒɪl bɒðm man] 'hole-bottom man.'

36 [ɒɪl bɒðmə] 'hole-bottomer.'

37 [pɒsts] 'posts.' OE *post*. .

38 [blɒks] 'blocks.' Probably from Fr *bloc*.

39 [ðaz tə bloː wɒn ɪ bits] 'you have to blow one to bits.'

40 [loːzɪz ɔːl ðat lɪft) 'loosens all that lift.'

41 [dɒgɪn ɶp] 'dogging up.'

42 [beənsɪz ɶp] 'bounces up.'

43 [ɪts ɒɪstɪd ɶp tət dɛlf ɪl] 'it is hoisted up to the delf hill.'

44 [wəkɪn ɶp] 'working up'.

45 [flatstn] 'flatstone.' ON *flatr* + OE *stan*.

46 [flagz] 'flags.' ON *flaga*.

47 [ɹɪvən bɪ and] 'riven by hand.'

48 [nɪkə] 'nicker.'

49 [dɛlfɪl] 'delf-hill.'

50 [stiː] 'stay.' ON *stige, stege*.

51 [dɛlf ɪl] 'delf-hill.' 'Delf' + OE *hyll*.

52 [fɛtɪld] 'fettled'. Origin obscure.

53 [skɹapɪld] 'scrappled.' Ultimately from OE *scrapian*.

54 [dɛlf ɪlə] 'delf-hiller.'

55 [skɹaplɪn pɪk] 'scrappling-pick.'

56 [skɹaps] 'scraps.' ON *skrap*.

57 [dɒg jɛd] 'dog's head.'

[58] [dɹɛsɪn] 'dressing.'
[59] [baŋkə] 'banker.' OF *banc.*
[60] [ə napɹən] 'an apron.' From OF *naperon.*
[61] [tlɒgz] 'clogs.'
[62] [jɔːks] 'yorks.'
[63] [ət skət ɛdʒ] 'at the skirt edge' ON *skyrta* + OE *ecg.*

GI' US PEACE

'Is it naah?' whisper'd t' trees;
'Maybe naah!' murmur'd t' wind;
'Happen naah!' burbl'd t' stre-am:
An' t' trees —
An' t' wind —
An' t' stre-am,
(In a queer wak'nin' dre-am)
Ga' voice to ther' thowts
In t' whisperin'.

'Ah'll goah!' said t' wind;
'Aye goah!' urged t' stre-am;
'Do goah!' begged t' trees:
An' t' quick wind went speedin'
Wheer bairnies ligged bleedin';
Mangl'd an' riven,
Stark-limb'd,
God-given,
Tip-toss'd childer.

Then foller'd wheer t' blast-guns
(De-ath's lakins) hed been;
An' wishfully skenned
I' warrin' men's een.

'Not yet!' gro-an'd t' trees
Foldin' deep into t' neet;
'Not yet!' purled t' stre-am
As it rullied fra t' seet.

Fred Brown (WR)

(1952)

lakins, toys; *een,* eyes

WENSLEYDALE CHEESE
T C Calvert

Little Miss Muffet, sat on a tuffet,
Eating her curds and whey.

How many generations of children have chanted this nursery rhyme? We who
have lived through the first half of the twentieth century are inclined to suppose
that we are infinitely superior to our ancestors, especially those 'ignorant savages'
of four to five hundred years ago. But are we, indeed, all we think we are? A few
minutes' reflection on such a commonplace article of food as cheese should bring
us down to earth, where we can respect and even admire our forefathers.

In peace their sacred ashes rest,
Fulfilled their days' endeavour,
They blessed the earth and we are blessed,
By what they did, for ever.

From the earliest years of recorded history we find that cheesemaking has been
the means of conserving the food value of milk for future use. The Old Testament
writers tell us that in those far-off days cheese was a common article of food.
David, the Shepherd King, was sent by Jesse, his father, to the battle front to
'carry these ten cheeses unto the captain of their thousands, and look how thy
brethren fare'. (I Sam: 17, 18). Homer, Aristotle and Virgil all refer to cheese in
their writings. The cheese that David took to the officers would in all probability
be made from ewes' milk, since his father was an extensive sheep-farmer — and
our first Wensleydale cheese was also made from ewes' milk, and the formula for
its manufacture was introduced into our Yorkshire Dales by the representatives
of the Church.

It was in 1144 that Earl Allen, the third Earl of Richmond, invited the Abbot of
Savigny in Normandy to send twelve monks to Yorkshire to pray for him and his
ancestors. He gave to these monks the northern watershed of Upper Wensleydale, west of Askrigg.

Up to this time the land in Wensleydale west of Askrigg was considered a waste,
but these twelve good men and true set about using it. They began sheep-farming.
They milked the ewes once a day, and whatever milk was left over after their immediate needs had been supplied they made into cheese. Some twelve years later

these early pioneers transferred their home to Jervaulx, lower down the valley, where they founded the beautiful Abbey, the ruins of which we can still see and admire.

For upwards of 400 years the brethren of this Cistercian order ruled their ever-expanding domain with dignity and splendour. But they were farmers as well as ecclesiastics, and they certainly knew the value of land, even of what some men would call bad land. The lowlands reared horses for the king, his courtiers and their armies, while the uplands were well stocked with sheep which were valuable for their milk, their wool, and finally their mutton. We think of the thousands of prime Wensleydale cheeses maturing in the cellars of Jervaulx. Yet we have no written recipe of how the wife of the herdsman made her cheese for the abbot. Probably it was lost in the final destruction of the abbey after the disastrous uprising known to us as the Pilgrimage of Grace, in which Adam Sedbar, the last abbot, took part and paid the price by losing his head. Yet although the abbot and his abbey were destroyed, the knowledge of how to make a good Wensleydale cheese could not be destroyed. Men and women born in the Dales had been taught the art of cheesemaking from childhood, and so the time-honoured craft was able to continue. Later on, cows, milk-producers in quantity, pushed the ewes into the background, leaving the sheep to the production of wool and the rearing of a better lamb. Hence right down to the end of the nineteenth century the bulk of the cows' milk in our Yorkshire Dales was manufactured by the farmers' wives into Wensleydale cheese.

Let us now look at one or two of their simple implements. First the 'cheese-kettle', a large copper pan holding anything up to twenty gallons, with a brass handle hinged over it. The milk was poured in and heated to a temperature that the cheesemaker tested by placing her elbow in the milk. Only the expert could tell the heat reaction necessary. At the right heat, 'keslop' was added. Now keslop was a broth prepared from a small portion of a salted and dried calf's stomach. Frequently the farmer had to kill a young calf specially for the stomach itself. The family ate the veal fresh or potted it for future use, but the stomach was taken out, washed, salted and dried. When the keslop bottle was empty, the remainder of the stomach was taken down from the nail in the kitchen rafters and a portion of it was then cut into small pieces and placed in a small pan of water on the fire and boiled for a considerable time. The liquid was strained from the boiled flesh, allowed to cool, and then bottled for future use. This liquid was used in small quantities, a spoonful or two being stirred into the warm milk. This set up a coagulation and produced the cheese curd. Small portions of the calf's stomach had to be boiled frequently, for the liquid soon went stale and rancid.

Next, the curd, which had risen to the top of the kettle, had to be broken down into the whey. This was done by a tool similar in shape to a tennis racket, the frame being made of strong copper or steel wire, and the strands making about a half-inch mesh were woven from hair pulled from the horse's mane or tail. After stirring the curd in the whey for a time, the whey was drawn off, leaving the curd in the bottom of the kettle. It was finally collected into a linen bag and hung from the rafters of the buttery overnight. Next morning the curd was taken down and 'murled sma' tev aboot the size o' lile taws' (marbles) and put into the 'chesford'. This was a cheese mould made of oak and bound together with copper straps. These chesfords were of two shapes, 'talls' and 'flats'. Talls were more popular for the long-keeping 'blue mould' cheese, while the flats were used for the quick-selling cheese.

Finally the 'sinker' was placed on top and the full chesford put in the press, where it stayed another day. Next, the cheese was knocked out of the chesford and placed in the brine vat. This vat was usually a large shallow bath, made of wood and lined with lead. The brine was a preparation of boiled water, to which salt was added while boiling. After boiling, the liquid was allowed to cool, and to test it for strength a new-laid egg was laid on the liquid. If the egg floated, the brine was at strength, but if it sank, the liquid had to be boiled again and more salt added. The cheese must not be fully covered in the brine, but about an inch of cheese had to show above the liquid. The cheeses were turned over each day for four days, by which time the curd had collected sufficient salt to 'cure' it and give it the salt flavour necessary for a good cheese.

After four days' steeping in brine, the cheese was taken out and placed in the cheese-room, which was often an airy room above the buttery lined with shelves or 'cheese traves'. Here they dried out and matured for two, three, or even six months. They were constantly inspected by the farmer's wife, and any cheese showing faults was weeded out and sold quickly, until towards Christmas nothing but the best was left, thus providing one of the popular delicacies of Christmas fare. Unfortunately the last fifty years have seen tremendous changes in the Wensleydale Cheese industry. Only two farmers' wives now make this cheese, and the great traditional industry has become a factory speciality. Space will not allow me to explain how science has come to the aid of the cheesemaker, or how the bulking of the milk from 50 to 100 farms has robbed him of the individuality peculiar to the farmhouse cheese. Yet I am convinced that dairy and creamery managers, as well as their cheesemakers, are in honour bound to maintain, and if possible improve, the product of this time-honoured craft, which was brought to our Yorkshire Dales by Norman monks some 800 years ago and has ever since been jealously and proudly upheld by the farmers' wives down to a generation ago.

(1955)

THE TECHNIQUE AND TERMINOLOGY OF STACKING AND THATCHING IN CLEVELAND
Bill Cowley

The craft of stacking and thatching offers a rich field for both the dialect student and the phonetician. It is an ancient occupation that has changed comparatively little in character during the last century or two; and it varies very little over the county and even over the country as a whole. True, in Scotland, because of the climate, they build small round stacks, such as I have heard referred to in Bilsdale as *chop-stacks,* which have 'Aboot yah looad tiv a stack'; whilst in the South, pride in the art of stacking seems already to have vanished. It is always a pleasure to get back across the Yorkshire border and see some workmanlike stacks again.

The present paper is only a preliminary study of the subject in a limited area, namely Cleveland and the adjacent parts of the North Riding. I hope to extend it later, and indeed to get further information from other areas here to-day. But as with other things, there must be no delay in this study, because the advent of the combine and grain storage bins will accelerate the dying out of old techniques and old terms.

One point gives food for thought: we now have expensive grain-drying plants and vermin-proof bins, whereas in the old days rats and mice were kept out cheaply by building the small round stacks on stone platforms. These are called *staddles* in parts of Cleveland Plain — hence Staddlebridge and Staddlethorp. Towards the hills and in the dales, however, the word used is *hemmels,* and people who use one of these terms seem to be quite ignorant of the other, though both use the word *staddlin* for the thorns and straw which make the *stack boddum* now that *hemmelsteeans* are no longer used. A seventy-year-old farmer from the head of Bilsdale said to me, 'When ah com eear fifty years sin, t' coorn emmels were vallied ti me at aboot ten shillings'. There are seven uprights or *standards* and seven flat or curved mushroom-like stones called *toppers* balanced on them. 'Wa put onny awd bits o' wood, awd stritchers an sike-like on' t' emmelsteeans, and then sum brakkins for staddlin'.' Another informant said: 'Yu'd still fahnd awd emmels i' t' coorner o' monny a staggarth. A good stacker's put hauf a daay's threshin on a cart-wheel; ther'd be hauf as big ageean at t' eeasins.'

Before going into detail about stacking terminology, I had better roughly explain the technique. Having got a sound bottom to keep the corn from getting damp from below, the sides are usually *sprung* to the eaves or *eeasins* so that the stack *dhrops dhry,* and then the top is well filled in so that any water which happens to

114

get in past one course merely runs down succeeding courses and out of the stack without ever getting where it can do real damage.

The operation of loading and stacking is one of the major operations of the farming year. A good farmer sites his stacks carefully and arranges his teams so that loads are always moving and the expert stacker is kept busy — on his knees — all day. One year our stacker wore out three pairs of trousers; and then we got him some leather knee-pads! Generally there will be two carts going. A forker in the field will fork up *shavs* (sheaves) to a *looadner* (loader), who will fork off his own load to the picker on the stack, who passes the *shavs* right way up to the stacker. The sheaves have short ends on one side sloping to long ends at the other, and much argument continues about which is the right way to stack them. Some build the body of the stack sloping out about equal to the slope of the bottom of the sheaf, long ends on top, giving a smooth well-sprung side, and reverse this on top, bringing the stack in similarly and getting a smooth top. Others say the long ends must always be on top to keep the stack dry. Others have the sheaves always on their sides, one layer pulled in one way and the next the other way, thus giving a smart patterned effect, like herring-bone. Stacking is rather like knitting, with each sheaf holding another in place, and each layer tying the one below. Nowadays a stack must be carefully calculated where possible to hold exactly half a day's threshing, as moving a threshing machine even a few yards takes a lot of time, with expensive labour standing idle. The little round stacks were all right for days when the flail was the threshing implement, but a much larger stack is necessary now.

A composite dialect picture, built up from several informants, in the dialect spoken in the North Riding between Stokesley and Swainby, which has intrusive elements from the moors, is as follows:

Fost of all yu've ti mek t'boddum — t'staddlin. Yu can't beeat thoorns for makkin' t' staddlin. It'd want ti be aboot three an a auf bi eight yards for hauf a day's threshing. That'd hod fower or fahve yakker — aye, six yakker if yu spring 'er weel. It'd bi t'seeam for owther woats or wheeat, 'appen a bit less for barley, if t'shavs is a bit less.

Then yu want a bit o' stthreea — onny awd stthreea 'll deea — on t' thoorns. A thin sthrinklin o' stthreea'll keep t'thoorns pairted fra t'corn.

Yu want ti start i' t' middil ti stack. Keep their 'eeads up and keep yu're middle full ti tonn watther. Neean o' t' eeads need be on t' grund. Rook three or fower up at yall end, or stook up t' middil, an' laay t' eeads o' yu're shavs on them. Mahnd, it dizzn't want ti be that full it starts ti slip o' yu'. Just work nicely oot fra t' middle, layin 'eeads on arses up ti t' bands, an' tak care ti get a good shap o' yu're fost ootsahde coorse. Then just carry on coorsin' yah waay an fillin t' other, arses up ti t' bands ivvery tahme, an' land end on t' top. Stack on yu're knees an' use yu're hands, nut a forrk — an' spring 'er weel, graw 'er oot — if ah build a stthreea stack ah'm fower batten wahde at t' boddum, but at t' eeasin ah's sivvn. A coorn stack wants ti be forivver wahder at t' eeasins seea it dhrops dhry. Yu want ti tak a bit o' pains wi it. Get doon atweean jags, whahl ther lowsin off t'rooaps, an' bray shavs in at's stickin oot. Ther'll be seven, eight or nine coorses ti t' eeasins, an' then yu've ti start ti fill. Fill 'er fahve tahmes — fra t' middil back ti t'ootsahde coorse eead, back ti t' middil an' back ti t' ootsahde coorse bands, and back ageean ti t' middil. Efther that, yu've ti laay yu're fost eeasin coorse. Yu're second eeasin coorse is t'warst ti gan roond. T' fost full coorse roon efther yu're eeasin is allus t' fullest. Efther that, tak 'er in — nut ti get yu're top ower brant, but keep 'er full or she'll tak watther. Fill yah waay an' coorse t' other.

A hay-stack should be seea full at t'picker yah sahde can't see t' stacker coorsin at t' other.

Nut two iv a hundred tops stacks oot wi shavs t' proper waay. If you tell 'em ti keep t' lang ends o' t' shavs on top, they saay it weeant hod that waay — but it'll hod watther t' other waay wi' t' short ends on top. T' watther runs off lang ends — it's a forivver betther waay.

If it reeaks eftther yu've topped it oot, yu've led it ower seean — it esn't bin riddy — yu've bin ower sharp givin t' coorn a rahde!

Put a pair o' props i owther sahde ti hod 'er, ti stiddy 'er — props is datal men, allus on their job. T'stack maun't whemmle ower — it might whemmle ower if it's heavy o yah sahde.

Here's a farmer's advice to a lad *looadin* carts: 'Yu allus want ti keep yu're middle full an' yu'll tak neea harm.' And the lad replies: 'Weel, maistther, ah's nivver 'ed it full sin ah com ti this spot!'

My informants on thatching, in addition to those already quoted on stacking, include Jack Lumsden of Farndale, a famous old craftsman in thatching buildings as well as stacks. Amongst other work he thatched the cricket pavilion at Escrick with heather cut from the Farndale moors. He used a *stinger,* or swallow tail, to *prod* straw into a roof, and a rake with wire nails ti *panch it doon.* He learned as a boy from an old travelling *theeaker,* David Hawnby. Jack often stopped *off skeeal* ti *sarve 'im,* and when he first tried himself, the old man said, 'Ah allus tellt tha, Shonnie, 'at that way o' theeakin was neea good. If tha dizzn't theeak seeam waay as ah diz, thi job's good for nowt — it'll blaw up i' t' fost wind at blaws.'

Thatching with heather was a new idea to me. Wheat straw is the usual medium, but near the moors or near marshes rushes are an even better choice. My Bilsdale farmer says: 'Wa allus theeak wi seeaves. Yah scoor fawd o' seeaves mak a threeav. Aye, ah've offens 'eeard: "Hoo monny fawd o' seeavs 'est tha gitten? We want fifty for a cart leead." Seeavs ton watther betther nor stthreea. They leeave t' coorn dhry as tunder. They're watther grown; an t' mair watther, t' betther t' seeaves. For stack prods ah've cutten monny a back-looad o' hezles — hard, lastin stuff — nowt leyke hezle pins for shoein sleds.'

For the usual technique with straw, which has first to be pulled or drawn to get it straight and one way with no loose bits of leaf on it, a composite picture is as follows:

Ti mak theeak for a hauf-day stack, yu' want aboot forty batten o' stthreea, saay three or fower threeave, wi' twelve battens ti t' treeave. Wa used ti draw theeak o' wet daays; yu run it atween yu're fingers or pull it through a gripe upsahde doon ti rahve t' ribbins off it. They'd hod watther. Yu'll git a loggin o' theeak oot of ivvery batten o' stthreea if its bin put through t' machine fair an' streyte. Noo we offens puts it on streyte oot o' t' batten an' use a cawmb ti rake each gang doon. Wa rake a yard doon an' then put prods in.

Afoor yu begin ti theeak, fost of owt yu want a good rigginbatten ti levil 'er up. If t' top isn't awver weel finished off it wants a wahde riggin-batten. A fowerteen-yard hay-stack 'd want tweea seven-yard riggin battens. Twist a bit o' stthreea roon ti fassen 'em.

A loggin an' a hauf o' theeak'll deea yah gang. If t' stthreea isn't ower good yu'll mebbie hev ti put a batten an' a hauf o' stthreea intiv a batten o' theeak.

Keep yu're prods up ower seea it runs t' watther off. If yu put 'em in doon ower, t' watther 'll run doon 'em inti t' stack.

If t' theeak's put on reet, a stthreea thickness 'll ton t' watther . Ti keep yu're bands streyte, yu mun hev yu're stee streyte seear yu're bands lie streyte alang yu're stowers. If yu're ladder's oot on't, yu're seean oot wi' yu're bands. Eftther yu've theeak'd it, gan roon wi' an' awd lye bleead or a sickle, an' knock t' lang ends off.

(1955)

117

THE TERMINOLOGY OF FENCES, DITCHES AND GATES IN THE VALE OF PICKERING

N A Hudleston

Enclosures for crops and stock have been known since the ancient Britons; the Anglo-Saxons hedged their villages; lords, monks and peasants enclosed intakes from the waste in the Middle Ages; enclosures for grazing created trouble for the Tudors; and the end of the last great series of enclosures for agricultural improvement, about 1750 to 1850, was (in our childhood) still nearly in living memory.

The art of fencing can thus be expected to have a vocabulary going back to Middle and Old English (and, in these parts, Old Norse) times. Fences are always with us; and they, and the words connected with them, change but little from one generation to another. These words are localised and thus give good examples of local dialect, more or less unaffected by the standard language, which in this respect hardly touches the farmer's form of speech at all. Mechanisation has scarcely affected them.

Let us glance at the different categories of local words in turn. Diagrams of many of the objects concerned are appended.

Clothing

Apart from your *warkday-clothes,* the only special personal equipment you need for hedging is a pair of good, stout, leather *mitts,* or mittens, in order to protect your hands from *prykelinz,* prickles. For *dikin',* ditching, you also want a pair of strong *gutterin'-* or *dikin'-beeats,* ditching-boots, made of either leather or rubber. Leather ones should be *clogged* with wooden soles, for this will make them *theet,* watertight.

Tools

The necessary tools include the *slasher* for trimming the hedges, the *bill* for cutting the thicker branches, the *mell,* of wood, for driving the *steeaks, stakes,* into the ground, the *gavelok,* iron crowbar, for making holes in the ground to hold the stakes, and the *stubbin-dig,* mattock, for tearing out the roots of the *thorn-bushes,* hawthorns. The *dykes,* ie ditches, are always dug out with the *speead,* spade.

Temporary Fences

For a temporary fence against sheep you can erect a wooden hurdle, variously termed a *sheep-reeal,* sheep-rail, *steck-bar,* or simply *bar,* or *tthraa,* tray or hurdle. To protect a young, growing hedge against cattle, you can put down a row of brushwood called either a *brash-hedge,* or a *ram-hedge.* And of course wire, too, is useful here.

Permanent Fences

There are two main classes of permanent fences: firstly, the *posst-* or *stoop-*, post, *and-reeal,* -rail; secondly the *steeak-,* stake-, or *stower-,* stake-, *and-topper.* The distance between the posts is termed the *room-steead,* -stead. As an obstacle across a *gap-steead,* gapstead, ie a permanent gap in a fence left for convenience, may be placed a *stap-reeal,* stop-rail. A *smoot-hole,* a permanent gap in a hedge to allow sheep to pass through, can be effectively barred with a *smoot-reeal,* -rail.

Hedges

Hedges are made of *wick-wood,* quick-wood bushes (especially hawthorn). The small seedlings are planted on the *cam,* ie the ridge or bank of earth removed from the ditch. After they have grown enough, they are *ligged,* ie the *stobs,* or *stubs,* viz. the upright stems, are cut half-way through low down with a bill and then laid horizontally along the line of the fence. These horizontals are known as *liggers.* To strengthen the hedge, *steeaks,* stakes, or *stowers,* are now driven into the cam. The liggers now send out *stuvens,* shoots, to form a more compact hedge. Later, when the hedge grows up, it is *slashed,* trimmed, with a *slasher;* in Yorkshire you thrust upwards with the implement, but strike downwards in Lincolnshire.

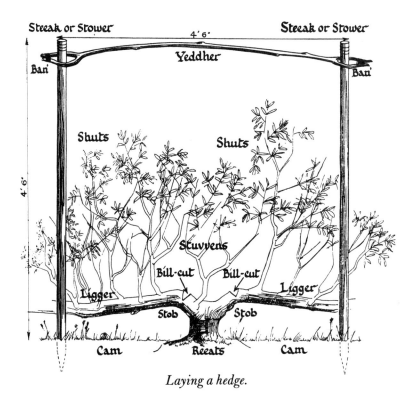

Laying a hedge.

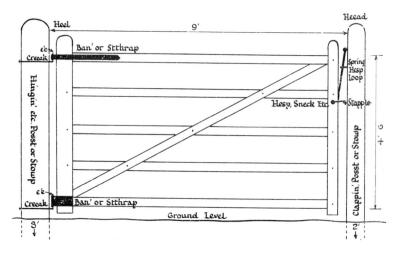

The gate.

If you decide, however, not to cut the young hedge right back to the bottom, ie *lig it*, but instead cut it back to half-height only, then you *fall-and-lap* it, or *stob-and-lap* it. Incidentally, to make the hedge still firmer, you *weave yeddthers* between the stakes placed in the hedge: these are thickish branches cut from the bushes in the process of *ligging* the hedge.

The roots of hedges, as well as of bushes and small trees, are grubbed out of the ground by *stubbing them up* with a *stubbin'-dig* or mattock. But the roots of larger trees can be *stub-felled, ie* torn out of the ground by severing the roots at one side and then pulling the tree over.

Ditches

Our ditches are called *gutthers*, gutters, and ditching is accordingly *guttherin'*. But we also speak of *dykes* and *dyking*.

Gates

Local *yats* or *geeats*, viz. gates, usually have five bars and only one cross bar (see diagram). They hang by the *heel* and fasten from the *head*. They hang from the *'ingin-*, hanging-, *slingin-* or *swingin'-posst, -stoop*. To attach the *yat to* the post, the heel has two *iron-bands* or *sthraps*, straps, one on the top bar, the other on the bottom. Each band has an *ee*, eye, into which fits the vertical pin of the *creeak*, crook. At the other end of the gate is the *yat-heead*, gatehead, which is provided with a *spring-hesp* to fasten in with a loop fixed on the *clappin'-post, -stoop*. For greater security, the *yat-heead* has also a *sneck*, *sneckle*, or *hesp*, the loose end of which is inserted into the *stapple*, staple, of the *heead-post*.

The gateway is called the *yat-*, *geeat-steead*.

(1958)

YORKSHIRE TERMS FOR EARWIG AND FOR THE MID-MORNING MEAL

Harold Orton

Some 130 replies, many from outside Yorkshire, were received in answer to the request for local words for *earwig* and *mid-morning meal taken at work between breakfast and dinner* that appeared in last year's *Transactions*. The request was given wider publicity in the local press, including the *Yorkshire Post*, the *Telegraph and Argus* and the *Darlington and Stockton Times*. We are most grateful for this enthusiastic response and wish to thank all our informants most warmly, and especially Northerner II of the *Yorkshire Post*, who was particularly helpful in stimulating inquiries among his readers.

Not all of the replies were usable, for they contained information that was too imprecise. We wanted the words in question actually localised. So to be told that a particular word was used 'in the West Riding' or again 'in Holderness' was far too vague for our purpose and consequently it had to be excluded from the maps reproduced below. However, most of the replies were truly instructive and our inquiry, thanks to our kindly correspondents, has undoubtedly achieved success.

Although the maps certainly reveal wide gaps, the general picture, in each case, emerges clearly. The *earwig* is in the North Riding a *twitch-bell*; but, in the East Riding, it is a *forkin-/forkie-robin/robber,* with *twitch-bell* as an occasional variant towards its border with the North Riding. On the other hand, the West Riding, at any rate at its centre, calls it a *twinge*. In North Lincolnshire we find *battle-twig,* which, as the map shows, just infiltrates into the West Riding.

The terms for the *mid-morning meal* similarly manifest a nice distributional pattern, and, again, one that is clearly based on the Ridings. Apart from the striking *dornton* in the west, we chiefly encounter *-o'clock(s)* (preceded by a numeral specifying the relevant hour, usually *ten*) in the North Riding. Nevertheless the Vales of York and Pickering in their use of *lowance* again demonstrate affinities with the East Riding, which employs this word with consistent regularity. Then, in the West Riding, we observe, passing from north to south, three main types, namely *forenoon drinkings, minning-on* and *bitin'-on,* the last two being rather curious formations compounded of a verbal noun and an adverb.

It would not be wise to press the evidence any harder, especially with such wide gaps in the information. Admittedly some of these might be reduced by including certain other words that have isolated occurrences, but we have preferred to omit them here.

The maps overleaf may now speak for themselves.

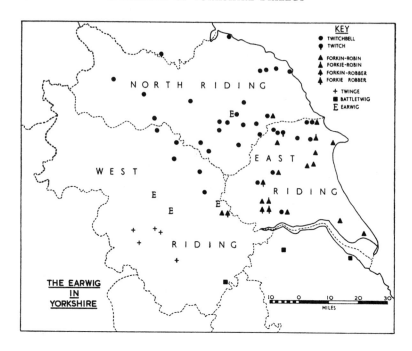

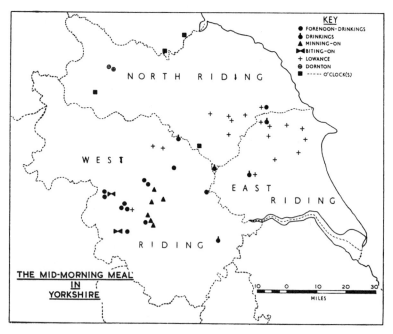

The earwig and the mid-morning meal.

To conclude, we append a few desultory remarks both on the wider distribution of our terms and on their etymologies, which are, however, far from clear. The sources of this information are, quite naturally, Wright's *English Dialect Dictionary* or the *Oxford English Dictionary*. The abbreviations of the county names are from the former.

Words for Earwig

1. BATTLE-TWIG. Found chiefly in E Midl Cos. Not in *OED*, but note BEETLE-WIG, first recorded 1595.
2. EARWIG. From OE *earwicga*, from OE *eare* 'ear' + *wicga* 'insect, beetle'.
3. FORKIN-ROBIN. Found n Cy, Yks, ne Midl Cos and Ches. Not in *OED*. On loss of *n* in *forkie-*, compare the local form *Robison* for *Robinson*.
4. FORKIN-ROBBER. Not in *EDD* or *OED*. Doubtless a simple variant of (3) above.
5. TWINGE. Found n Cy, Yks, Lan and Ken. First recorded 1790. From *twinge*, vb 'pinch', from OE *twengan*.
6. TWITCH-BELL. Found n Cy, more especially Nhb, Dur, Cum and N Yks. Not in *OED*.

Words for Mid-Morning Meal

1. BITIN'-ON. Found Yks, Lan and Der. From BITE vb, OE *bitan*, and adverb ON.
2. DORNTON. Not localised in *EDD*, which, however, also records *dortor*, *down-dinner*, *downdrins* and *undern*, all with the same sense. The source of *undern is* OE *undern*, 'third hour of the day', ie 'about 9am', and this is doubtless the source of *dornton* as well as of the other curious forms mentioned above.
3. DRINKING, FORENOON DRINKINGS. The former is found in n Cy, e Midl Cos, Lan, as well as Ken, Som, and Dev, but the latter only in W Yks. Self-explanatory.
4. LOWANCE In gen dial use in Sc and Engl. A shortening of *allowance*, fr Fr *louance*.
5. MINING-ON Recorded Yks only. Not in *OED*. It is tempting to connect the first element, with the Northern English verb *min*, 'to remind', from ON *minna;* and thus to suggest that the word originally meant 'reminder' (of something to come).
6. -O'CLOCK(S).
(A) TEN-O'CLOCK(S). Possibly a distributional distinction exists between the singular and the plural form. According to *EDD*, the singular is found in Nhb, Dur, Cum, Wm and Der. Our correspondents report the plural at Sleights and Staithes (both E Riding) and Darlington; and the singular at Tollerton (nr York) and Dallowgill (nr Ripon). But in the absence of much fuller information, it seems wiser for the present not to stress the difference.
(B) ELEVEN-O'CLOCKS. Found Sc, War and Som. Our correspondents report it at Stockton-on-Tees. [Incidentally *EDD* records *elevener* in Sc, Dev and Cor, *elevens* in Wor, Glo, Suf, Ken and Dor, and *elevenses* in Suf and Ken. But many people would probably be willing to believe that the last-mentioned form *elevenses* is nowadays much more widely distributed all over the country].

(1958)

A NOTE ON EQUINE TERMS IN YORKSHIRE
J Fairfax-Blakeborough

Yorkshire played a very conspicuous part in the evolution of the Thoroughbred horse. Prior to the Thoroughbred the county had its own indigenous breed — the Cleveland Bay (originally known as the 'Chapman Horse'). Yorkshire time out of count has been famed for its horse-breeders, and its horsemen, as well as for its horse fairs, which were amongst the most important in Great Britain for hunters, coach-horses and horses for the land. It is not unnatural, therefore, that our dialect is rich in words which had their origin in the stable, the stud and the field, and gradually became part of everyday conversation in which the horse had no part. There is a very old saying 'Shake a bridle on a Yorkshireman's grave and he'll get up and steal a horse', whilst George Borrow, in *Romany Rye,* wrote: 'By no manner of means permit a Yorkshireman to get up into the saddle for if you do it's 3 to 1 he rides off with your horse. He can't help it. Trust a cat among cream, but never trust a Yorkshireman in the saddle of a good horse [at a fair].'

The Yorkshire dialect term for a Thoroughbred is *bleeadhoss* (blood-horse). Every Thoroughbred in the world descends from one of seventy-eight foundation mares and three Eastern (Barb, Turk or Arab) sires. Almost all these foundation mares were located in North Yorkshire. Many of them were 'running galloways'. According to the *Oxford English Dictionary* the word *galloway* is from the Scottish district of that name but this is doubtful. The term *gallower* is still regularly applied to a small horse of 14 to 15 hands. Often a *gallower* showing a blood strain, or more than usual quality, is called a *tit* or *blood-tit*.

It is quite possible, if not most probable, that the Cleveland Bay Horse, which was the foundation of the Yorkshire Coach Horse, was evolved from exactly the same type of mare as the foundation of the Thoroughbred. When roads were too bad for vehicular traffic, Yorkshiremen chose the stoutest of the well-bred gallowers for pack-horse work, and produced a breed first known as 'Chapman Horses', because they were so much used by the chapmen of that day. Like the first race-horses, these Chapman Horses were of pony size. Like the racehorse, Chapman Horses had a dose of Eastern blood. This cross with Arab, Turk or Barb in both cases 'nicked' extraordinarily well in the evolutionary stages but was entirely dropped after a century. Both the Thoroughbred and the Chapman or Cleveland

Bay (as now known), gradually grew in height, though the Cleveland Bay, whilst having the density of bone and quality of the Thoroughbred, was bred with a stockier type in view—what is called in Yorkshire *'A lot o' hoss in a little room'*.

The Cleveland Bay breed was found so plastic that when roads improved it produced the best coach-horses, the fastest walking horses for the land, the stoutest hunters, the best trappers — indeed, what is claimed for it today, that it is the best general utility horse in the world. During my lifetime the Whitby Agricultural Society retained in its show-catalogue the old description 'Chapman Horses'. Although bred throughout the county, Cleveland and the Vale of Pickering have always been the main supply areas of Cleveland Bays.

Here, at random, are a few equine terms in Yorkshire dialect in addition to those already quoted:

ROOADSTER. The name given to the breed now known as the hackney.

HOSS-HAY, HORSE-HAY. Hay well got, free from dust, with a good smell, as opposed to that of poorer quality, which is known as *stirk hay*, ie hay for cattle.

COCKTAIL. A half-bred horse, or one with a thoroughbred strain, but not eligible for entry in the General Stud Book.

WINGEY. A horse which is of uncertain temperament, which in temper *yeyles oot* (ie makes a howling noise), *scools* (ie lays back its ears), *shows t' white of its een*, or *clicks up a leg* ready to strike.

MUCK-SWEEAT. A horse which has been so hurried that it is in a lather and is bringing both sweat and dirt out of its pores and coat.

STALLED. A horse which has had too much corn given it and refuses to eat.

OWERFEEACED, OVERFACED. A horse which has been yoked to draw too heavy a load, or one which has been so overfed that it is *stalled*.

STOTTING, or GANNIN' CRAMMELLY. This describes a horse which moves badly. It may be not quite sound, or may have thin-soled feet.

COWT. A young male horse.

COWT FOOAL, male foal.

DOG HOSS. A horse which *tons orkerd* (ie turns awkward) and refuses to do its best.

YAWD. A roadster, a horse of inferior breeding. Often used in a derogatory sense. An old (c1750) Sinnington Hunt song tells of followers being mounted on *'Awd yawds and blood tits'*.

STAG. An unbroken gelding. In 1435 Peter, the chaplain of Ingleby Arncliffe, was fined for allowing his *stag* to feed with the lord's horses in the pastures below Alexander Hill.

GEEASE- (or PARROT-) GOBBED, GOOSE- . Applied to a horse with the top jaw longer than the bottom one, thus making grazing difficult.

PRAD. A term (usually derisive) for an old horse.

PRADDLE. Applied to the action of a horse with bad legs.

TONNED-OFF (-AWAY). Turned out to graze. If away from home it is *gysted.*

MISTETCHED. Mis-taught, not broken in properly. A runaway horse, an undependable animal, or one with bad manners.

GREEN HORSE. Used of a horse that has still much to learn about the job it is intended for.

JIBBER. A horse which is given to refusing to start, or to running backwards.

NEEA MOOTH, no mouth. A horse which does not respond to the reins, which pulls, or is difficult to guide.

DEEAD YA SAHD OF ITS MOOTH, dead one side of its mouth. Is applied to a horse that does not respond to the rein on one side.

TAK T' REEAST, take the reest. A horse *taks t' reeast* when it refuses to move backwards or forwards.

STRUNT. The first few inches of a horse's tail from the vertebrae.

NAG. Although often applied indiscriminately to all equine breeds, the term in Yorkshire connoted a small horse for riding as distinct from using in a cart, or agricultural horse. So recently as 1892 a 'pure bred nag stallion' (entered in Hackney Stud Book) travelled in the Ganton district of Yorkshire.

NOWT BUT A KNACKER. Referred to a horse in very poor condition, fit only for the knacker's slaughterhouse.

WETTING A HORSE'S HEAD. In Yorkshire, when a horse is shod for the first time, the owner stands treat at the village pub to all those congregated at the smithy. They drink *'Good luck ti t' young cowt, or meer'*, as the case may be.

FADGE. To ride at the slowest pace a horse can trot.

HOSS-CORN. Oats.

BAITING. Usually applied to feeding a horse when on a journey, or away from home.

(1959)

AH'M COMIN' BACK ...

Ah'm comin' back, Ah'm stalled o' t' leets;
  Ah'm sick to t' deeath o' City streets;
An' t' City ways, Ah's nivver leearn –
  Ah'm comin' back, to th' hills ageean.
Ah'm comin' back – ther's nowt else fo' 't–
  Mi belly warks wi' this mad lot –
Ah'm comin' back, to t' wind on t' fells,
  To t' cotton gress, an' th' heather bells.
Ah'm comin' back, mi thosst to sleck
  I' t' peeaty wine o' th' Ewden Beck,
Mi heart to warm, an' sowl to fill,
  Wi' t' seet o' t' stars thra Hartcliff Hill.

Ah'm fain for t' tang o' peeat ageean,
  For t' scent o' t' gorse an' t' ling,
For t' seet o' t' lapwing on her peeak,
  An' t' moorcock, low on t' wing.
Mi heart, it's set i' th' upland ways;
  An', reyt daan i' mi booans,
Ah'm one gret wark for th' Heigh
    Lad Ridge,
  T' Crow Chin, an' t' Glory Stooans.

Gordon Allen North (WR)

(1958)

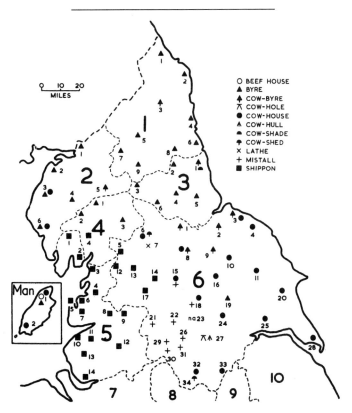

*A map illustrating an article on dialect names for the cow-house by Stanley Ellis,
in the 1962 Transactions.*

YORKSHIRE AILMENTS
Gwen Wade

This talk is not to be a learned exposition of matters medical but a few brief notes on the Yorkshireman's attitude towards '*t' ills o' t' flesh*', given by me in the hope of stimulating your memories and producing expressions and anecdotes of a like nature from you. My contribution will consist for the most part of 'modern instances' which have come my way during my years of ambulance work in the Ripon district, and I am trusting that we shall hear some of the 'wise saws' of Yorkshire medical history from you.

Yorkshire ailments? You may say that they are much the same as 'foreign' ones, but are they? *Ah'm noan so sewer.* Even if the Yorkshireman does not exactly enjoy poor health, he is apt *to mak' a reet job on it.* Everything stems from the fact that we in Yorkshire have a unique point of departure from the norm or, rather, a unique norm from which to depart. This is the Yorkshire state of health — *middlin'*...

Mr Austin Hyde, in his play *Home Cured*, has told us that there are three grades of *middlin'ness.* I would claim four for the West Riding, namely *pretty middlin'*, *middlin'*, *nobbut middlin'* and *nobbut varra middlin'*.

The man who boasts of being *pretty middlin'* would assuredly be passed by the insurance doctor as a first-class life. He whose avowed state is *middlin'* may either be a perfectly hale but cautious fellow, who does not wish to tempt Providence, or he may be suffering from a mild attack of *brownchitis* or maybe *belly-wark.* One such sufferer commented that he '*didn't reckon nowt to yon' teea an' coffee — they rots yer booits'*. He put safety first and drank beer to his breakfast. Or the sufferer may have been '*Havin' a bit o' bother wi' his varra couarse veins'*, or even '*with his various veins'*, though the latter is generally a feminine ailment.

The woman who tells you she is *nobbut middlin'* will likely go on to describe to you at length the details of a recent visit to her doctor for her gastric stomach: '*At's bin natterin' me summat chronic. Eh! An' I wor dowly! I'd t' ditherum-dotherums all o' t' dea' an' I kep' on gettin' them flutterin' birds an' t' doctor says ti me, he says...*'

Should a friend report of *t' wife's mother* that '*Shoo's nobbut varra middlin'*', it is simply another way of saying that the old lady is *nobbut just an' just*, or *taperin' off an' nigh on ready for sahdin!* Dr Bishop, in *My Moorland Patients*, tells of a woman who was *real proud cos her mother 'd 'ed five reasons for deein': 't' rheumatics, t' heart disease, t' dropsies, t' neuralgy, and t' chronic'.*

But think on '*at there's variations in t' riewls even i' Yorkshire. There wor one awd chap — a Highsider he wor — 'at wor nigh at Deeath's door wi' t' pneumonia but he would 'ev it he wor wick es a lopp an' 'He woren't bahn be lugged dahn t' stairs bi a couple o' lasses, nawther'. We had to let him walk at the finish. Another awd lad 'at wer ligged up a cat-stee aboon t' bar-parlour iv a country pub 'd likely be sufferin' wi bronnical asthma. When his mates coom in ov a neet, they'd shaht up tiv 'im: 'Ha's tha blowin', Tom, lad?' An' he'd skrike back: 'Ah aint' blowin' no-ha' — Ah'm reet bad'*. But these examples are extremes—exceptions to the even tenor of our mediocrity.

There was an old lady who was *all of a shack-a-doddle, 'cos Ah'd getten penicillin determinitis an' they'd insulated me for fower deays'* — an interesting etymological point here: in modern Norwegian to insulate is *isolere*, so why not the reverse in Yorkshire — *insulate* for *isolate?*

The most fascinating and fantastic ailments are always those which have been described to us by our medical attendants. *'An' t' doctor tell't me'* is a prelude to great marvels both anatomical and pathological. *An' he said: 'No, Mrs Dixon, it's not brokken, it's nobbut a frackssher'.*

What we should like most to hear from you is old prescriptions for cures which are tinged with the black of magic: *'Nah, yer want to give it some ivy off 'n a holly-bush'*. They were probably most efficacious cures as *vide* the success of the co-operation of the physician and the psychiatrist to-day.

But there are two sides even to the psychiatrist's couch. A Bradford lad of a very low mental grade was a member of a searchlight unit early in the war. Like many of his kind, he was possessed of a keen money-sense and after a prolonged bout of pilfering from his hut-mates, he was sent before the Command Psychiatrist. On his return he was eagerly questioned: *'Well lad, an' ha' didstha go off?'* His reply: *'Whya, t' chap weren't reet iv' 'is bloody 'ead; yer cud tell that bi t' daft questions he axed yer'.*

But back to magic. I give you this authentic West Riding cure for *arthuritis* and you can adjudge it black or white: *'Yer gets a black cat an' yer shuts it up i' a dark room an' yer chases it rahnd while it's in a white lather an' then yer scrapes off t' lather an' rubs it on t' affected part'.* And that is about as near the bone as I am prepared to go!

(1959)

ON T' SURFACE

Days, afters,
Through the neet,
Ther's a seathin' quiet
Along t' main street.

T' mornin' steams,
T' pit-head monster simmers,
As it gulps t' pit-men
Like a lion its dinners.

It's nivver 'Good mornin',
But 'All reight, Bill?'
'Sam!' 'Nah, Jim',
'Okay, Will?'

Or else t' silent nod,
That's t' usual greeatin':
The' goa abaht ther business,
Noa fussin' wi' meeatin'.

Ther's a steady throb;
T' noise from t' coil-lurries,
T' owd ten-past t' hour,
But nob'dy 'urries.

T' pit-buzzer mooans,
T' tractors shatter,
Milkdrays drooan,
'eead-scarved women natter.

But all this is rare,
An explosion i' t' calm.
It lasts for one minute,
Then quietens dahn.

Nigel Leary (WR)

(1960)

POT O' ONE

From t' varry day mi life begun
Ah've allus bin a pot o' one,
An' up till t' time 'at it mun end
Ah didn't think 'at Ah sud mend.

Sin' fust Ah left mi babby-pen
Ah've bin ower-mindful o' missen:
Ther's nawther care ner choice ner fun,
No sharin', for a pot o' one.

But oh, dear lass, tha's ta'en mi heart
An' shocked mi little warld apart,
An' pot o' one's no use to me
Now Ah'm so much in love wi' thee!

Ah can't abide thee aht o' seet,
On pins abaht thee, day an' neet;
Ther's nobbut one thing we can do:
Lass, sal we be a pot o' two?

An' if it pleases t' Lord above,
Through joy an' sympathy an' love,
I' time together, thee an' me,
We's happen mak' a pot o' three.

Ian Dewhirst (WR)

(1965)

pot o' one, originally referring to a pot used by woolcombers to keep their combs warm, the phrase means a person not fond of company, unwilling to share.

130

LAMBIN' STORM

'*Cheddy-yow! cheddy-yow!*'
That wur mi gaffer's cry
To ewes oot on t' brant hill
When lambin' snaws wur nigh:
I' Grannie's garden crocus floored
An' daffies made a show;
'*Cheddy-yow! cheddy-yow!*
Think on, we'll see mair snaw.'

'*Cheddy-yow! cheddy-yow!*
Tho' birds is singin' sweet
Spring's not here by a lang chalk,
For sure it isn't reet
For flooers to bloom while t' lambs
   is dropped',
An' he wud call his ewes,
'*Cheddy-yow! cheddy-yow!*'
An' bring in his twa coos.

That inklin' o' mi gaffer
Wur reet, for sure eneuf
T'wind wud rise, clouds wud lower
An' weather wud be rough,
Then he'd be up on t' brant hill
To drive his ewes fra' harm,
'*Cheddy-yow! cheddy-yow!*
Heer cooms t' lambin' storm!'

Dorothy Una Ratcliffe (NR)

(1961)

brant, steep

Dorothy Una Ratcliffe.

KING'S SQUARE, YORK

Ah laay thoo's tewed wi' traipsin'
   t' toon,
An still thoo's gotten time ti spare?
Why, thoo mun gan an' git a rest
On yan o' t' seats theer i' King's Square.
A choch yance stood on t' varry spot,
Near-hand wheer t' traffic's throng
   i' t' street;
There's shady trees an' floowers noo,
Wi' pigeons feedin' roond thi feet.

Think on, an' lewk straight for'ard like,
There's gabled hooses, awd an' high,
Wi t' Minster showin' ower t'roofs,
Sa grand an' grey, agean t' blue sky.
Thoo maun't be feared thoo'll loss
   thi bus,
For ivvery quarter t' bells'll chime.
Aye, it's a handy spot ti rest …
Happen thoo'll come another time.

Kathleen Stark (ER)

(1962)

THOWTS I' SPRINGTAHME

Come on, tha's surely had enough
O' dowly winter dumps!
It's spring ageean; up-end thissen;
It's tahme tha stirred thi stumps,
Or else tha ween't desarve to see
A lahmestun wall ageean,
Or curlews ower Langstrothdale
Wheer t' air is keen an' cleean.

Aye, keen enough, Ah'll bet it is,
Up amang t' fells an' gills!
T' gre't aat o' dooars — Ah know,
   Ah know;
'There's cowd i' them theer hills'.
Ay, theer it is, Ah'm gettin on;
Ah can't goo on for ivver
Roamin' abaat on t' tops as if
Ah still were young an' clivver.

Nay, drat it, if Ah haven't gooan
An' set missen agate
Thinkin' o' Oughtersha' an' Cray,
An' watterfalls i' spate!
Ah dooan't know 'at its all that far;
A bus 'ud just do t' trick.
Ah'll 'lift up me een to t' hills' ageean.
Na wheer's me walkin'-stick?

F A Carter (WR)

(1963)

NIGHT WORKER

*(Many night workers in Yorkshire textile mills are employed from
6pm to 7am —even today.)*

He sets off lahke a ten-yer-owd,
At fahve i' th' afternooin,
Whistlin' fit ta brusst hissen,
An' singin', ar — but sooin —
Sooin, i' t' valley bottham,
Daan i' t' chimley reek, an' t' sooit,
He shuffles inta t' mule 'oil,
Hawf isleep, thra t' yed ta t' fooit.

At four at t' morn, i' t' mulegate,
Sammin' t' threeds up, reyt an' left,
I' t' 'lectric glare, an' t' frussins,
An' feelin' hawf a man, at t' best,
He looks for t' fosst grey leet o' day
Wi' een lahke vestry pegs,
An' nawther rythme na reason,
Nobbut shuther, i' his legs.

At knockin'-off tahme, thick i' t' yed,
He stum'les aat, i' t' cowd,
An' thinks o' nowt but whom an' bed
Whal crossin' t' factory fowd;
He's een for nawther t' trod na t' gress
Whal stracklin' back, up th' hill—
A walkin' winteredge, nooa less,
A lad 'at's had his fill.

Gordon Allen North (WR)

(1964)

sammin', gathering; *frussins*, bits of thread, fluff; *trod,* path;
winteredge, clothes horse

SMOKELESS ZONE

Ther's an order cum aart —
We've to do as we're teld;
An' burn wat we're ordered;
Wi' t' fahrsahde they've mell'd.

We hevn't to burn coil,
T' fresh air to mahr;
But wat Ah'st miss moast,
'll be t' picters in t' fahr.

Fred Brown (WR)

(1963)

THE DIALECT OF FILEY
A Selection of Terms Concerning Fishing and the Sea
J D A Widdowson

The Filey district has received some attention in the past from a few well-known writers, notably George Shaw in his book *Filey and its Fishermen*, the works of Canon Cooper, the famous 'walking parson', and a number of smaller publications. All these have tended to concentrate on folklore and local history and there has been no large-scale systematic study of the dialect until recent years. Indeed, when one realises that Shaw's book, which may be regarded as the definitive work on the area, was published in 1867, it would seem that Filey has received less attention than might be expected.

Even though the town has been a popular seaside resort since the mid nineteenth century, the many visitors seem to have made comparatively slight inroads into the local speech and customs until very recent times. Even thirty years ago the fishing community of Filey was still comparatively closed, and when I first went to live in the area some twenty years ago the situation was much the same. At that time a detailed survey of the dialect, representative of the informal local speech, would have proved rather difficult for an outsider to undertake, although a native speaker might well have found it a much easier task. The gradual breaking down of the barriers of class and custom which was greatly accelerated by the Second World War made it much easier for an outsider to attempt a survey of such speech when my own research began in 1958. Traces of the traditional conservatism and independence still remain, but all the local people interviewed, most of whom were over sixty years of age, gave generously of their time and went out of their way to assist the work. Many were conscious that the dialect is gradually slipping away along with the traditional crafts and customs, and this awareness often proved a great help during the survey. I owe a special debt of gratitude to all those who took part in the survey and especially to my friend Mr George Waller who is an authority on Filey and its history.

The dialect itself is broadly similar to general East Riding speech, though it retains many distinctive pronunciations and items of vocabulary especially with reference to fishing and the sea, in spite of the decline of the inshore fishing in the last fifty years. The comparative isolation of the town has led to its becoming something of a relic area until quite recently. During the last thirty or forty years the constant influx of visitors and various social adjustments have brought about the encroachment of a northern Regional Standard pronunciation upon the area as a whole. The present-day dialect indicates that two possible phonemic systems, one related to Received Standard, and one representative of the traditional local speech, exist side by side in the area. This has resulted in an unusually wide range of phonetic variation. For example the word *stone* may be pronounced [stiǝn], [stɪǝn], [steǝn], [stɛǝn], [stɔ:n], [stɔǝn], [stɔɷn], [stuǝn], and the choice is not always conditioned by the social context. To some extent, in common with many other English dialects, a measure of bilingualism exists in the area. Speakers may adjust their pronunciation according to circumstances. For example a speaker may vary his pronunciation and also some of the words he uses according to whether he is speaking formally to a stranger (or someone he regards as a superior) or speaking informally to his family and friends. The development of what Filonians call 'a Saturday night voice' alongside the more traditional mode of speech is often the subject of ridicule in local anecdotes.

The following selection of terms concerning fishing and the sea represents the substance of a paper read at the annual general meeting of the society at Sheffield University on the 26th March 1966. It is drawn from tape-recordings and impressionistic transcriptions made between 1960 and 1966 as part of the general survey of the Filey dialect referred to above. Pronunciations are given in broad phonetic transcription, variants being separated from each other by commas. The following abbreviations are used: OED, *Oxford English Dictionary*; EDD, *English Dialect Dictionary*; n., noun; v., verb.

[Editors' note: in the interest of clarity, the list of dialect terms and their phonetic equivalents is reproduced directly from the original pages of *Transactions*.]

BARMSKIN		[ˈbaːmskɪn] An oilskin; specifically an oilskin apron worn by fishermen.
BAY		[bɛː], [bɛɪ], [bɛə]
BEACH		[biːtʃ], [bʉɪtʃ]
BEETING		[ˈbiːtɪn] Making or repairing nets.
BLASH		[blaʃ] A sudden squall of wind and rain.
BLEG		[blɛg] The sea bream.
BLOATER		[ˈblɔːtə(r)], [ˈblaːətə(r)], [ˈblɔɷtə(r)], [ˈblɔːətə(r)]
BOATBUILDER		[ˈbʉət̯ʔbɪldə(r)]
BOATHAND		[ˈbʉətand]
BOW	n.	[baɷ], [bɔɷ], (bou)

1. The forward section of a boat.
2. The curved strut of a crabpot made of briar or cane.

BOWL		[baɷl] A small spherical buoy attached to fishing nets.
BRAID	v.	[brɛːd], [brɛəd] To make or mend nets with a mesh and needle. In Filey it is usually applied to the making of crabpots as distinct from nets.
BREEZE		[briːz], [briəz], [brʉiz] In addition to its normal meaning of "a light wind" this word often refers to a strong wind, squall or gale.
BULKSHEAD		[ˈbɒlk̯ʔsɛd]
BUTT		[bɒt̯ʔ] The halibut.
BUOY		[bʉɪ]
CAG		[kag] A small cask, a keg.
CAGE		[kɛːdʒ], [kɛɪdʒ], [kɛədʒ] A crabpot.
CANVAS		[ˈkanvɪs]
CARGO		[ˈkaːgə(r)]
CASTENED THING		[ˈkɛsn t̯ʔ θɪŋ] The third marker buoy on a fishing line; it consists of a metal bowl attached to an anchor by a line and is thrown out or "cast" along with the baited line.
CAVE	v.	[kiəv] To separate old bait, seaweed and other unwanted material from a used fishing line: to clean fishing lines after a fishing trip. cp. CAVE v.[4]: "to separate chaff and empty ears from corn" OED.

CHAT		[tʃat?] A very small haddock; usually in the combination "chat haddock" cp. CHAT sb.⁴ "a small potato" OED.
CLEW		[klu:] The lower corner of a sail. It is found in the phrase "from clew to earing" (see EARING below) which means "from top to bottom, completely."
CLINCH	v.	[klɪnʃ] To lift with winch and chains.
COALFISH		[ˈkuəlfʃ]
COBLE		[ˈkɔbl̩] The traditional local fishing boat with high prow and deep keel used for fishing up to approximately fifteen miles offshore.
COMIC SINGER		[ˌkɔmɪk? ˈsɪŋə(r)] The name given to a stiff, dead fish, often one which is "throat-hung," and which rises from the water with its mouth gaping wide when the fishing line is hauled.
CONGER		[ˈkɔŋgə(r)] The conger eel.
COOKHOUSE		[ˈku:kʉus]
CRIB		[krɪb] The box-like rectangular sections situated aft of the engine in a coble. They are separated from each other by crib-boards and the fish is thrown into them when it has been caught.
CRIB-BOARDS		[ˈkrɪb buədz] Movable boards separating one crib from another in a coble.
CROWN		[kru:n], [krɔun], [krʉun] The curved section of an anchor between the flukes.
COILING		[ˈkɔɪlɪn]
CUTCH		[kɔtʃ] The commercial name for the catechu used in the tanning or barking of nets and lines.
CUVVINS		[ˈkɔvɪnz] Periwinkles, the common sea-snail.
DAG		[dag] A strip of coarse material wound round the palm of the hand to protect it when hauling fishing lines.
DODGING		[ˈdɔdʒɪn] Avoiding bad weather at sea, as in the phrase [ˈdɔdʒɪn fə bad ˈwɛðər] "dodging for bad weather."

DOOR [diə(r)] The opening in a crabpot through which a crab can be taken after it is caught.

DOWLY [ˈdaɒlɪ] Used in reference to weather: dull, gloomy, overcast.

DRIFT [drɪft] Driftwood and similar material washed ashore by the sea.

EARING [ˈɛərən] A small rope which fastens the upper corner of a sail to the yard. It occurs in the phrase "from clew to earing" (see CLEW above) meaning "from top to bottom, completely."

FACING [ˈfiəsɪn] A piece of oilskin used to cover the newly baited line after it has been coiled on to the skep.

FATHOM [ˈfad̪ðəm]

FLAMBEAU [ˈflambɔː] A fire-signal, beacon.

FLITHER [ˈflɪd̪ðə(r)] The limpet, used for baiting fishing lines.

FLOOD [flɒd], [fliəd] The flood tide.

FLUKE [flɒuḳʔ] The sharp triangular point at each end of the curved lower section of an anchor.

FOOTING TREE [ˈfiəṭʔn̩ triː] A piece of timber in the lower part of a coble against which an oarsman could press his feet when rowing.

FORECASTLE [ˈfuəkasl̩]

FORESHORE [ˈfuəʃuə(r)]

FOY [fɔɪ] A salvageable wreck.

FUNNEL [ˈfɒnɪl] The metal chimney of a boat's engine or stove.

GARTHANGLE [ˈgaːθaŋl̩] A staff or pole, usually with a metal prong at one end, used for hauling fish aboard; a gaff.

GLAZY [ˈglɛːzɪ] An oilskin coat.

GRADE v. [grɛːd], [grɛɪd], [grɛəd] To drag with grappling hooks. cp. GRAITH sb. 7 EDD.

GRAVING FORK [ˈgrɛəvɪnfɔrk] A long-handled implement with three thin tines used for digging up sandworms.

GUERNSEY [ˈgɛənsɪ] A thick woollen pullover worn by fishermen.

GURNARD, GURNET   [ˈgɔnɪt̬ʔ], [ˈgɔnət̬ʔ]

HADDOCK   [ˈadək̬ʔ], [ˈarək̬ʔ]

HALIBUT   [ˈɔləbɒt̬ʔ]

HARBOUR   [ˈa:bə(r)], [ˈaəbə(r)]

HATCH   n. [etʃ] The cover of a hatchway on board ship.

HERRING   [ˈɛrɪn]

HOOK   [u:k̬ʔ], [iək̬ʔ], [ʉuk̬ʔ]

HORIZON   [ˈɔrɪzən]

INWIRE   [ˈɪnwaɪə(r)] Narrow wooden bar which helps to brace the timbers of a coble below the level of the thwarts. cp. INWIVER sb. EDD.

JENNY   [ˈdʒɪnɪ] A small skate.

JOWL   [dʒaɔl] A sea swell.

JUMBO HADDOCK   [ˌdʒɔmbɔ: ˈadək̬ʔ] A very large haddock.

KEDGE-ANCHOR   [ˈkadʒˌaŋkə(r)] A small anchor.

KELK   [kɛlk̬ʔ] The spawn of a female fish.

KITTIWAKE   [ˈkɪtɪwɛ:k̬ʔ], [ˈkɪtɪwɛɪk̬ʔ]

LAND-SAILOR   [ˈlandsɛələ(r)] A humorous or contemptuous term for a landsman; a land-lubber.

LAUNCH   v. [lanʃ]

LAUNCHER   [ˈlanʃə(r)]
1. A man employed to help launch a coble.
2. A heavy block of wood used to prevent the wheels beneath a coble from moving while the boat is pushed off them into the water.

LEAD   n. [lɛd] A plumbline. Often heard in the phrase [ə kast ə lɛd] "a cast of lead" when the plumbline is thrown overboard to test the depth of water.

LEAK   v. [lɛk̬ʔ]

LIGHTHOUSE   [ˈli:tɒus]

LOP   [lɔp] A condition of the sea's surface when the water is choppy and small waves are breaking continually away from the shore.

139

LORD	[lɔ:d] A patron who owns a coble and employs fishermen. In former times the patrons were often members of the aristocracy but are usually wealthy businessmen nowadays.
LOW	[laɷ] A small, thin plaice.
MACKEREL	[ˈmakrɪl]
MAINBRACE	[ˈmɛənbrɛəs]
MAUND	[mɔ:n(d)] A basket used for holding bait and carried on the back by bait-gatherers. It is no longer in use at Filey.
MEET	n. [mi:t̬?] A bearing between two points as a means of navigation.
MESH	[mɛʃ], [maʃ]
MOORING	[ˈmuərɪn]
MOP	[mɔp] A very small codling.
NAB	[nab] A projecting cliff, headland or promontory.
NOSEBAND	[ˈnuəzbən] A length of line attached to the front of a skep.
OARS	[wɔz], [ɔəz]
OAR WASH	[wɔr ˈwɛʃ] The blade of an oar.
OCKY	[ˈɔkɪi] Material used for tanning or barking nets and lines; ochre.
OFFSIDEMEN	[ˈɔfsaɪdmɛn] Men who fished in yawls further from the shore than those in cobles.
OILSKIN	[ˈɔɪ(ə)lskɪn]
OLD HEN	[ɔ:d ˈɛn] A type of large black-shelled clam.
OYSTER	[ˈɔɪstə(r)]
PILOT-TROUSERS	[ˌpa:lət̬? ˈtru:zɪz], [ˌpaɪlət̬? ˈtru:zɪz], [ˌpaələt̬? ˈtru:zɪz] Trousers of heavy blue woollen cloth formerly worn by fishermen.
PLAICE	[plɛ:s], [plɛɪs], [plɛəs]
PLEASURING	[ˈplɛʒɔrɪn], [ˈplɛʒərɪn] Going for a pleasure-trip in a boat; taking someone for a pleasure-trip in a boat.
POND	[pɔnd] A compartment filled with water in which fish are kept alive on board ship.

PORT		[puːt̪ʔ], [puət̪ʔ]
PORTHOLE		[ˈpuətuəl]
POT	n.	[pɔt̪ʔ] A crabpot.
POT	v.	[pɔt̪ʔ] To catch crabs in a crabpot.
POUND	n.	[paɷnd] An enclosure for fish on board ship.
PROD	n.	[prɔd] A long boathook.
PRODUCE	v.	[prəˈdɷus] To supply (a ship) with provisions.
PUP		[pɷp] A young fish.
QUAY		[kiː], [kaɪ] Used specifically as an abbreviation for Bridlington quay instead of naming the town itself. The second pronunciation is the more common.
QUEENY		[ˈkwiːnɪ] The queen oyster.
RATCH	n.	[ratʃ] Sailing on a tack; a tack or "reach"; cp. RATCH sb.³ OED.
RATCH	v.	[ratʃ]
		1. To sail on a tack; to "reach".
		2. To draw out, stretch in a figurative sense; to exaggerate.
RAZOR-BILL		[ˈrɛɪzə bɪl]
ROKY		[ˈruːkɪ] Misty.
ROVING		[ˈruəvɪn] Fishing in any area at random; fishing with no set berth.
ROW	v.	[raɷ], [rɔɷ] (Propel a boat with oars).
ROWLOCK		[ˈrɔlək̪ʔ]
SAIL	n. v.	[sɛːl], [sɛɪl], [sɛəl]
SALT FISH		[ˈsɑːt̪ʔ fɪʃ], [ˈsɔːt̪ʔ fɪʃ], [ˈsɔɷʔt fɪʃ]
SAND-POKER		[ˈsand ˌpɔːkə(r)] A beachcomber, especially one who searches for coins in narrow crannies at the base of the cliffs, using a stick to poke away the pebbles. See SCRATTER below.
SCARER		[ˈskɑːrə(r)] The sea-anemone.
SCOTCHMEN'S SKINS		[ˌskɔtʃmənz ˈskɪnz] An old-fashioned float made of skin and attached as a marker to the fishing lines.
SCOUT		[skuːtʔ], [skʉutʔ] The guillemot.

SCRATTER ['skratə(r)] A beachcomber. See SAND-POKER above.

SCRATTING ['skratɪn] Beachcombing; especially searching for coins by scratching away loose pebbles with a stick.

SEABOOTS ['si:bu:t̬ʔs], ['si:biət̬ʔs], ('suibiət̬ʔs]

SEAGULL ['si:gɒl]

SEATHORN ['si:θɔ:n] A type of starfish.

SEINING ['si:nɪn] Fishing with a seine-net.

SHEET [ʃi:t̬ʔ], [ʃiət̬ʔ] [ʃuit̬ʔ] A rope, attached to the lower corner of a sail.

SHOAL [ʃɔɒl] A number of fish swimming together.

SHRIMP [ʃrɪmp], [ʃrɛmp]

SIDE-STICK ['sa:dstɪk̬ʔ] A short piece of wood used for measuring the size of mesh in the making of a fishing net.

SILE [sa:l], [saɪl], [saəl] Young herring.

SKANE v. [skiən] To cut shellfish out of the shell before using them as bait.

SKEEL [ski:l] A water-cask.

SKEETS [ski:t̬ʔs] The iron shoes or runners over the wooden forefeet of a coble. The skeets protect the runners when the boat is being moved on land.

SKEP [skɛp] A circular piece of basket on the flat surface of which fishing lines are coiled after they have been baited.

SLANG-BANG [slaŋ 'baŋ] A tangle of fishing-lines.

SLENK [slɛŋk̬ʔ] A very thin fish.

SLIP [slɪp] An apron used by fishermen when baiting lines, cleaning fish, etc.

SLIPWAY ['slɪpwɛ:], ['slɪpwɛɪ]

SMEAR n. [smiə(r)] The edible intestine of a male fish.

SMOCK [smɔk̬ʔ] A loose-fitting outer garment, usually brown in colour, worn by fishermen. The smock was often tanned along with the nets and lines and is sometimes referred to as a [ba:k 'smɔk̬ʔ] "bark smock".

SMOLT [smɔlt̬ʔ] A young salmon.

SNOOD		[sniəd] A short piece of line attaching each hook to the main fishing line.
SOLE		[soəl]
SOUTH-EASTER		[soðˈiəstə(r)]
SOUTHER	v.	[ˈsodðə(r)] Said of the wind: to blow from a southerly direction.
SPA-ING		[ˈspɔ:(w)ɪn] Going for a pleasure trip in a boat; taking someone for such a trip.
SPAR		[spa:] A mast, yard or boom of a sailing ship.
SPOUT		[spu:t̯ʔ], [spɒut̯ʔ] The funnel-shaped piece of net through which a crab enters a crabpot. It is widest at the outer edge of the pot and narrows on the inner side to prevent the crab from escaping.
SPRAG		[sprag] A young codfish.
SUN-DOG		[ˈsondɔg] A section of a rainbow; a small rainbow.
SWAMP	v.	[swamp] To fill (a boat) with water causing it to sink.
TACK	n.	[tak̯ʔ] Food in general.
TAFFLE	v.	[ˈtafl̩] To ravel, entangle.
TAILBAND		[ˈtɛəlbən] A short length of rope attached to the back of a skep.
TANGLES		[ˈtaŋlz] Seaweed.
TEDDY, TEDDY BEAR		[ˈtɛdɪ], (ˈtɛdɪ bɛə(r)] The name given to a small codling which is often a mottled brown in colour.
TEGGY		[ˈtɛgɪ] The lesser weever, a type of stingfish.
TELL-PIE		[ˈtɛlpa:], [ˈtɛlpaɪ] A hermit crab.
THOFT		[tɔft] The thwart of a rowing boat.
THOLE		[θaɒl] A vertical pin on the wale of a coble which slots into an aperture in the handle of an oar and acts as a pivot during rowing.
TIDE		[ta:d], [tɑ:d], [taɪd], [taəd]
TIDEWAY		[ˈta:dwɛ:], [ˈta:dwɛə]
TIMBER		[ˈtɪm(b)ə(r)]

TOW   n. [taɷ] A rope used for towing, a tow-line. Also the rope attached to a crabpot for hauling and lowering it, often referred to as [ˈpɔt taɷ] "pot tow".

TRAP   [trap] The pouch of a salmon net.

TRAWLER   [ˈtrɑːle(r)], [ˈtrɔːlə(r)], [ˈtrɔələ(r)]

TROT   v. [trɔt̯ʔ] To fish with a trot-line, i.e. to leave a baited line on the beach overnight and retrieve the catch when the tide ebbs.

TROUT   [truːt̯ʔ], [trʉut̯ʔ] The name given to the salmon-trout caught in Filey Bay.

TWINE   n. [twaːn], [twɑːn]

WADMENZ   [ˈwadmənz] Stockings made of heavy white wool, worn inside sea-boots. Although this word is known at Filey the local people always claim it is a Flamborough word. The more common local term is [ˈbiət̯ʔ-stɔkɪnz] "boot-stockings".

WALE   [wiəld] A piece of timber extending horizontally round the top of the sides of a boat. In a coble it forms a ledge on the upper edge of the planking and extends from stem to stern.

WARFISH   [ˈwaːfɪʃ] The razor-fish.

WARP   n. [waːp], [wɔːp] A rope used for hauling or moving a ship in harbour.

WATERTIGHT   [ˈwatətɛɪt̯ʔ]

WELLINGTON   [ˈwɛlɪt̯ʔn]

WESTER   [ˈwɛstə(r)]..A sou'wester.

WETHER   [ˈwɛd̯ðə(r)] The barb of a fishing hook.

WHEELHOUSE   [ˈwiːluːs], [ˈwiːlɷus], [ˈwiːl us]

WHELK   [wɪlk̯ʔ]

WINDWARD   [ˈwɪndəd]

WING   [wɪŋ] A projecting section of a fishing net, especially a trawl-net, on one side of the main section.

WOLF, WUFF   [wɷf] Catfish.

WRACK   n. [rɛk̯ʔ] Seaweed.

WRECK   n.   [rɛk̰?]

YARD   [jaːd]   A spar slung from the mast and supporting a sail.

YAWL   [jɔːl], [jɒᴈl], [jɔəl]   A fishing boat larger than the coble though of similar design and equipped with sails.

(1966)

SUPERMARKET

A little wire basket —
Tempters on t' shelves —
It cums a bit cheeaper
When yer help yerselves.

A packet o' biscuits —
A nahce fancy cake —
Fill up yer baskets!
Ther's noah need to bake.

Line up at t' counter —
They tot up yer score —
Yer've got what yer needed,
An' happen a bit more.

—————

Ah remembered t' owd shop
Wi its cleean sanded floor,
An' buckets an' brushes
Hung swingin' near t' door.

Yer joined in wi' t' gossip,
An' monny a joake,
When whiskery old Sam
Tipped yer flaar into t' poake.

Old Sam hed noa baskets,
Nor slick shiny till;
But noa chromium-platin'
Could match Samuel's goodwill.

Fred Brown (WR)

(1967)

145

YORKSHIRE STEEL TERMS TODAY
Peter Wright

Recently, helped greatly by Yorkshire Dialect Society members like Mr Ben Calton of Stocksbridge, Mr T E Haynes, senior metalwork lecturer at Sheffield College of Education, and employees of United Steel and other companies, I have been collecting Yorkshire steel terms. They were gathered partly in the comfort and quiet of people's homes, and partly from visits and interviews amidst the deafening noises of giant presses, cranes and furnaces.

Although the industry, centred on Sheffield, covers a small area on the map, it embraces a vast language area with many branches each quite specialised. The press-forge man is unlikely to know many terms well known in the foundry, and the worker in the electric-arc melting shop is in a sub-industry, with a different set of words, from the blast-furnaceman. The fact that the steel industry is comparatively modern is no drawback to the language collector, for it certainly isn't a case of racy dialect being submerged in a general, uninteresting, technical vocabulary. In such a fast-moving industry the steelworker has to think and communicate at least as quickly as the countryman. (There is, in fact, a special way of cupping your listener's ear to talk above the din of machinery.) As new processes appear, new words are needed to describe them and, where the technical terms seem too long or too learned for the man on the shop floor, he will change them or invent his own. He must talk.

All along, distinctions, expected and unexpected, abound. *Smelting*, 'reducing the metal from its ore', differs in meaning as well as a mere letter from *melting*, the later process of making iron or steel. The iron bars about four feet long into which the ore is smelted are called, with something approaching a farmer's affection, *pigs*, and the larger ones *sows*. This latter was once the word for the large channels feeding the smaller ones — hence the name — but is now used for what are formed in the channels. Formerly there was much dodging to avoid unloading *sows* because they were so much heavier, but the operation is now done on a pig-casting machine.

The main parts of a blast-furnace, as shown on the diagram, are:

1. *Skip* (small wheeled container to charge the furnace); 2. *'Opper* (hopper, container for receiving the ore and passing it into the furnace); 3. *Throit*, 'throat'; 4. *Stack*, 'chimney'; 5. *Belly* (widest part of the stack); 6. *Bosh* (container round the belly); 7. *Mantle* (to support the stack); 8. *Bustle pipe* (distributing hot blast); 9. *Tweeaz* (*'tuyères'*, nozzles through which the air enters the furnace); 10. *(H)earth*;

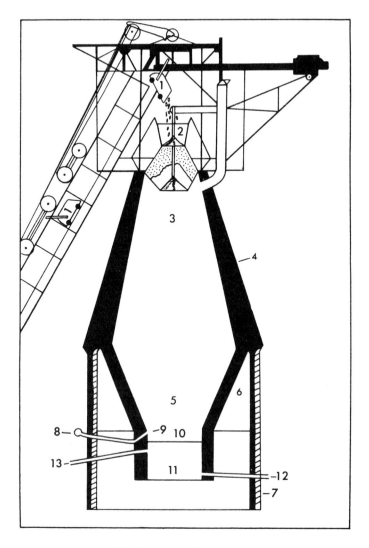

The parts of a blast-furnace.

11. *Bottom*; 12. *Slag-oil* or *slag-notch* (the place where the cinders etc come out); 13. *Tap-oil* (small opening through which the metal is run out).

Among so many words of Anglo-Saxon or Germanic origin it seems unusual to have *tweeaz*, 'tuyères', but even here steelworkers have twisted the pronunciation away from the French type *twee-airs*. Other odd names occur like *bear* for a lump of metal left in the hearth when the furnace is emptied. This is another animal name, like *pigs* and *sows* above, the metal perhaps being likened to a bear in a pit. Another curiosity, unknown to the *Oxford English Dictionary* or *The English Dialect Dictionary*, is the *go-devil*, a bucket of coke hung in the throat of the old blast furnace to light the escaping gas. Moreover, the blast-furnaceman never pours metal but *casts* it from the furnace into the ladle, or later *teems*, 'pours', it from the ladle into the ingot mould. Again, he has his own expressions for stopping or reducing the operation of the furnace. These include *banking* or *banking down* (adding fuel but reducing the air supply, as one does by putting *slack* on an ordinary domestic fire), *blowing down* or *steadying down* (gradually decreasing the blast), and *blowing out* (closing the furnace for repairs to the lining).

Frequent differences occur between book language and that of the shop floor. For the cupola, the type of casting furnace, although in Sheffield the pronunciation *kyoopala* is gaining ground, *kyoopalaw* is still preferred, as it was in 1893.

The metal put into an open-hearth furnace, which in technical books is usually the stock, becomes on the shop floor the *charge*, because *stock* refers to the ingots etc kept in the section of the steel mill called the *stock-bay*.

Ingot defects have various names, for instance the *roke*, into which a surface blowhole rolls out; *lap*, a discontinuity on the surface where the steel *laps* or curls over on itself; *hot clink*, where slag adheres to the ingot; *hot tear*, where the ingot comes slightly apart in being rolled; and *clod shut*, where part of the surface metal has solidified during teeming.

Terms used around the press forge include *porter bar* (an iron bar suspended from a crane for handling the ingot), held by a *burden chain*; *swage tools* (for bending and shaping the ingot); a *dye* (a four foot metal container for upending it and impressing a design upon it); *wemblies* (wide moulds introduced at the time of the Wembley Exhibition); *pickling* (dipping bars into sulphuric acid to remove scale); and *slinging* (moving ingots around by crane — to sling in the sense of hurl them, even if possible, would be sheer madness!). Also there are *dogs*, yet another animal name. According to Brandt's *Manufacture of Iron and Steel*, they are spikes in the floor for moving the ingot, but by *dogs* Yorkshire steelmen, who ought to know, mean mechanical grabs for awkwardly shaped ingots where a sling would be impossible.

A press-forging team is led by the *codder*, and there is a corresponding verb, eg *he's codding today* (of a deputy doing the work of the leader). The team includes a *stockman*, responsible for each ingot entering the *shop*, the area where the team work; an *assistant slinger* who helps him; a *clayman*, who makes a *length lath* to determine the size of job required for the press and puts this lath on the ingot; a *press driver*, who manipulates the ingot for size; a *crane driver*; and a *scaleman*, who keeps the press clear of scale. There is also the *handyman*, who keeps the shop clean: he is not called *labourer* or *sweeper-up* because then he would not qualify for a special piece-work bonus. But the gentleman in the team with the most remarkable name is the *back-tonger*, the second-in-command. He formerly stood behind the press forge with a pair of tongs to keep the ingot square, but now, his tongs having disappeared, just signals to the crane-driver to keep it in position. Other occupational names are *teemer*, 'man who pours out the molten metal', *tenter*, 'first hand in a cupola team', and in the rolling mill the *roller* (responsible for size and section), the *shearer* (in charge of cutting), and the *floorman* (the shearer's assistant).

Electric-arc furnace work is a branch of the industry so new that it has barely had time to manufacture its own terms. So far its most noticeable features are the tendencies to shorten technical words and give them more homely names — *pressure cooker* for the electric-arc furnace, *sticks* for the electrodes, *puller-out*, 'fume-extractor', *lid* for both the furnace roof and a safety helmet, *dally*, 'dalofrit' (to mend the furnace), *connies*, 'economisers' (to stop heat escaping between electrode and roof), *bricks* for refractories and *dipper* for pyrometer, *blacking*, 'graphite dust', and *whiting*, 'lime'. Also disconcerting is the way normal names refer to enormous objects. For example, *pens* for scrap are the size, not of sheep-pens, but of about four railway waggons; a *charging basket*, far different from, say, a shopping basket, is a metal container holding about ninety tons; and *button hooks* are the curved ends of crane arms to hold gigantic metal ladles.

In the foundry a host of tools exists, such as the *stirrer* for stirring the melt and the *skimmer* to skim off its impurities; the *chill*, a piece of cold metal put into the mould to harden it at that point; the *rapping bar* for making the mould, and *venting rods* and *vent wires* to let air into it; *sieves* and the coarser, bigger *riddles*; and *trumpets* and *tundishes*, vessels for different ways of pouring into moulds. The many types of ladle are accompanied by a variety of names, from *shanks*, 'hand ladles', and *two-man ladles* held and turned by two men, to enormous crane-ladles called simply *pots*. Popular etymology is keen to explain some of these words, eg *strickle* (the instrument to smooth the outside wall of a mould) is thought a newish word from 'strike it level', whereas it probably goes back to the Anglo-Saxon *stricel*, an instrument for smoothing corn in a measure.

General dictionaries note some steel words and not others, for example, known to the *OED* are *spark arrester*, *tap-hole* and *sill* (the ledge in front of it), *soaking pit* (a firebrick-lined hole for cooling ingots), and *skelp* (steel strips for making into tubing); but not *wind-belt* (reservoir of air in the cupola), *tapping-pit* (next to an electric-arc furnace to draw off the metal), *stripping-stools* (for holding ingots), *slag-oil*, or even its more 'refined' equivalent *slag-hole*.

Even when the steel is about to leave the mill, curious names are not finished with. It may be loaded on to lorries by a *wharfman* at the *wharf* or *loading dock*, 'loading bay', although no river or canal is in sight. Of the major British industries, farming and fishing include more old words, building language seems more straightforward, textiles has its share of curiosities, and mining expressions have a tremendous variety; but words in the steel industry are as fascinating as any.

(1966)

THE INNKEEPER

Breekfast? Why lass, Ah's nut 'ungery,
Ah nivver thowt on for ti eeat.
An Ah's breeat as a bullace this mornin',
When Ah owt ti be deead o' mi feeat!

Last neet — there'll be nivver nowt like it,
If Ah live tiv a hundhred an' ten.
Ah've bin chaanged owerneet somehoo, Mary,
An' Ah's capped hoo it happened, an' when.

Thoo'll recall that young couple fra Nazareth:
We'd nowheer ti put 'em i' inn:
Well, Ah fun 'em a plaace doon i' coo-shade
— Bud weather was desperate thin:

Sooa, when Ah'd all visitors sattled,
An' thoo hard asleeap i' thi bed,
Ah lowsened aud Jess frev her kennel,
An' wended mi way doon ti shed.

It was clearer nor dayleet i' fowdyard:
Ommost midneet it was — moon at full.
Nut a glimmer frid hooses i' village,
An' snaw covered grund, soft as wool.

They'd ed nowt ti eeat ti ma knowledge,
So Ah browt 'em a bite an' a sup,
An' some oil i' case lamp wanted thrimmin',
An' happins, ti lap bairn up.

Then Ah tended ti coos, an' ti Jenny,
— An' Ah've nivver knawn cattle si calm.
Then Ah browt some cleean sthraw doon for manger,
Just ti mak seear at bairn was warm.

Ah deean't think they nooaticed me scarcelins,
As Ah rawmed aboot sidin' spot through.
They wor taen up wi' lewkin' at bairn
— An' it mother es same name as thoo!

Sike a wee, conny thing it was, Mary,
Poor bairn! Ommost lost amang sthraw!
… But Ah couldn't distorrb 'em mich langer,
So Ah left 'em an' stood oot i' snaw.

A still neet it was — sthraange an' quiet,
As Ah leeaned up agen dooar jamb …

Then Ah fancied Ah heeard soond o' music,
As thaw stars was all singin' a psalm!

At fosst — well, Ah thowt Ah was dhreeamin':
But they'd heeard it at pinfowd an' all,
An' Ah seed 'em come runnin' doon hillsahde,
An' makkin' their way sthraight ti stall!

It was Rewben, an' Shep, an' young Davy,
They'd bin up at top tentin' sheeap.
They wor towld ti come doon intid village,
Wheer they'd finnd lartle bairn asleeap.

Noo, sthrangest of all was aud Rewben:
Leeavin' lambs nobbut yistidda born!
But all he would say when Ah axed him —
'The Lord'll tak care o' 'is awn!'

Well, summat was dhrawin' me, Mary,
So Ah went in wi' Rewb an' his men.
We stood a bit lewkin' at bairn …
But Ah hardlins knaw what happened then.

We went doon on oor knees theer i' staable,
Awhahle mother took bairn ov her knee.
An' she crooned a soft lullaby ower it,
Tahme we knelt: Rewben, Shep, Dave, an' me.

Noo, God's bairns is all on 'em lovely,
— Why oor awn was a bonny, wee thing.
An' Ah play wiv 'em, noss 'em, an' love 'em —
Yit we knelt like we would tiv a king!

Sooa that's why Ah's nut varry 'ungery:
Ah'd like ti walk hills all day lang.
— Bud we've visitors' vittles ti see tiv,
Varry seean we'll be booath on us thrang.

Bud fosst, walk wi' me doon ti coo-shade:
Ah feel some day, when we've getten aud,
We'll be glad we leeaked efther that bairn,
An' fun it a plaace oot o' caud.

Arthur Jarratt (ER)

(1968)

bullace, wild plum; *tentin',* watching over; *thrang,* busy

151

WHA WOD A THOWT IT?

Ah stood o' t' station platform, an' Ah wor glad that oor faythers wor safe an' soond i' the' graves, an' edn't lived ti see syke an' a seet.

Ah thowt o' all t' fooaks 'at used ti swarm on ti this 'ere platform, an' noo it seeamed ti swarm wi' ants, an' ti feel as deead as a graveyard.

The' wor fooak 'at used ti gan bi t' train teea an' frae the' wark ivvery day, farmers an' the' womenfooak went ti t'market ivvery week, an' t' bairns, fresh as daisies, went o' the' Sunda'skeeal trips, an' the' com back wi' sticks o' rock, an' buckets an' spades, ready for the' beds.

Monda' wor Market Day, an' t' igh leet o' t' week for t' farmers. Women took baskets o' fresh butter, an' grand broon eggs, the'd be up afoor day leet ti get t' butter chonned afoor t' sun gar up, an' the' cooked it wi' ice cawd watter oot o' t' well. Toons fooaks allus favour a good broon egg, an' yer can't beeat a few good Rhode Island Reds, the' used ti knaw the' 'ens them farmers' wives. When the' all gat inter t' carriage, the' wor lively talk ower prices, profits an' losses, them farmers 'ed a twinkle i' the 'ee, the' seeamed ti thrive o' them losses. Station maister wore a tippy cap on 'is 'eead, an' gold braid 'ov 'is cooat, bairns wor a bit freetoned on 'im, 'e wor a bit stiff like, same as t' skeeal maister an t' parson.

T' goods yard wor allus thrang an' all, farmers browt all the' stuff ti' station, taties, beet, an' corn, an' the gat off waggin looads o' tillage an' feedin' stuffs. The' used pole waggins i' them days an' teeams o' fower 'osses, full o' mettle, an' the' took some 'andlin. The' wor a clerk i' t'office, an' ootside two poorters an' two signalmen, an' ivvery yan on 'em took a 'and i' keepin' station reet up ti t' mark, flooers wor bloomin' all doon t' platform an' i' t' tubs alangside an' all, an' all t' staff wor fair prood on it.

Ah stood theer an' gawped, rusted metals, winders brokken, nettles an' rubbish ivvery wheer, Ah cud a' bluthered an' reeared. Ah nivver thowt Ah should a' lived ti see syke an' a seet.

F E Jackson (ER)   *(1967)*

HITLER IS A BAD UN!

Durin' t' Warr Ah kept this big blue budgie. Joey, Ah called him. T' time Ah fun aht he could speyk wor one day when t' gas-man called, an' ses 'Good mornin', Missus', but Ah didn't answer him for Ah'd summat burnin' i' t' oven an' Aw wor just lewkin' to see what it wor. When t' gas-man wor goin' he ses, 'When Ah cum in, Missus, tha didn't say owt, did ta? Well, summat did. Summat said good mornin'.'

Ah ses, 'Aw've a budgie, but Ah didn't knaw he spak.' So Ah ses, 'Good mornin', Joey', an' he ses, 'Good morning! Good morning!' like a proper little gentleman — lovely big blue budgie, he wor. 'Good morning! Good morning!'

Well, after that he gat to say all soarts. He used to say, 'What're yer doin' nah, Enid?' — this wor a little lass Ah used to minnd of a mornin' while her mother wer warkin'. Shoo wor nobbut three, an' Ah used to gie her mi button-box to laik wi', an' when Ah codn't hear t' buttons rattlin' Ah used to say, 'What're yer doin' nah, Enid?' Soa then, Joey used to say, 'What're yer doin' nah, Enid?' as plain as owt. He used to say, 'Pretty Jean has goan to schooil' an' all — that wor mi little niece — 'Pretty Jean has goan to schooil.'

Aw hed to hev a gert big green blinnd at t' winder i' them days, for t' black-aht, an ivvery mornin' Aw hed it to winnd up. Allus, when Ah wor winndin' it, Ah used to say, 'Hitler is a bad un!' Aye, ivvery mornin', 'Hitler is a bad un!' as Ah wor winndin' t' blinnd up. An' it worn't lang afore Joey wor sayin', 'Hitler is a — ' an' then he'd stop. Just 'Hitler is a — . Hitler is a — .'

For wiks Ah tried to get him to say 'bad un', but he wodn't, though he'd say 'Hitler is a — . Hitler is a — 'mony a time a day. Ah thowt happen he codn't say t' letter 'b', but he said 'Little Boy Blue' plain eniff (though Ah nivver gat him to say 'Come blow up yer horn'). He sahnded t' letter 'b's wonderful i' 'Little Boy Blue'.

Soa Ah gat to think he wor a reight Hitler man, wor Joey. He wodn't call him a bad un at nowt. Just 'Hitler is a — . Hitler is a — .'

Well, one mornin' Ah were feelin' reight aht o' sooarts, an' when Ah wor winndin' t' blinnd up, Ah doan't knaw hah it wor, but it just slipped aht, an' Ah just ses, 'Hitler is a *bugger*!' Ah nobbut said it once, tha knaws, it just slipped aht 'cause Ah wor feelin' aht o' sooarts, an o' course Ah wor in o' mi awn.

But t' next thing Ah knew, Joey wor sayin', 'Hitler is a *bugger*! Hitler is a *bugger*!' as clear as a bell. Ah codn't shut him up at nowt, an' he wor allus sayin' it, reight through to t' end o' t' Warr!

Ian Dewhirst (WR)   *(1968)*

BEN TURNER

(1863-1942)

John Waddington-Feather

One of the most colourful figures the West Riding produced at the end of the nineteenth century, and one of the early members of the Yorkshire Dialect Society, was Ben Turner, later to become Alderman Turner, Mayor of Batley, and eventually Sir Ben Turner, MP, Minister of Mines.

His early life runs parallel with that of many other Yorkshiremen of his time who started life in very humble circumstances and subsequently became famous. He was a contemporary of Professor Joseph Wright, and like Wright (to whom strangely enough he bore a strong physical resemblance later on in life) he knew near poverty for long periods of his youth and early manhood. He also started life in the mills like Wright as a half-timer. He went to work at the age of ten as a piecener, helping the warp-dressers to prepare their warps for the looms. In his autobiography, *About Myself* (1929), he recalls:

> We had to go to school one half-day and the mill the other half-day. One week we started work at 6am and went on till 12.30pm with a half-hour for breakfast. We then had to go to school from 2 to 4.30pm. The opposite week we went to school at 9am until 12 noon, and to work from 1.30pm to 6pm. It was a bit cruel at times when on the morning turn at the mill, for it meant being up at 5am, getting a drop of something warm, and trudging off to the mill a mile away. In winter it was fearful.

Sir Ben Turner was born at Holmfirth in 1863, but at an early age went to live in Huddersfield. Part of his elementary education he received from an old handloom weaver, who, self-taught, gave music lessons to the neighbouring millworkers' children. The weaver spoke only in dialect, like his charges, and the young Turner's first love for dialect literature came through music, for dialect songs were set to tunes and Ben Turner's father was very adept at singing in dialect. His father also used to bring home penny dialect broadsheets which were so popular in the nineteenth century and formed a principal source of home entertainment in West Riding textile villages and towns. It was natural, therefore, that Ben Turner should later turn to the dialect when he tried his hand at verse-writing.

As Ben Turner was brought up in a politically conscious household, his energy and interests soon veered towards politics, in which he played an important part during his lifetime. Ben's family had a tradition of radical socialism. His father's uncle was tried at York Assizes as a Luddite and his own father was an active worker for trade unionism throughout his life. It was from his father that Ben Turner inherited the single-minded independence and extreme sensitivity to unfairness and injustice which characterized his political career. From his mother, it would seem, he received the tact and openmindedness which made him famous in settling industrial disputes and respected as a magistrate. In his autobiography he gives us a vivid account of the price his family had to pay for its part in running union affairs in the 1870s:

> My first glimpse of a strike was in Holmfirth in 1872, when I was nine years of age. My father was one of the strikers and a union committee man as well ... I went and watched the processions of strikers as they marched round the district or went the six miles' walk to the mills at Huddersfield. The dispute pay was four shillings per week, and my mother had to allocate so much bread per day for the seven of us, and often we were hungry. Sometimes my aunt would give us a 'buttershive' or 'treacleshive' (ie a slice of bread with butter or treacle on it) and these were looked upon as gifts from heaven. At times we would get a turnip or some big potatoes ... Another aunt gave my mother some dripping, but it had gone 'reezed' (rancid) and I turned against dripping for many a year afterwards.

When he grew up, Ben Turner threw himself wholeheartedly into the trades' union movement, becoming chairman of the TUC in 1928; but he did not neglect his education nor lose his love for dialect. He regularly attended classes at the mechanics' institute after work three or four evenings a week, and he would walk miles to hear lectures, listen to good music concerts and see dramatic productions by actors the calibre of Sir Henry Irving. He began to write dialect poems, and in one marathon sitting of twenty-seven hours during the textile dispute of 1925 he kept up the morale of his colleagues by reciting dialect poems. One of his fellow committee men on the union negotiating committee of that dispute was Philip Snowden, later to become Chancellor of the Exchequer. Snowden was himself an enthusiastic writer and speaker of Yorkshire dialect, and he and Turner were close friends. When Turner, who was MP for Batley from 1922 to 1931, was standing as candidate for the 1924 election, Snowden sent the following poem to him:

Philip Snowden to Ben Turner

Tha'rt a bit of a poet thisel, Ben,
Soa Aw think Aw'll send thi a rhyme,
Just to wish thi luck and to say ha' mich
Aw want thee to win this time.

For tha's been tried and tested i' Parliment,
An' tha's proved a reight good chap;
Tha's allus spokken and voated for them
'At were not i' Luxury's lap.

We want noa taxes on food, lad,
Ner on cloathes ner shoon ner leet,
Tha's a better plan ner that, Ben,
For keeping t' hoam fires breet.

Soa Aw hoap at Batley an' Morley,
An' Ossett an' all the rest,
We'll stick to Ben and return him,
Fer he's one of our very best.

Turner mentions in his book what a fascinating speaker of dialect Snowden's mother was in his home village of Cowling, just beyond Keighley. He says:

The Yorkshire dialect poet, Professor Moorman, was so charmed with the old lady and her dialect talk that he had her to speak into the phonograph and the record is put away for future students of languages to hear a hundred years hence.

(I don't know what has become of the recording Moorman made of Mrs Snowden, but the society still has in its library valuable recordings of Philip Snowden reciting dialect stories and proverbs, along with other speakers throughout the county; recordings which were made in the 1920s.)

In a chapter entitled 'Poetry and Politics', Sir Ben Turner details his own efforts at journalism and dialect writing. He published two collections of verse, mainly in dialect, called *Pieces from a Yorkshire Loom* (1909) and *Collected Rhymes and Verse* (1934). Most of his verse forms in dialect are traditional ones and they are far and away better than his efforts in Standard English. Like other social writers of his time, Ben Turner's dialect verse will be remembered for the insight he gives a contemporary reader into industrial and living conditions at the end of the nineteenth century. This is not to say at all that his verse lacks appeal as poetry. He writes, for example, a blatantly propagandist poem called *Slumland*, attacking the appalling housing conditions in many West Riding towns. Yet in this poem is a masterly satirical paradox:

T'sun varry seldom finds 'em,
It peeps in nah and then,
But daily darkness blinds 'em,
An' breeds some owd young men.

and he can also pen a beautiful lyric, *Bonny Mooin*, which has some very effective imagery and metaphor in stanzas like:

Bonny breetness up i' th' heavens,
What a pleshur 'tis to see
Thy full face wi' loines so wrinkled
Lookin' dahn o' th' world an' me.
When tha comes wi' dim faint aghtloine,

Wi' thi neb cap cockt i' th' sky,
Awm fain glad 'cos then Aw knaw, lad,
Tha'll be bigger by an' by.

Like nearly all the other notable dialect-writers of the nineteenth century, his efforts at verse in the standard language are little more than doggerel. Dialect verse is quite definitely his forte, and dialect poems about town life rather than the country contain his best work. However, his interest in dialect-writing was not confined only to verse, for, as a journalist, he frequently wrote dialect sketches and thumbnail portraits of local characters in the *Huddersfield Examiner* and the *Northern Pioneer*, under the pseudonym Ike Longtung. Many of his poems were first printed in our own *Transactions*, and a very informative article by him about nineteenth-century dialect almanacs appeared in the YDS *Transactions* for 1932, the year after he was knighted. He also lectured widely throughout south Yorkshire on dialect topics.

His activities in politics brought him into contact with many famous national figures. George Lansbury, Beatrice and Sidney Webb, Ramsay MacDonald and George Bernard Shaw were all friends he made through his support of the Labour Movement. He had a deep and personal friendship with Keir Hardie who frequently stayed at his house when he visited Yorkshire; and the Pankhurst family were also very friendly with him.

In 1920, Ben Turner visited Russia with the first delegation of the Labour Party and TUC. It was on this visit he had a memorable interview with Lenin, with whom he disagreed strongly on the violence and bloodshed he had used to effect the Communist Revolution in Russia. A lifelong pacifist, Turner hated violence in any form and told Lenin bluntly that he disapproved of Soviet revolutionary methods. Lenin answered that the Russian Revolution had achieved its end, therefore bloodshed was justified; and he went on to forecast that England would have bloodshed before she had a socialist government. In his forthright way, Turner replied:

I don't think so. I believe I know as much about my people as you do about yours, and I know well enough that your methods are not those of Englishmen. I don't say we won't have a revolution — we have one every five years — but our weapon is the ballot-box.

The relationship between George Bernard Shaw and Ben Turner was a particularly close one after they first met at the foundation of the Independent Labour Party at Bradford in 1893. Turner went as a delegate from the Batley Labour Party, and Shaw went as one of two representatives of the Fabian Society. Shaw was at first refused admission to the inaugural ILP Conference, and Turner was one of the delegates who voted against his admission as an executive member of the conference. As a result, the delegates to the conference were treated to an address by Shaw from the visitors' gallery on the reasons why he and his fellow Fabian should be accepted as full delegates. Shaw's oratory earned him admission as a full delegate the same evening.

From that time onwards the friendship between Shaw and Turner grew. During Ben Turner's 1922 campaign for Parliament, he wrote to Shaw asking him to come up to Batley and speak for him. Shaw replied, saying he regretted he couldn't come as he was already fully booked up. He added at the foot of his apology a typical Shavian postscript: 'PS. A message from me is dangerous. You have no idea how some people dislike me. GBS.'

Perhaps, from a literary viewpoint, the most interesting correspondence Turner had with Shaw was when Shaw was writing his play, *St Joan*. In a letter dated 27th June, 1923, Shaw writes:

Dear Ben Turner,

Will you just scrawl for me on the enclosed card the names of a few published stories in north country dialect, and pop it into the post. Your own preferably.

I am writing a play about Joan of Arc; and it is no use making the girl talk like Dr Johnson: I must devise some sort of dialect for her; and as she was north country I want to found it on our north country talk. My own dialect, being Irish, is not available. I know nobody who will understand what I want as well as you.

Don't give yourself any trouble beyond writing the titles: I know how you curse the postman.

ever

G Bernard Shaw

Ben Turner sent him the Yorkshire dialect books and he received a reply from Shaw on July 2nd, which goes:

The 12 books have just arrived—Twelve thousand thanks.

The worst of Dialect Societies is that they are too much taken up with out-of-the-way words and pronunciations: some of them think that when they have written a story in university English, and then misspelt it and spoiled the grammar a little, they have produced Yorkshire dialect, or whatever other dialect they are after. But what I am after is the construction of the sentences, the music and dramatic emphasis of them. All that can be got without going outside Johnson's Dictionary; and it will fit Joan of Arc as well as Jenny of Otley.

Have you noticed that Lady Gregory and all the later modem writers of Irish-English have given up the old phonetic spelling of the Victorian comic writers, and use conventional spelling always? However, don't answer until we meet some day.

GBS

Five years later, in 1928, when Ben Turner was writing a few autobiographical notes for a newspaper, he wrote to Shaw asking if he would object to Turner's using the correspondence about *St Joan*, but omitting several lines from the letter which he thought were confidential. (Perhaps it was Turner's tactful way of not upsetting his fellow Yorkshire Dialect Society members!) Shaw readily gave his consent and wrote back on the 3rd March, 'By all means use the letters: I shall be proud. There is no need to cut anything out. Now that I have forgotten all about St Joan I find the sentences you have crossed quite interesing.'

Just which sentences Turner crossed out is unknown. Possibly they were those indirectly referring to the Yorkshire Dialect Society, for from Shaw's cryptic observations he clearly thought, mistakenly, that what the YDS published in the 1920s was bogus dialect. Nevertheless, it is interesting to learn from this correspondence that St Joan's speech is based on West Riding dialect, and that Shaw took such pains to give her a character like that of a West Riding dialect-speaker. It is a feature which comes out strongly in the dialogue of the play; not least in St Joan's flashes of dry humour. Indeed, the whole character of Joan, her independence, her grit, her anger at injustice and intolerance, her intense patriotism leavened with a desire to promote the fuller brotherhood of man, and, perhaps, most of all, her marked regionalism in speech and manner, are just the traits Ben Turner possessed.

(1969)

RAININ' AGIN

It's rainin agin, Ah's fed up on 't,
We've nivver a day bud it rains;
T' watter's fair silin off t' roof tops
An foamin away doon t' drains.

Ah presses mi nooase up ti t' winder
Ti watch t' raindrops splatter on t' pane;
By heck, hoo Ah wish it 'd stoppit
Soa Ah cud laik oot i t' lane.

Oor Mam says Ah've got ti stay insahd,
In case Ah gets cawd i' mi heead,
Bud Ah'd rather purron mi wellies,
An goa oot an paddle insteead.

Hey up! Ah reckon it's slackin',
It's nut arf as ard as afooar,
Mi Mam lewks reet busy i t' kitchin,
Soa Ah'll try an sneak oot o t' dooar!

'What's that, Mam? Purron mi
   top coat?'
Aw heck, Ah mun as well stay in,
Bi t' tahm Ah gets on all t' clobber
It's boond ti bi rainin agin!

Michael Park (NR)

(1972)

159

WHEN AH WOR A LAD

Ah wish Ah wor a lad ageean —
By Gum! Ah'd mak it crack!
Ah'd laik as long as it wor leet,
An' come 'ooame mucky-black.

Ah'd nivver waste a minute on 't;
Ah'd be i t' street all t' day,
Cos me an' t' lads we'd nooan bi stuck
For summat fresh to play.

We'd appen be Red Indians,
Or gangsters fightin t' p'lice,
Wi watter-pistols, dustbins lids,
An' a gun an' caps apiece.

Wi gangs, an' dens, an' bogey-rides
Us lads were nivver stalled;
But t' mothers said: 'Nah, then.
    Think on!
Just come in when tha's called.'

Aye. In them grand short-trahsered
    days,
We'd appiness galooare …
By Gow! To be a lad ageean!
Ah couldn't ask for mooare!

Arnold Kellett (WR)

(1972)

T' TELE

T' art o' conversation's deead,
Gone fer ivver nah, Ah'm fear'd,
All sum fowk ev i ther eead
    Is t' tele.

Yer nivver see barns laikin' nah,
The've lost that spark o' life somehah,
The're all sat watchin Children's Hahr
    On t' tele.

No tin-can rallies i' t' back street,
An pawsin' t' tin-can aht o' seet,
The're cahred theear i' t' hahse all neet
    Wi t' tele.

No bows an' arrers, whips an' tops,
No gawpin hahrs i' all t' spice shops,
The're rushin 'ooam ter t' *Top o' t' Pops*
    On t' tele.

Unched up i' t' chair i' t' dim awf-leet,
Till t' little white dot's aht o' seet:
Sum nivver miss a single neet
    Wi t' tele.

The' watch it till it urts ther eyes,
An' though some think Ah'm nooan
    ser wise,
At leeast Ah knaw wheear t' off-switch lies,
    On t' tele!

Glyn Whiteoak (WR)

(1972)

COUNTRY CHRISTMAS

Christmas in t' farm 'ouse,
All fettled and clean;
There's a feast on yon table
'At's fit for a queen;
A gurt buxom turkey
Wi t' trimmin's ter come,
An' a champion puddin',
An' sauce laced wi' rum;
Aye, ther's cheese, an ther's spice-cake
An' summat ter sup —
By gum, lad, tha'll bust
If tha doesn't give up!

Christmas in t' mistal,
All shabby an bare,
All stinkin wi' cow-muck —
An t' cattle just stare,
As much as ter say:
'Ther's nowt 'ere for thee!'
But ovver in t' corner —
Na then — dosta see?
Ther's a lass wi 'er babby,
All snuggled in t' 'ay;
Yon grand little Jesus
On t' first Christmas Day!

Arnold Kellett (WR)

(1973)

ALL CHANGE ...

Noo things is allus changin',
   They'll nivver be t' seeam ageean,
They've meddled wiv oor Rahdins
   An gi'en 'em a different neeam.

They pinched a bit o' Cleveland —
   An teeak it wiv sike ease! —
Then lumped it all tigither
   Ti join it up ti Tees.

Ower it t' west they've teean some
   A bit o' Yorkshire grit,
They nivver sud a deean't
   We'll e ti bahd wiv it.

T' West Rahdin's shifted ower —
   An' gin a bit away,
Whahl t' Eeast is knawn as Umbersahd —
   Yis, even Bolliton Bay!

Bud what aboot that new spot?
   That Rahdin' they call t' sooth?
Why did thoo ivver ear sike
   Frae a Yorkshire mooth?

Ah wonder when they've finished
   What men o' aud wad say.
At what they've deean ti t' thriddins
   In oor modern day?

Sydney Martin (York)

(1973)

161

Dr Wilfrid J Halliday, president of the society from 1964 to 1974.

BLETHERSKITES

Ah hev two timepieces,
An nawther on 'em match,
Yan's a girt alarum clock,
T' ither's a lahtle watch.

T' alarum clock varies wildly,
Bud t' bell rings lood an fine,
T' wristwatch ligs theer quiet,
Bud it keeaps perfect tahm.

T' world hes monny talkers,
An quiet fooaks thoo'll meet,
Bud, him at shoots oot loodest
Is rarely t' yan that's reet!

Michael Park (NR)

(1973)

THE OLD TEXTILE WORKER

Ah've powled through mulegates up ta t' knees i' brokken ends an' fluff;
Ah've fettled t' cairds i' t' scribblin' 'oil 'til t' greease gate through ta t' buff;
Ah've treddled t' sheds thra morn ta neet, i' booits worn daan ta t' welts;
Tubed-up spindles; looaded creels; splahced rim rooapes; mended belts.

Ah've slopped i' t' sooap i' t' scaarin' 'oil; an' chooaked i' t' dye 'oil's stinks;
Trullied t' beeams thra t' warpin' frames ta t' looms on flooars lahke
    skatin' rinks.
Ah've trodden t' blend i' t' teeasin' shed, chucked in t' shoddy, watched it fall;
Steeamed t' bobbined weft for t' shuttles, ar, an' tewed wi' th' healds, an' all.

Ah've hugged full pieces on mi rig as heavy as missen;
Hawked cops abaat i' t' crutch o' th' airm 'til Ah could hardly sken.
Ah've piecened; wovven; fettled; teeased; an' worked i' t' jerry 'oil;
An' once — when they wor fast for men — Ah shooled ten ton o' coil.

Ah've whistled at mi wark, an' sung; dreeamed monny a rooasy dreeam:
Thar on thi own i' them mad 'oils o' noise an' stink an' steeam.
An' when at last it's ovver, an' tha's getten t' pension book,
An' tha sits up theer on th' hillside, an' tha gi' es th' owd mill a look,
It caps thee yahr tha's managed it, ta strackle through ta th' end
Baaht deein' off, cuttin' thi throyt, or traipsin' reight raand t' bend.

Gordon Allen North (WR)

(1974)

'oil, hole, small room; *heald,* heddle (on a loom); *hugged,* carried;
sken, see (with difficulty)

NOTES ON THE WEST RIDING
DIALECT ALMANACS
B T Dyson

Yorkshire dialect almanacs were annual publications in 'prophetic' almanac form
written entirely in the Yorkshire dialect. They are, I believe, unique to the industrial
West Riding.

There is very little written about these almanacs, and in the few articles which
exist there are, in fact, errors. The most important article was written by Professor
F W Moorman, Professor of English Language, Leeds University, from 1909 to
1919, who was also editorial secretary of the Yorkshire Dialect Society. His position naturally lent great authority to what he had to say:

> A West Riding dialect literature seems to have arisen first of all in Barnsley
> and Sheffield in the fourth decade of the nineteenth century. Between 1830
> and 1834 a number of prose 'conversations' entitled *The Sheffield Dialect:*
> *Be a Shevvild Chap* passed through the press. The author of these also pub-
> lished in 1832 *The Wheelswarf Chronicle,* and in 1836 appeared the first
> number of the *Shevvild Chap's Annual* in which the writer throws aside his
> nom-de-plume and signs himself Abel Bywater. This annual, which lived
> for about twenty years, is the first of the many 'Annuals' or 'almanacs' which
> are the most characteristic product of the West Riding dialect movement.

It seems strange that these characteristic products should have been so long neglected
as objects for study. Federer produced a bibliography of most of the almanacs in
Transactions of the YDS (1901); but that was incomplete, and, in the case of the *Bairnsla*
Foaks' Annual, shown to be wrong by EG Bayford in *Transactions* (1925). Federer
had made a useful start. An article on dialect almanacs printed in *Transactions* for 1931
is merely a run-through of the names of some almanacs and their composers.

Usually, when almanacs are mentioned in the county magazines and newspapers, it is with unabashed and uncritical nostalgia. This sort of thing:

> It is a pity that nearly all those Yorkshire almanacs which once burst upon
> us each New Year, brimming with cheerful verse and mournful prophecies,
> have vanished. They were *homely* little productions, full of the works of
> budding Wordsworths and Tennysons.

That was in the *Yorkshire Evening Post,* sometime in the 1960s. There is not the
opportunity here to discuss the contents of the almanacs critically, but verse is
the least part of the almanacs, and apart from some by Hartley in the early *Clock,*
it is certainly the worst part.

Margaret Ottley in the *Dalesman* magazine offers her impression of an almanac:
There is a comforting, *homely* air about the word 'almanac', a suggestion of
lamplighters, knife-and-fork teas, and cosy fireside evenings in a pre-radio age.
This is probably true of some later almanacs, but if the best of the West Riding
almanacs only fitted either of these descriptions then they would be best forgotten.

It was James Burnley of Shipley, himself the author of *Saunterer's Satchel*,
writing in Dickens's periodical *All The Year Round* at a time when the almanacs
were flourishing, 1875, who made the first relevant comment:

> Of late years there have been issued from the local press a large number of
> almanacs and comic pamphlets written wholly in dialect. Dialect almanacs,
> witty and racy though they often are, are not adapted for the uninitiated
> reader; they can only be appreciated by the people who belong to the soil
> where they have been produced, and, therefore, can never be accepted into
> the literature of the country.

It is reasonable to ask why we should bother to study almanacs now. The historian's answer is fairly clear, and admirably expressed by Kitson Clark in the 1960
Ford Lectures on Victorian England. Writing about 'ephemeral literature' he says
that:

> the drama, the songs, and above all the novels and magazine stories (here I
> add the material in our dialect almanacs), although wildly distorting mirrors,
> nevertheless reflect something, they reflect the mind of the people who liked
> to look into them. The generalisations men accept about life, the morality
> which commends itself to them are in some ways reflected in the plays they
> see, in the songs they sing, in the stories they enjoy.

The dialect almanacs are the nearest thing we have to a genuine 'working class'
literature written by working people (extraordinary working people maybe); consequently they embody the ideas of the contemporary 'man-in-the-street' much
more closely than the material presented in the wider circulated but less personal
magazines. They are confirmatory rather than source material for the social historian. The student of literature is far less likely to find them useful, for the almanacs
have little humanising influence, and are certainly not vehicles of civilizing ideals.

For the dialect student the almanacs contain an enormous vocabulary, which
can be placed in a fairly definite local setting, and of course in a definite period. If,
as Sheard thinks (*Transactions* 1945), decay in dialect is represented by loss of
vocabulary rather than in sound changes, then the almanacs are essential source
material. Moreover, in some slight degree, it is possible for present-day speakers
of dialect to gain some idea of the speech of the defined locality at a time when
dialect was used naturally on the bench and in the dock; in the pulpit as well as
the pew.

The 1830s and '40s were decades marked by a tremendous growth in the reading
public. The 'ordinary man' was coming into his own, the period produced the
mechanics' institutes, a passion for reading was a notable feature of the time. 'Popular

Nineteenth Century
Comic Dialect Almanacs

CRUICKSHANK'S COMIC ALMANAC

PUNCH ALMANAC

SHEVILD CHAP'S ANNUAL

BAIRNSLA FOAKS' ANNUAL AND POGMOOR OLMENACK ─ ISAAC BINNS ── TOM TREDDLE-
EDITOR   HOYLE JUNIOR

T'FROGLAND OLMENAC

BOME MILN

BACK AT MOOIN

OLMENAC

TOMMY TODDLES'S

NIDDERDILL OLMINAC

BAG O'SHODDY ?

CLOCK ALMANACK

SWASHLAND OLMENAC

? T'CODDY MILN

? T'OWD ORIGINAL CODDY MILN

FRONT O' TH' SUN

BEACON

HOWORTH, COWENHEEAD & BOGTHORNE ALMANAK

LEEDS LOINERS'

? MAYPOLE

SAUNTERER'S SATCHEL ── YORKSHIREMAN'S

WEYVERS' AWN

1890
89
88
87
86
85
84
83
82
81
1880
79
78
77
76
75
74
73
72
71
1870
69
68
67
66
65
64
63
62
61
1860
59
58
57
56
55
54
53
52
51
1850
49
48
47
46
45
44
43
42
41
1840
39
38
37
36
1835

Culture' raised its head, cheap magazines appeared; *Chambers Journal* and the *Penny Magazine* among them. The tone of these latter was moral and scientific, and very much a part of the industrialisation of the people. The organic agricultural community was rapidly becoming an organic industrial one with the consequent shift of the ways and needs of life. The literature of the era reflected, and in some cases guided this change. According to the Hammonds in *The Age of the Chartists*, a witness before the 1836 Select Committee on Arts and Principles of Design patronisingly asserted:

> Every Saturday I have the satisfaction of reflecting that 360,000 copies of these useful publications are issued to the public, diffusing science and taste and good feeling, without one sentence of an immoral tendency in the whole.

Then came Eliza Cook's *Journal*: very moral and serious. This kind of magazine had to compete with periodicals which contained, according to one witness before the Select Committee on Public Libraries in 1849, 'rubbish replete with moral contamination'. Cheap periodical literature was produced especially adapted to the evident tastes of the 'working classes'. In mitigation it should be noted that humour was another feature of the 1830s as represented in the *Pickwick Papers* which started to appear serially in that decade. Against that sort of background, here too hastily sketched, the dialect almanac was created.

In 1834 the duty on almanacs was withdrawn. A fact not often recorded, but in the first *Punch* almanac of 1841 we can read, with good eyesight or a magnifying glass, that 'Punch, on behalf of the British Nation acknowledges the boon, and presents the country with a guinea's worth of wit for 3d'. The withdrawal of the tax was an even greater boon for the West Riding dialect writers — our first almanac came out before the Punch. But the fear of a further tax was always present, and this was expressed by Hartley in 1871, for he believed:

> ... it's a bit ov a treat to be able to ease one's mind once i' th' year, an' just to let fowk know what yo think abaat things, an' to have a shot at th' follies one sees abaat em. Bob Lowe [then the Chancellor] hasn't taxed almanacs, for a wonder, soa a body can have a cut in cheap.

The first dialect almanacs did not carry any advertisement because the duty on these did not disappear until 1853. (But what adverts when they came: 'Latest American Invention. The very last thing is a patent paper shirt ... cost 25 cents, warranted perspiration proof, and wears three weeks without washing if only properly got up with the Glenfield Starch.')

The first almanac to appear in England after the repeal of the duty was *The Comic Almanack* of 1835. It was:

> an Ephemeris in jest and earnest / by Rigdum Runnidos, Gent. / Adorned with a dozen of right merrie cuts, / pertaining to the months, / sketched and etched by George Cruikshank, / and divers humorous cuts by other hands. / London: Imprinted for Charles Tilt, / Bibliopolist, in Fleet Street.

A comic almanac was something new. Whether this almanac had any influence upon Charles Rogers, our first dialect almanac writer, is open to speculation, but

similar features, especially the illustrations, can be found in the *Bairnsla Foaks'*
Annuals.

It is probable that the first almanacs were constructed by the Greeks of Alex-
andria in the time of Ptolemy to assist in their study of astrology. The almanac
gave them accurate knowledge of the state of the heavens. In this sense the primary
function of the almanac was prophetic. Incidentally when, at the end of the
eighteeth century, the almanacs omitted the column about the moon's influence
upon parts of the body it is recorded that most of the copies were returned.
Prophesying was an integral function of the popular almanac:

> Old Moore reckons to profisy a bit ... an' I allus think he acts varry wisely
> by puttin it o' th' last page; for when it's new yo cannot tell whether it'll turn
> aht true or not — an bi th' time yo get to know, it's soa mucky 'at yo cannot
> read it. (*Clock* 1867)

The next function of the popular almanac was to give the dates of important events
with a calendar of days and months, and information about the moon and about
eclipses. I hope to show how the dialect almanacs modified these essentials.

In 1830 came Abel Bywater's first dialect production, *The Wheelswarf Chron-*
icle, to be followed in 1836 with his *Shevvild Chap's Annual.* During the early part
of last century there were current movements which disturbed and frightened
many people. There was Reform agitation which continued throughout the
century and is a frequent subject of almanac pieces. There was pressure to have
slavery abolished. There was industrial unrest because of the introduction of new
machinery. William Hone was publishing pamphlets attacking the Government
and the Monarchy. In 1829 the Earl of Winchelsea issued a letter charging the
Duke of Wellington with 'intending to introduce Popery into every department
of the State'. Methodism was gaining ground in Sheffield and elsewhere in the
North. The old order was not only changing, but to some showed every sign of
crumbling.

Abel Bywater was concerned about all this, and his pamphlets and annuals
were written in an attempt to defend, and have restored, the *status quo* in politics
and religion. The sale of his works is evidence that he reflected the thoughts of
many working men at that time. Bywater never minced his words; maybe it was
because of this that he was constantly having to change his printer and publisher.

B R Dyson in his article in *Transactions* (1932) writes that Bywater's pamphlets
satirised the evils of drink, laziness, Owenism and free-thinking.

To appreciate the tone of Bywater's writings, observe him on drink, a subject,
of course, which almanac writers used later in a humorous way, or in a mildly
critical manner, but never as the 'Shevvild Chap' writes. (This piece was written
before the magic-lantern lecture).

Usually in this same harsh fashion Bywater wrote about:

The Impudence of Popery.

When Will t' Reformers Beeat Conference?

The Shevvild Chap's Letter to t' Mester at Methodist Conference,
highly seasoned.

And in 1852 the Annual was headed:

Another Rod Pickled for Priestcraft.

Often the articles took the form of a dialogue between Sheffield workmen, or their
wives; and on some occasions, in a friendly but critical vein, with an Irishman. The
dialogue form provided a convenient framework for dialect writing, both serious and
comic, because it places the emphasis on expression rather than description.

Here the essential question arises — Why write in dialect at all? Why not use
ordinary English that everybody can understand?

I don't think there can be a satisfactory conclusive explanation, and no reasons
were ever given by the writers themselves.

(a) The reader seems to feel that he is one of a select company listening to someone
speaking in his own private language. Dialect helps one immediately to identify
with characters of one's own social class, and therefore with persons sharing one's
humour, prejudices and outlook.

(b) Certain ideas can be put forward in dialect which might seem very unsophist-
icated in plain English; conversely, dialect is a help in bringing high-falutin' notions
down to earth.

(c) Many of the 'digs' in the almanacs down to the middle of the century were
aimed at the newly settled Irish; so maybe dialect was used to keep the feelings
expressed about them 'in the family', as it were. With this notion goes the one of
stressing the difference and superiority of the readers.

(d) It might just have been an attempt to keep dialect alive — there was a real interest in
dialect as is shown by the number of glossaries printed during the century.

Whatever the reasons for writing in dialect, in 1838 Charles Rogers of Barnsley
issued a pamphlet:

Sum thowts abaat doins e Bairnsla ant Crawnashun Day,
be Tom Treddlehoyle, Will Weft an Ben Bunt.

Our first comic dialect writer was learning his craft. In 1840 came:

The Bairnsla Foaks' Annual an onybody elsas at ive a mind,
for t year of our Lord 1840, be Tom Treddlehoyle.

There were two more issues similar to this one but none of these contained a
calendar. It was not until 1843 that Rogers published *The Bairnsla Foakes' Annual
an Pognoor Olmenack*. This was in almanac form, and tax free. It had to pay its
way from sales because initially, as has been said, the almanacs carried no advertisements. Although Rogers had no connection with the weaving trade, like many
others he chose a pseudonym for that trade which had become so important in
the West Riding. Coal mining might never have existed as far as our writers are
concerned.

The almanacs were completely urban in character. They marked the final break
from the agricultural nature of society. Very seldom is there even a furtive glance

back to that 'Golden Age'. It seems to me that the almanacs assume a society in which there are inevitably masters and men; a state of affairs seldom criticised, but rather complacently accepted. Though written by literate members of the 'working class' the almanacs are not what Empson would call 'proletarian literature'. Hartley's poem *Bite Bigger* and its like are not the material of social revolution.

There are no agricultural connections. The only concession to farming — small holding — in the almanacs was the occasional syndicated insert which gave such information as the gestation period of pigs. Even the countryside was seldom alluded to. The West Riding comic almanac was a product of a settled industrial community.

Professor Moorman in the quotation at the start of these notes said that 'all of these almanacs conform more or less to the same pattern, as it was first laid down by the founder of the dialect almanac, Abel Bywater of Sheffield in the year 1836'. This statement never appears to have been challenged. But it is not correct. Bywater did not write an almanac. He wrote an annual pamphlet which did not give phases of the moon, dates, nor contained any of the essential features of an almanac previously mentioned. Bywater, with few exceptions, did not write humorous articles. The fact is that the style of all comic dialect almanacs was set by the *Bairnsla Foaks' Annual*, which in turn took its form from the popular Zadkiel's and Old Moore's.

The dialect almanacs were all octavo; a convenient and economical size. With very few exceptions they consisted of fifty-six pages. Type was used to fit the page, so that often the lower part was written in such small type it was most difficult to read. Apart from the headings there were sometimes more than three type sizes and faces on one page.

Rogers began his almanacs with an address to the reader. This prologue remained an essential feature of all the dialect almanacs which followed:

Well, ah do declare, hah time duz slip on, ta besuar. Wha, it nobbut looks like tuther day sin ah wrate yo befoar, it duzant hacktly; an here we ar, poppin into annuther year, az thowtless az a donkey goin past a guide poast.

(*Bairnsla Foaks'*, 1844)

Oh yes, it's me; I' m heear ageean, as t' flea sed tot jam pot as it wiped it eelash wi' a bit a cobweb; an thare's anuther yeear gooan ...

(*Weyvers' Awn*, 1907)

Six yeear owd today — six goin i seven! Ah can scarce believe possible. Yet it's true. This is mi sixth yearly almanac, an afooar t' ink o' this here un gets fairly dry ah sal be sattlin misen darn at mi owd kitchin table to start anuther.

(*Bob Stubbs* 1912)

Following the prologue was the almanac proper. Sometimes it occupied two facing pages, at others only one page for each month. If on one page: the month

(eg Jenewery, Febrewery etc) and underneath this the necessary 'Day breiks …
Twileet ends', with the times of these events. All naturally in dialect. We learn:

In 1868 theare al be two eclipses at sun. T' furst al be an annular eclipse at
sun Febrewarry 23rd; it al begin at seventeen minit past eleven it fornooin,
an end at twenty-five minit past five it afternooin, bud yo'll net be able ta see
it awther at Dawgreen, Pudsa, or Wibsey Bank Fooit …

The days and dates were in columns to the left of the page, then, with important
dates interspersed, came snippets of dialect, mainly humorous, chiefly brief:

OWLBECK FEEAST — Owlbeck fowks, an Leeds Loiners, be careful.
Dunnot feeast wol yo mack yorsens poorly. Eit an drink e moderation.

LEE FAIR — Ommost everybody goas to Lee Fair.

Ther's BATLEY & MORLEY (OWD) FEEASTS horse flesh in abundance, an horses baht flesh e proportionate numbers. Ther's traders to tempt
yo to buy ther live stock, an geese e full feather — an innumerable flock.

Hah one thing brings up another, said t' doctor when he gav his patient an
emetic.

Milk begins ta go saar in a neet. — Yis, but a little mind, remember, goaz
saar in a seckand.

These pages in later almanacs often carried longer, more tedious stories, and at
the end of the century verses in and out of dialect were used to fill them.

Hartley in the *Clock* used two facing pages — the left-hand one for the calendar
and notable events, the right-hand one for his 'Rambling Remarks' for each month.
Bob Stubbs in the *Yorksher Awmynack* dealt the *coup de grace* to this part of the
almanac with a terse:

New Moon [date]   Month   Full Moon [date]

which was followed with a dialect story of many pages, unrelated to the month.

The remainder of all the almanacs now — after 1900 — was filled with stories of
very uneven quality; often of great length ie up to twenty pages for each. Only occasionally did the writers now deal with topical issues of political or social interest.

To return to Rogers. From many of his original articles it could reasonably be
suggested that he was poking fun at those 'serious' almanacs, Zadkiel's and the
like, possibly from an awareness of the force of scientific interest among ordinary
people. There are many examples of Rogers' 'scientific writings', One example:

Wilmot Weatherpeg, a man ov great skyescrakope knowledge an under-
standin', though not much noatist be modern filosofers, tells us 'at Eclipsas
at Sun or Mooin iz causd or browt on be stray or lost winds cumin e contackt
we wun edge on am an dubblin' am up.

This he states without giving an 'opinion a me awn consarnin it'. The style parodies
the serious writers of the 1840s; note the careful use of alternatives to give an
impression of thought and precision. The paragraph from which this piece is
taken maintains the tone rather cleverly. (*Bairnsla Foaks'*, 1844.)

Five years later Rogers takes Zadkiel's 'Predictions' for his target giving us:

PREDICKSHANS	FULFILLMENT
Alarmin fires, railway	Betty Brittoner, a
accidents, an menny foaks	Chorley, freetand wit
injured be fire an iron.	saand ov a railway
June.	whissal, wal sho bate
	hur tungue end off.
	A couk flew aght a
	Susy Sitfast's fire
	reight into hur pockit,
	an burnt a pincushin,
	three cotton balls, a
	huzzif, an melted hur
	thimal end off.

Rogers later makes play with the mythologies of the period, and takes a look at some human foibles and failings after the manner of Andrew Tooke's *Pantheon*. One assumes that the readers of the almanac knew of this, or a similar, work. The style is catechistic:

'Is that Venus? Yes, that is Venus, the goddess of love ... vile promoter of impudence and lust ...' Tooke.

Rogers has:

Q.   Who wor Simon Snakeoil?

A.   A native a Pudsa, an' a understrapper in a manufacturin consarn; but who tried to raize hizsen to a heigher situashun be poisonin hiz maister's ear agean them at wor aboon him, an' tellin a ivvery little matter at he saw goin' on abaght t' plaice. This went on wal hiz noase grew to a greas-horn; an', bit way a faather punishment for hiz deceat an' interfearance, he wor cumpelld to go an hiz hands an' knees it hoppan streets, an' grease wheel-barra trunals at rate a five an' twenty a day.

This kind of writing was not repeated in the almanacs as they gained popularity.

From the examples already quoted it might be gathered that the writers delighted in words — in puns, riddles, odd word forms — as if they had just discovered them. Words and the humour in their use:

Wot macks joiners better ta do bizness we than onny boddy else? Becos thare plane-deal-in men. Pare yer corns if yov a mind; but reckaleck theal noabdy catch me pairin mine, for I've wun up a me little toa, an it's plenty.

Hieraglyphic   Loweraglyphic.

Fearful Larnd.

Skyologer an' Weathergishan.

The almanacs had perennial subjects: Leap Year, April Fool's Day, Christmas,

New Year, and of course in the mid-nineteenth century Valentine's Day which always had a page devoted to it:

> Febrewery 14th. Thear wor a lot a skoil lads wunce, when they wor aght laikin', screamd an' made a great noise. T' maister, thinkin at sum on em wor hurt, ran aght at skoil an sed to em, 'Wot's amiss?' 'Wha' sed wun at lads, as reddy az cud be, 'It's a yung wuman at's niver been marrid.' (Rogers)

There were also favourite topics for the saws:

> Appearances are deceptive ... 'Mind ya saddle t reit hoss.

> Caution ... 'Knaw wot thart doin afoar tha tacks thi barra back'.

There were also hypocrisy, baldness, justice, patience which gave us epigrammatic sayings such as were in vogue at the time. Some of the sayings epitomised the rules for leading the 'good' life according to the then current standards — standards often ridiculed today, but none the less generally sound. In fact one striking feature of the almanac was the moral tone of much of the writing which occasionally tends to leave one with the feeling that some of the authors were 'holier than thou' types.

On drink the views were ambivalent; a writer would apparently condemn drinking in one passage, and appear to condone and extract some humour from it in another. Never, by the way, as harshly as Bywater did:

> One cold New Year a chap at Ossett hevin' been varry drunk t' neet afore, an' beckin' off went tut pump ta sup, an when he wanted ta tack his maath away, he fan it aht he cuddant for he wor frozzen tut spaat. Az he cuddant manage ta hug t' pump abaat wi' him he wor forced ta stop wol sumbdy com by, an' wol they gat a saw an cut t' lead spaat off ...

The *Bairnsla Foaks' Almanac* was alone until 1852 when the *Frogland Olmenac* was issued in Leeds, Frogland being the byname of an area in Dewsbury Road:

> T' Frogland Olmenac, an' Leeds Loiners' Annual,
> containin' ivvery Thing 'at's nawn an' a monny
> Things 'at izzant. Be Harry Frogland, Hisquire.
> Leeds. John Cooke.

This was the first of the few almanacs which consisted of only sixteen or twenty pages. There were twelve issues. There is no evidence of who wrote it; and like the next almanac, *The Bome Miln*, by J Firth, seems to be unobtainable:

> The Bome Miln Olmenac, an Bradfurth an West Riding Annewal.
> Be Timothy Shoddygul, Esq., MP For Bome Miln, nane so far
> off a Clackheaton.

1855 to 1858, printed at Cleckheaton, Sheffield and Bradford in turn.

So until 1862 only three dialect almanacs had appeared. That year marks the Great Age of the dialect almanac. With the introduction of much advertising matter the almanacs became more economically sound. One which shows as much the influence of Punch as of Treddlehoyle, was *Tommy Toddles's Comic Olmenac*.

From 1862 this was written by J Hamer (this man might have been responsible for the *Frogland*). Then in 1865 until its end in 1875 it was written by J Eccles.

STANSFELD & SONS, ALFRED ST., BOAR LANE, LEEDS.

1,000 Tons Bars & 1,000 Tons Bolts and Nuts always in stock.

Prices on application. See advert. in centre of Book.

Iron & Steel Merchants, Manufacturers of every description of Bolts & Nuts.

Hartley's *Clock Almanac* came in 1867. This is the most famous of them all, and, because so many thousands of each issue were sold, is the most readily available in its entirety. The first copies, containing 'Th First o th Soart', 'Bite Bigger', 'Duffin Johnny', 'Th Battle o Tawkin' and 'Pill Jim's Progress', were very good of their kind. The contents were all anthologised by Hartley himself.

Initially the *Clock* had yellow or blue paper covers, cost 2d, and the contents were printed on the cover. In 1872 the red and yellow cover, the word 'Clock' in Punch-style figures, and the picture of Mally and Grimes made its debut. The initials *S B del* (drawn by) make it unlikely that Hartley designed it as some writers have asserted. The *Clock* in its way demands greater attention than can be given here, but in all essentials it is a direct descendant of the *Bairnsla Foaks' Annual*.

Between the years 1870 and 1881 there were eighteen West Riding dialect almanacs published. Obviously among so many the quality was very varied, and some deservedly lasted for brief periods.

Arthur William Bickerdike, a teacher of music from Halifax, wrote the *Beacon Almanac* 1873-76 (four issues). It contained indifferent material:

A pey hoil — a sooart ov juvenile club or hotel.

Fer th' root ov all brutalisin, drinkin' an' crime

seek aat th' permanent peyhoils an' burn 'em daan.

Bickerdike's purpose in writing the almanac was to advertise readings of his own dialect writings, and his profession.

The *Maypowl Almanack,* also from Halifax, was another which only managed a few issues. Its main contribution was an account of the:

Grand dimmunstrashun a Luddenden an' Luddenden Fooit

Henpickt Club — with the club rules.

The almanac part of this was a syndicated one. Federer doesn't list it.

The Morley and Ardsley district produced an almanac which enjoyed one issue — not surprisingly for it had Christmas Day entered on the 26th December.

The almanacs entirely in dialect which follow are *Saunterer's Satchel,* by James Burnley; *Weyvers' Awn or Pudsa Annewal edited be Sammy Bruskitt* (John Middlebrook); *Bob Stubbs' Yorksher Awnynack* — 1904 to 1927?. This latter almanack and the *Chimney Nook* from 1903 were Christmas offerings and effectively reduced the almanac and calendar to a minimum. All the later almanacs were for 'thousands o' fowk 'at's fond ov listenin to a few yarns spun i' th' homely owd twang' (Sol Darrell, 1906 *Chimney Nook*). They concentrated on stories and short pieces which could be used for recitals; many of their contents were collected and published in paper-backed booklets for that purpose.

Among the nineteenth century almanacs were four, of sixteen pages each, which were published and printed in Batley. The first, in August 1861 — not a Christmas affair — was the *Dewsbre Back at Mooin Olmenac,* bi Mungo Shoddy. The layout of this and the other three is copied from the almanac parts of the *Bairnsla Foaks'.* It is mainly concerned with events of the previous year, written entirely in dialect and well larded with moral comments. The standard of the political comment is typified in this:

> It's gotten to be reight feshonable for some ov them gurt chaps to come ovver to see us, nah days. We've hed a chap called t' viceroy ov Egypt, an t' Sultan o' t' Turks, an' lots ov others. It looks varry nice an' friendly on both sides, an' we owt to be so wi chaps aht ov other countries; bud I think they owt to bring ther dinners wi' 'em. (1868)

A slightly better almanac was *T Bag o Shoddy Olmenack an Bundel ov Wisdum.* ('A scrapin off at shoddy hoil floor ov witty sayins; containin fizzick 'at al do 'em moar gooid nor a five shillin bottal a onny quack's medsin. Be Uriah Waketea, Teicher at ABC Class at Carnla Munda Schooil.') Waketea was Isaac Binns, who also contributed to the *Clock,* and for the years 1876 to 1883 he kept the *Bairnsla Foaks* going until Tom Treddlehoyle Junior took over. By comparing the vocabulary of the *Back at Mooin* and *T Bag o Shoddy* we can detect differences in the pronunciation of some words between two very adjacent districts, namely Batley and Dewsbury.

There were two more local almanacs from the Batley press which came out simultaneously. They were *T Coddy Miln Annewal* be Peter Suteall, and *T Owd Original Coddy Miln.* The rivalry is obvious in the titles for the Coddy Miln was the dividing mark between Batley and Birstall. Both were similar in content, taking the framework of the *Bairnsla Foaks'.* The striking difference was that Suteall favoured Birstall:

Ah dussent knaw hah it is at Batla new steam fire engine is called t' Littel
Gem unless its becos t' gem's sa littel wol noaboddy sets mich vally on it.

Whereas the writer of the *Original Coddy Miln* has a bit about noted men in Birstall which includes:

One at they call Jerry Skinflint who cleans his boots six times ovver at Monday, an' then they do for every day. He wears one polish off it a day, an sez at it saves plenty a bother an' trouble.

Like most almanacs begun during the 1860s and '70s they had a steady sale for about ten years and then disappeared. When popular, though, they had quite a success.

These local almanacs concerned themselves more with current topics than did the larger circulated ones. The articles are slightly humorous but have an underlying serious intention. The Franco-Prussian War is under discussion:

'Nanny:- This war iz a serious thing; they say 'at thev killed aboon fower million fowk.

Peggy:- Ay, it iz a shockin' thing; it ad bank ahr berryin' club.

Nanny:- Ah think at we're all reit wi a varry gooid Queen, at fowk sez is a dacent, clean an tidy body.

Peggy:- Wa, an soa sud awther a us be if we'd sooap fun for nowt ... an then, shoo's two wesherwimmin.

Nanny:- Wah, of course shoo owt ta be wi that.

Peggy:- Ay, an they say at shoo's spendin brass alaad at ad aboon keep me.

Nanny:- Wah, then.'   (*T Owd Original Coddy Miln* 1871)

Another of the Batley writers expressed views which must have been fairly common in the Heavy Wollen District. His opinion was:

In Batla 99 aht at hunderd al shaat aht 'yolla for ivver'. Ther wor one Blue at t top a Batla Carr at hed a nice garden full a yolla an red poasies, an he hed em all pooled up, an he willant eit butter, ar cheese, he sez heel hev nowt ta do wi owt at's yolla if eh can help it.

An then ther wor t meetin i Hide Park e Jewly 1866 that wor a thing at owt ta be remembered bi t blues, as t sine a summat withaat thers a olteration afore long. Ye twelve shillin a week gaffers, look aht! Might hez been reit this last munth ar two, but reit al be might afore long.

Twelve years later another Batley writer expresses his views; he was a Tory. He begins by writing about the wars at the time (1878) and his concern then was with the local mill owners, but he puts his word in for the ordinary man at the end:

Reit enuf trade is, an has been bad, bud it mud a been war. War is a terrible calamity, bud all trades doant suffer thro war. Brummagem chaps an blanket manifacturers profit bi it ... But feitin is a subject at's noan so palatable for yor humble sarvent. Ther's moar pleasure e eitin nor feitin, onny day it week. It's better for a country to hev a government turnd aht o office (even if it's a Toary government) nor what it wod be to begin a feitin awther wi t Russians or t Turks. England hez plenty to do, if sho'll nobbut look at hoam. Ther's national debt at tacks plenty a keepin warm, an a revenue to raise every year at t snuff tackin, smokin an drinkin pairt ot community booast so mich abaht helpin to sam together. Ther's one bit a legislation to do, whatever else is done, if t Toaries mean to bid up for a renewal ov t nation's confidence. Allahin me to judge, I can tell all statesmen, boath real an sham, at a varry deal o dissatisfaction shews itsen e districts ahtside ot limits a boros, all becos honest, hard workin, peeaceable, ratepayin an law abidin haaseholders are deprived a ther fair share a parlymentary voatin pahr.

He even advocates 'full voatin pahr to boath male an female'.

To end, just one other political feeling, and one of the reasons earlier mentioned for using the dialect. In the 30s of last century Irish people had come into Batley to take the work of strikers in the shoddy mills. Later there was a great fear of a Fenian invasion, and the feelings about the Irish were expressed in dialect. No Irish immigrant would read a copy of *T Bag o Shoddy*. At this distance of time away from the events it would be unfair to say that the fears of the people were irrational, to them the fears were real, and I think the writings were an attempt to laugh at and laugh off a very worrying state of affairs. Some of the pieces are really atrocious in their strong feelings, and only in those do any of our writers approximate to the tone of Bywater's utterances. Just some of the more moderate:

> The Irish 'al be happen takkin a fit ta land i t country sumdy, an then we sal see ah ahr muffin shooiters go on. On St Patrick's day some fowk wor expectin t Irish swimmin abaht i t streets i peggi tubs, i Inglish blooid.

(The Rifle Volunteers were formed in 1859 as a sort of Home Guard against a French invasion. They were duly dubbed 'Muffin Shooiters' in the Dewsbury area and were looked on partly seriously and partly as a joke, much like 'Dad's Army'.)

The problem about the Irish became so acute that the most ridiculous things were said about them:

> Ah've just gottan ta hear at t kolera's expected daily i Bradfurd, an t tahn cahncil hev oerdered ivvery Irishman ta be weshed a t tahn pump ivvery mornin, weel scrubbed wi a besom, an lastly dredged wi MacDougall's disinfectin pahder.

I hope that these brief notes show that the dialect almanacs are rather more than the homely little productions misremembered so nostalgically by the writer quoted earlier. They are a unique and brief outburst of intense interest to the social rather than the literary historian.

(1975)

BARNSLEY DIALECT IN EVIDENCE
Cedric Sellers

This is not an account of dialect in Barnsley speech today, but is an extract from the reporting of one of the worst tragedies in the history of that town and of the nation, the Oaks Colliery disaster. Details are taken from a report entitled *Narrative of the events connected with the explosions of December 12/13, 1866 (HM Inspector of Coal Mines — Home Office Report Number 18467)* and printed by E Moxon, Barnsley. The incident was all the more tragic in that men engaged on rescue work were killed in a violent explosion on the second day.

The inquest report presents an interesting insight into the social structures and customs of the time. For example, the comment that amongst the spectators was Mr John Normansell, the secretary of the South Yorkshire Miners' Association. (Imagine the situation if the union secretary today could only act as spectator.) The reporter thought it sufficiently noteworthy to record that 'during part of the day "several ladies" were in court'. The desperation of the 'orphan' child is illustrated in the evidence of Jane Jackson who said that John Jackson was not her child but had been brought to her by her own children and as no-one had claimed him she had adopted him. Naturally enough in an enquiry of this kind there were many references to purely mining terms and a list of the more common ones is attached. However, there are enough uncommon or disused terms together with the everyday speech of the people to interest us here.

Mr Mammatt, the colliery surveyor, was first questioned and he was asked by the HM Inspector of Mines, 'Have you been able to ascertain how many workpeople were in the mine on the day of the explosion?' He replied, 'About 300. There were about 130 colliers with sets of tools. Each of these sets of tools would have one and some two *hurriers*.' Hurriers were young boys and men, whose job it was to keep the collier supplied with *corves* into which he filled his coal and the hurrier would take the full corves out of the working place where they could be transported away. It is thought that at this period the hurriers were employed by the colliers and not by the Oaks Colliery Co, and that many of the boys would be the colliers' own children.

The Inspector of Mines asked, 'With regard to the mode of working the coal, did you use powder or wedges?' He was told, '*Wedges* entirely'. A little later he was to be told that 'blind powder was used in the stone drift'. The colliery surveyor was asked about the examination of *goaves* and he said that this work was carried out by '*fire-triers*' or deputies. Further questions for the surveyor related to quantities of ventilation and as a part of this he said, 'At a distance of 150yds, about 15,000 cubic feet of air goes up No.2 "*jenny*" per minute.'

Several under-officials, workmen and a boy were called and during the questioning a measure of the awe of workmen's understanding of what was taking place comes out in the evidence of one Robert Cadman. Cadman said, 'I went down in the second *draw* after the accident'. He told of the persons who travelled into the pit before him and then related what he saw: 'I saw some "dead uns" and some "*wick* uns" an' all.' He then told the court the names of the men he had seen alive and added 'and the lad [Marshall] you "tried" yesterday'.

There is a hint of the use of second names when William Charlesworth tells of going into the pit along with William Barker (alias Sugden) and Thomas Needham. He stated, 'When I got to the bottom I found the *box-hole* but had no light. We went where we heard a cry and found three boys alive. I went round the box-hole feeling under the *settle*.' There were no doubt many moving stories and incidents. This same witness gives his account of meeting the *furnaceman*. 'We afterwards went to the *cupola*, and whilst in the drift, about fifteen yards from it, met with George Tasker, furnaceman. He was standing still on one side, holding a *spragg* in his hand. I said "Halloah!" ' The coroner, 'Never mind what you said. What did you do?' Witness, 'Why, we were forced to speak to him. We afterwards pulled out the fire. There was a little fire on the back of No.1 furnace and fire all round No.2 but none in the middle. After we had pulled the fire out we sat down and waited perhaps ten minutes to see if it kindled up again. There was some air there coming direct from the *downcast* shaft. After a while the fire brightened up a bit and we pulled it out again. We *sammed* the cat up from the *flags* and took it with us to the bottom. The cat was lying dead just where the man said he had been laid, but it did not appear to be burnt or scorched.' Earlier Tasker in evidence had said, 'I lifted my head up after I was knocked down and saw the kitten spinning round, like a "whirlwind", and making a noise. I got hold of it with my arms, I then went to sleep.'

Charlesworth was called to give evidence again and this time when questioned about air doors he went on to say, 'There are two doors pretty *nigh* to the downcast, top side of the old north level'. A little later he goes on to explain that he and Barker (alias Sugden) went back to the engine plane to *Billy Wood's jinney*. This last expression is interesting in that it identifies a person with a length of roadway. It has been common in the mining industry in the past to identify the leader of a team of men who have carried out a major construction in this way by naming the site after him. Explaining what they had done and where they had been, Charlesworth went on to say, 'We might have got about fifty or sixty yards when we found some stuff nailed to some *puncheons*. These were boards about five or six inches broad and nine feet long.'

Charlesworth was questioned about the emission of gas in the places where the men worked and he went on to explain that from time to time there were small quantities of gas. He then went on to say where they did find gas. 'That was in the *break* behind the face. They always had to go there for *packing*. They were never allowed to take a lamp behind the *clog*s. He then gave testimony of his experience. 'I have *wrought* in the Barnsley Bed of coal over thirty years. I have got from a *trapper* up to being a *deputy* or *fireman*.'

The next witness was George Frost, a miner, whose evidence followed similar lines to that of Charlesworth. He describes the scene they found underground and makes unusual use of the word *sadly* when he said 'The stools and cans were upset and *sadly* smashed.' George Minto, an underviewer at Barnsley's Mount Osborne Colliery used the expression again to indicate the severity of the burning. He said, 'We went through by Thomson's boxhole where we found many bodies *sadly* burnt.'

Not surprisingly the evidence of the officials is not so rich in dialect expressions as that of the workmen, nevertheless they are interesting to compare and do quote a fund of mining terms. John Platts, an underviewer at Wharncliffe Silkstone Colliery, went to the Oaks Colliery on the first day of the disaster. Like others who gave evidence he explained in detail what he saw. He stated that in the drift they found thirty-four bodies and went on to relate, 'The whole of those in the drift were not burnt, but appeared to have died from the *after-damp*.' He later said, 'I went down the slant about thirty or forty yards, but found that the *choke-damp* was so bad that I could not get any further.' Elsewhere in the evidence this man refers to *fire-damp* in the *goaves*, whereas Minto the underviewer at Mount Osborne Colllery speaks of *goaf*.

James Marsh, a miner, colourfully described the events of his excursion underground on the day of the explosion. He uses the word *tumbled* when clearly he means 'fall of roof' and *fall* when he means 'pile of debris'. He said, 'We went a little further and found the pass-by had tumbled in. We went over the fall and found a lad (dead) lying under a donkey. Barker said he had two sons further on and we tried to get to them, but had to turn back as the air was so bad. We then got into the back travelling road and left the bodies of the two lads at Jones jinney as Barker failed there and we had to get him out.' Presumably by failed Marsh was saying in a gentle way that the man had broken down emotionally.

Earlier it was suggested that the hurriers were employed by the colliers direct and this seems to be reinforced by a statement by William Gibson, a coal miner who was giving evidence of having worked at the colliery prior to the explosion. 'While I worked in the pit the ventilation was very bad at my place. My master, Andrew Barker, complained of the gas ... I was set on as a hurrier to Barker.' Barker was obviously a known character for when another collier relates the meeting of a deputation with Mr Dymond, the colliery's managing partner, William Ward said, 'We saw Mr Tewart and Mr Dymond together ... We reported that Andrew Barker had stated ... that he had been knocked up in about three and half hours. Mr Dymond said that Barker must have been "beering".' The witness said that the deputation went down the pit with Mr Tewart and Mr Dymond and on visiting Andrew Barker's working place had said Barker did not seem fit for work with getting drink. The company lawyer: 'He had been on the spree for two days, had he not?' The company cashier was called to give evidence about the deputation's meeting with Mr Dymond. The statement that the cashier's books were open to all at the colliery comes somewhat as a surprise!

Attempts were made to identify the first cause of the explosions and a deputy WIlliam Stephenson was questioned about shotfiring in the *stone drift*. He tells of having fired three shots that night but there is a touch of humour in his description of an earlier shotfiring incident when the shothole had been charged and set by workmen and obviously a short fuse was used. 'He fetched me to light a shot, and I went to light it. When I lit it I had to gallop!' During the questioning Stephenson dropped out several good dialect expressions including, 'I got *anent* where the drift was being made', and a reference to the drill hole, 'It must have *brussen* the bottom out partly.' Perhaps his most meaningful comment was that made in reply to the foreman juror who questioned him about the shotfiring operation. Juror, 'Did you ever notice how far the fire seemed to come?' Stephenson replied, 'No, I did not look, I kept my head out o' t' gate.' He went on to say that after putting powder and fuse into the shot hole, 'then a bit of straw made like a ball to take all the loose powder down with it'.

Was Stephenson tired by the questioning or harrassed? He seemed to have answered well to this point and then the reporter writes, 'the witness, who appeared 'nonplussed' created much laughter by his attempts to make his language intelligible.' Stephenson was not quite finished and went on to explain that the lower end of the shot hole seemed to have bursted out. He added that gas lamps in the pit bottom were sometimes blown out by the shotfiring. There is an interesting use of the word *chair* by the lawyer Blackburn when he asks Stephenson the question, 'Have you known the working of the *chair* put out the lights near the bottom of the shaft.' It is surprising that this word should be introduced by a lawyer, although fairly common, when the colliery carpenter had used the more general synonymous term *cage* in his evidence. The lampman also spoke of the 'waft of the cages which sometimes blew lights out near the pit bottom'.

The colliers, famed for sticking together in times of trouble, seem to have maintained a common front on this occasion. One must suspect that there were instances where they sought to get the better of the questioner. For example, when William Wood was asked by a juryman, 'Can you tell us anything that you either saw or did that is worth hearing further?' He replied, 'I don't think I can, for I wasn't there.' Surely, William Youle, a lamp cleaner, spoke tongue in cheek when he said, 'I don't think there was a man or lad in the pit who would have done such a thing as pick a lock.'

The management of the colliery seems to have been singularly adventurous, having earlier tried a cutting machine and piped methane from the workings and used it to light the roadways in the pit bottom. Without too much detail there are indications that the workforce was organised with mention of a meeting at Hoyle Mill and a deputation to meet the manager. Undoubtedly the language of the management and the men identifies them with their own profession and era.

Glossary of words appearing in the report

AFTERDAMP. The noxious gas resulting from a colliery explosion. This *afterdamp* is called *choakdamp* and surfeit by the colliers and is the carbonic acid gas of chymists. (Hodgson — *A description of Felling Colliery.*)

ANENT. Concerning. (OE has *on efen* — 'on a level with'.) (*OED*)

BAHN. Going . In evidence Richard Hunt said, 'they were bahn to fire the shot'.

BEND-UP. To bend away. Signal given in coal mining to intimate that the cage is to be brought to bank. (*EDD*)

BENKS. (i) A vault in a mine. (ii) A section of a pit allotted to several colliers. (*EDD*)

BOARD-GATE. Cf *Board,* also written *bord.* A working-place or passage in a coal pit, excavated at right-angles to the line of clearage. (*EDD*)

BOX-HOLE. Underground office or meeting place. Cf *Box* — a benefit or friendly society possessing a common box. (*EDD.*) A local friendly society. (*Nicholson*)

BRATTICE. A portion, either of wood or strong hempen sheeting placed in the shaft of a pit etc for the purposes of ventilation. (*EDD*)

BREAK. A place of discontinuity in the coal seam such as a slip, fracture or cleat. The surfaces are in contact or slightly separated. The term is also applied to a fracture or crack in the roof beds as a result of mining operations. (*Nelson*)

CHAIR. The frame used for drawing up materials and men from the mines. (Mawe)

CHOKE-DAMP. See *after-damp.*

CLOG. (i) A log of wood. 'Yulelog' called 'Yule clog'. (*EDD*). (ii) A log of wood used as a stool. (*EDD*). (iii) Mining — a sledge loaded with stones and dragged round by the gin, to which it acts as a brake. (*EDD.*) In fact, in this case, it is thought to refer to a piece or pieces of wood used as roof support on the edge of the *goave.*

CORVE. A basket of pined hazel rods in which coals were formerly brought to the surface of a coal pit. (*EDD*)

CRIBS. (i) A circle of wood wedged tight in a pit shaft, to make a foundation for walling when the strata are loose. (ii) The lining of wood or iron put round a pit shaft to dam back the water in water-bearing strata. (*EDD*)

CUPOLA. A smelting house or furnace. A ventilating furnace. (*EDD*)

DEPUTY. A minor colliery official. (*EDD*.) The man who lays the plates and sets the timber for the hewers and has charge of a district of the mine.

DOWNCAST. The shaft down which fresh air passes into a mine. (*EDD*)

DRAW. One complete traverse or wind of the cage through the pit shaft. Cf *Draw* (of ore) — ore underground ready and waiting to be drawn up the shaft. (*Kirkham*)

DRIFT. A passage or tunnel driven into the ground either to explore or reach the coal etc. (*EDD*)

ENGINE PLANE. A road on which the tubs are hauled along by ropes from a stationary engine. (*Nicholson*)

FIREDAMP. Light carburetted hydrogen gas. (*Nicholson*)

FIREMAN. In this context he is thought to be referring to the under-official post of shot-firer or shot-lighter. (The man responsible for igniting the shot.)

FIRE-TRIERS. Cf firetrying — searching for fire damp. (*EDD*)

FLAG. Flat slab of rock for paving. Pavement made of these. (OED)

FURNACE-MAN. Cf *furnace* — a large fire used for ventilating purposes in a mine. The man who attends to the ventilating furnace. (*EDD*)

GETTER. A man employed in breaking down the eoal which has been previously kirved. (*Nicholson*)

GOAF. Also in form *goave*. The space left in a coal mine after the whole of the coal has been extracted. (*EDD*)

HANGER-ON. Cf *hanging-on* — a place in the shaft where tubs are taken out and put in. (*Nicholson*)

HURRIER. Cf *hurry* — to transport or convey, especially to transport coal from the face of the working to the bottom of the shaft. 'A horse hurries coals' (W Yks). Hence *hurrier*, a person, generally a boy, who pushes the coal *corves* along the colliery roads.

INTAKE. An inhalation, a drawing of breath. The airway along which the fresh air is conducted into a mine or district. (*EDD*)

JENNY. Also *jinney*. A gravity operated haulage system. In this case *jenny* is the roadway on which such a haulage probably operated.

LEVEL. A drain or gallery in a mine. 'The sinking to shafts is followed by the driving of levels.' (*EDD*)

MOTTIES. A small information disc. 'Allowances for explosives, drills and motties — per ton 0s. 1d.' (*YMA*) Synonymous with 'token' which *Nicholson* describes, 'A piece of metal, tin or leather having stamped into it some distinguishing mark by which the owner may be known. It is from 1½ to 2 inches long, by 1 to 1¼ inches broad and either oval, round or oblong.'

NIGH. Near. Extensive with 'nighest', 'nighly', 'nighish'. (*EDD*)

OVEREAST. An arrangement carried overhead for the purpose of ventilation. Specially applied to an *air-crossing* (*EDD*.) (*Air-crossing* = an arched way of wood or bricks by which one current of air is carried over another or the same current after having traversed its district or panel of workings. (*Nicholson*)

PACKING. Cf *pack* — a rough wall to support the roof of a mine and to form a roadway for air. (W Yks.) 'The elder Danforth then came up, and seizing Grice by the throat pushed him against a pack.' (*Yorks Evening Post* 24/2/1899) (*EDD*). Hence p*acking* — the material and debris used to make a pack.

PUNCH. Cf p*unch* — a pit prop. (*EDD*)

PUNCHEON. A pit prop, a support for the roof. (*EDD*)

RAPPED. Cf *rap* — to knock up, arouse by knocking. To signal to the banksman at a colliery. (*EDD*)

REEKING. Cf *reeky* — smoky, smoking, fumes, smell. (*EDD*)

RUNNERS. Cf *runner* — an iron plate at the side of a fire to contract it and save fuel. (*EDD*)

SADLY. This is taken to mean 'excessively'. The text referred to *sadly* smashed and *sadly* burned. Cf *sad* — bad, ill, in bad health, very bad. (*EDD*)

SAMMED. Cf *sam* — to gather or scrape together, to collect, pick up. Generally used with 'together' or 'up'. 'He sammed up a stone' (*Tom Treddlehoyle's Bairnsla Annual*, 1847). (*EDD*)

SETTLE. A bench with high backs and arms. (*OED*)

SPRAGG. A short prop of timber used to support the roof of a mine, while the men are at work under-cutting. (*EDD*.) To prop up, support.

STONE DRIFT. A tunnel driven through strata adjacent to the coal. (*EDD*)

STOPPINGS. Cf *stopping* — (i) A wall built into an excavation in a pit to give direction to a current of air. (ii) The blocking up of disused roadways. (*EDD*)

SUMP. (i) A portion of the shaft below the working level where water collects before being pumped to the surface. (ii) That portion of the shaft kept a yard or more in advance of the drift or pit. (*EDD*)

TRAPPER. Cf *trap*. A ventilating door in a pit. (*EDD*) Hence *trapper*, a boy employed to attend to the trap-doors of a mine. (*Greenwell*)

VIEWER. The manager of a colliery. 'Officials and men have each their duties clear and unmistakable. They rank much in the following order: viewer, under-viewer, overman, back overman, deputy, hewer etc.' (*EDD*)

WEDGE. An implement for splitting coal, firewood etc A sharp or flat pointed iron or steel tool used for splitting and breaking coal or stone. (*EDD*)

WENDING. To turn around. To go; to walk. (*EDD*)

WICK. Living — a dialect form of 'quick' as in the prayer book version 'the quick [live] and the dead'.

WROUGHT. Worked, laboured, performed, struggled. (*EDD*)

References & Abbreviations

EDD. J Wright (ed), *English Dialect Dictionary*, Oxford, 1898-1905.

GREENWELL. G C Greenwell, *A Glossary of Terms used in the Coal Trade of Northumberland and Durham*, London, 1849.

KIRKHAM. N Kirkham, *Derbyshire Lead-Mining Glossary*, Leamington Spa, 1949.

MAWE. Mawe, *Minerology*, 1802.

NELSON. Nelson, *Dictionary of Mining*.

NICHOLSON. W E Nicholson, *A Glossary of Terms used in the Coal Trade of Northumberland and Durham*, Newcastle, 1888.

OED. H W & F G Fowler, *The Concise Oxford Dictionary*, Oxford, 1950.

YMA *Yorkshire Miners Association, NUM (Yorkshire Area) Price Lists and Agreements*, 1947.

(1981)

MI STICK O' RHUBUB

Ah saw it on t' stall in t' markit,
Limp, thin an wizzened as owt.
'It's rhubub!' t' man said, 'Fresh
   an' juicy' ...
It looked like a bit ev owd roap!

Wi grew rhubub in t' gardin, near
   t' closet,
When tha wor nobbut a lad.
Mam cut it wi' t' carver, fer stewin',
An chucked t' leaves on t' compost
   fer Dad.

Wi ett it wi' custard, all runny.
'It does thi blood good', Mam
   telled me.
'Fer t' ate it i' Spring gets thi workin'...
What working? Ah nivver could see!

Nah t' rhubub's i' cans i' some places,
Else frozzen i' lumps summat 'ard,
T' wir better when straight aht o'
   t' gardin
Dipped i' sugar ... an' ett i'
   t' back yard!

Doris Beer (WR)

(1989)

185

THE LYKE WAKE DIRGE
Bill Cowley

It is thirty-three years since the *White Rose Garland* was edited by two distinguished members of the YDS, Wilfrid Halliday and Stanley Umpleby. A few — but only a few — items in their collection and notes now require re-appraisal, and one of them is the *Cleveland Lyke Wake Dirge*.

In 1949 the *Dirge* was known only to a few dialect and folklore experts and some music lovers. In 1943 Britten had already composed his *Serenade, Opus 31, for tenor, horn and strings*, expressly for Peter Pears and Dennis Brain, which included a magnificent rendering of the *Dirge*, with music as haunting and powerful as the words themselves, which were Sir Walter Scott's version. This was published by the Decca Record Company (SXL 6449) in 1970 with Barry Tuckwell playing the horn and Benjamin Britten himself conducting the London Symphony Orchestra.

Meanwhile in 1955 I had suggested the forty-mile challenge walk across the North Yorkshire Moors which became known as the Lyke Wake Walk because on the first crossing, in darkness and storm, amongst the deep ling of Wheeldale Moor, we recited the *Lyke Wake Dirge* to the startled grouse.

> This yah neet, this yah neet,
> Ivvery neet an all,
> Fire an' fleet an' cannle leet,
> An' Christ tak up thy saul.

> When thoo fra hence away art passed,
> Ivvery neet an all,
> Ti Whinny Moor thoo cums at last,
> An' Christ tak up thy saul.

> If ivver thoo gave owther hosen or shoon,
> Ivvery neet an' all,
> Clap thee doon an' put 'em on
> An' Christ tak up thy saul.

> Bud if hosen an' shoon thoo nivver gave neean,
> Ivvery neet an' all,
> T' whinnies'll prick thee sair ti t' beean,
> An' Christ tak up thy saul.

If poetry in origin is magical incantation, then this is high poetry, which especially with Britten's music will chill the spine, and which can only be fully appreciated by those who have done the Lyke Wake Walk! In the past twenty-five years over 100,000 people have done this, and most of them will have read the *Dirge*, or even heard it sung.

The *Dirge* in fact has become very well known, with three or four folk-singing groups each having their own version. It has been sung on radio and television many times. The Fettlers give a rendering — a rather flat one on the Yorkshire Pilgrimage record PIL 1002 (Yorkshire Tourist Board). The Lyke Wake Club has three versions on tape (not for sale). It is strange to think that this ancient funeral dirge has now almost become pop music!

The *White Rose Garland* pointed at *A Yorkshire Dialogue* (1673) as the first example of modern dialect poetry, which is fair enough. There can be no doubt however that the *Cleveland Lyke Wake Dirge* in one form or another is very much older. In 1686 John Aubrey wrote, 'The belief in Yorkshire was, among the vulgar (perhaps is in part still) that after the person's death, the soul went over Whinny Moor and till about 1616-1624 at the funeral, a woman came and sang the following song ...' Richard Blakeborough recorded an instance of the *Dirge* being sung in Kildale about 1800. The Cleveland historian Ord notes that in 1684 the whole village of Runswick 'except one house sank in the night. Great loss of life must have ensued had not some fishermen been engaged at the time in waking a corpse' and so gave the alarm. In the Cotton MS Julius VI is a letter written to Sir Thomas Chaloner (1564-1615) about alum, but also including this:

> When any dieth [in Guisborough] certain women sing a song to the dead body reciting the journey that the deceased must go, and they are of beliefe (such is their fondnesse) that once in their lives yt is good to give a pair of newe shoes to a poore man, forasmuch as after this life they are to passe barefoote through a greate launde full of thorns and furzen, except by the merite of the Almes aforesaid they have redeemed thereof forfeit: for at the edge of the launde an oulde man shall meete them with the same shoos that were given by the party when he was living, and after he hath shodde them he dismisseth them to goe through thick and thin without scratch or scathe.
> [The same chatty letter includes the fascinating information that Guisborough people 'are altogether given to pleasure, scarce one good husband among them, day and night feasting, making matches for horse races, dogg running, or running afoote in a field called the Deer Close'.]

The Lyke Wake Dirge is clearly well-authenticated in Cleveland over many centuries. It can scarcely have been peculiar to Cleveland. Though known versions are Christian on the surface, the folklore is pagan, very ancient, and very widespread, with connections in Norse and Hindu folklore, and even amongst American Indians. Of course the idea of a soul having a difficult journey after death is a natural one. Canon Atkinson in a *Glossary of the Cleveland Dialect* (1868) gives copious notes on the Dirge and its connections, especially with the Norse *Hell-way* and *Hell-shoon*. The idea of the Bridge of Death also exists in many folklores:

> Fra Whinny Moor when thoo mayst pass,
> Ivvery neet an' all,
> Ti t' Brig o' Dreead thoo cums at last,
> An' Christ tak up thy saul.

Scott found an old legend of Sir Owain that had this verse:

> The brigge was high as a tour
> And as scharpe as a rasour,
> And naru it was also;
> And the water that ther ran under,
> Brend of lighning and of thonder
> That thocht him michel wo.

There is a Muslim version, and a Burmese one, and a link with Scandinavian boat-burnings or boat burials, and with 'Who pays the Ferryman?'

According to Atkinson, 'Fire an' fleet an' cannle leet' referred to the Cleveland custom that a fire had to be kept burning and a candle lit in the room where a corpse lay. (A coffin, with a candle superimposed and two Ordnance Survey symbols for howes — ON *haugr,* burial mound — are the Lyke Wake Club's badge.) *The White Rose Garland* interpreted 'fleet' as being floor, or house-room. I prefer Atkinson's suggestion that it is the Cleveland word 'flet' for sparks or live embers, continuing the poetic imagery of the whole line. Irene Sutcliffe's *Drouthy Deed* in the *Cleveland Anthology,* about 'tentin ti t' swiddens', or burning off the ling, illustrates this word beautifully:

> Wa'd bont a bit mair nor wa aimed to,
> Wa war flowtered wi' t' reek an' wi' t' flet

Atkinson quotes another folklore source: 'The Norse colonists of Iceland carried fire round the lands they intended to occupy in order to expel the evil spirits — and that the dead may not come again, the palliasse they died on must be burnt and live embers be thrown after the funeral procession'. In *Forty Years in a Moorland Parish* Atkinson records frequently finding charcoal from what he believed to be mediaeval graves in Danby churchyard, as also in all the Bronze Age burial mounds he excavated on the moors. Such mounds — Flat Howe, Loose Howe, Shunner Howe, Simon Howe, Lilla Howe, Burn Howe — are our guiding marks right across the Lyke Wake Walk. There is always a strong feeling on these moors that one is walking not only through distance, but through time. I do not think it too fanciful to suggest that some of the imagery of the *Dirge* goes right back to those Bronze Age funeral pyres on our high moors, and that when we sing it, echoes come from 4,000 years ago.

188

Bill Cowley, 1915-1994.

The White Rose Garland also includes *A Dree Neet* which Richard Blakeborough found in an old manuscript dating from at least 1750. These too are powerful, even frightening, verses using much of the same imagery as the *Dirge* — an applied version of it, so to speak:

> T'war a dree neet, a dree neet,
> As t' squire's end drew nigh,
> A dree neet, a dree neet
> Ti watch an' pray an' sigh.

> Bud lahl deeath recks hoo dree t' neet be,
> Or hoo a sowl may pray;
> When t' sand runs oot, his sickle reeaps,
> A gannin sowl can't stay.

189

> T'war a dree neet, a dree neet
> Ower Whinny Moor ti trake,
> Wi sheeanless feet ower flinty steeans,
> Thruff monny a thoorny brake.
>
> A dree neet, a dree neet,
> Wi' nowt neeaways ti mark
> T'gainest trod ti t' Brigg o' Dreead,
> A lane lost sowl i' t' dark.

This particular squire had no good deeds to aid him, too many wronged women behind him:

> An roond t' cannle tweea tahms ther cam
> A dark winged moth ti t' leet,
> Bud t' thod it swirled reet inti t' fleeam
> Wheer gans his sowl this neet.

It is obvious that the *Dirge*, and all the imagery connected with it, has always made a powerful impression on people's minds. It still does.

Note. The word *lyke* or *lich* for a corpse does not seem to have been used in Cleveland, at least in recent times, except in the compounds *lyke wake, lich-gate* (where the corpse was rested on entering the churchyard). Some English dictionaries also give *lich-owl*, the screech owl, supposed to foretell death. AS *lic*, ON *lik*, German *Leiche;* a (usually dead) body.

CLEVELAND LYKE WAKE DIRGE

Richard Blakeborough's version with slight amendments and revised spelling.

> This yah neet, this yah neet,
>   Ivvery neet an' all,
> Fire an' fleet an' cannle leet,
>   An' Christ tak up thy saul.
>
> When thoo fra hence away art passed,
>   Ivvery neet an' all,
> Ti Whinny Moor thoo cums at last,
>   An' Christ tak up thy saul.
>
> If ivver thoo gav owther hosen or shoon,
>   Ivvery neet an' all,
> Clap thee doon, an' put 'em on,
>   An' Christ tak up thy saul.

Bud if hosen an' shoon thoo nivver gav neean,
    Ivvery neet an' all,
T' whinnies'll prick thee sair ti t' beean,
    An' Christ tak up thy saul.

Fra Whinny Moor when thoo art passed,
    Ivvery neet an' all,
Ti t' Brig o' Dreead thoo cums at last,
    An' Christ tak up thy saul.

If ivver thoo gav o' thy siller an' gowd,
    Ivvery neet an' all,
On t' Brig o' Dreead thoo'll finnd foothod,
    An' Christ tak up thy saul.

Bud if siller an' gowd thoo nivver gav neean,
    Ivvery neet an' all,
Thoo'll doon, doon tummle towards Hell fleeams,
    An' Christ tak up thy saul.

Fra t' Brig o' Dreead when thoo art passed,
    Ivvery neet an' all,
Ti t' fleeams o' Hell thoo cums at last,
    An' Christ tak up thy saul.

If ivver thoo gav owther bite or sup,
    Ivvery neet an' all,
T' fleeams'll nivver catch thee up,
    An' Christ tak up thy saul.

Bud if bite or sup thoo nivver gav neean,
    Ivvery neet an' all,
T' fleeams'll bon thee sair ti t' beean,
    An' Christ tak up thy saul.

fleet, sparks, embers; *yah*, one; *neean*, none; *beean*, bone; *bon*, burn.

(1982)

GOOISE GREASE AN' BRAHN PAPER

When it gets rahnd ta t' backend, winter dunt seem so far off, does it, an' t' other day Ah fun missen thinkin abaht t' owld-feshioned winters when Ah wor a nipper. (Appen it wer walkin ower t' owld spots at set me on.)

I' them days we didn't ev jabs for flu an' 'oopin' cough, but wer mothers did t' best they could ta keep off t' coughs an' cowlds, an' owt else 'at wer goin'. They couldn't afford to ave us poorly any mooar than they could elp. They'd t' doctor bills ta pay then, tha knows, an' t' medicine ta pay for an' all.

At t' first sign of a peff, or a sniffle, aht came t' camphor begs. An' it didn't matter 'ah much we begged an' pleaded, t' denged things were pinned on ta wer vests. Just in case ther's a few young uns 'at knows nowt abaht camphor begs, Ah'll explain. T' camphor wor i' blocks, abaht an inch square, an' 'appen abaht a quarter of an inch thick. Mi mother med little begs aht o' bits of owld wool vests, or jerseys, or summat o' t' sooart, an' popped a piece o' camphor in each one. Then t' begs wi t' camphor inside were pinned ta wer vests — wi a safety pin.

If anybody bumped ya on your chest, sometimes t' pin came undone, and then ya 'ad a prick ta add ta your misery, cos as sooin as t' other kids cottoned on 'at ya were wearin' camphor, they didn't 'alf torment ya. Tha sees, as sooin as t' camphor warmed up, it began ta smell — that wer t' idea like — t' fumes were supposed ta clear your tubes an' keep t' germs at bay. It were on its way aht when Ah were a bairn, an' t' few 'at did 'ave to wear it didn't 'alf cop it from t' others in t' class.

Nah, if ya did get a bad chest, ya were rubbed wi' camphorated oil, aht of a blue bottle, wi' ridges dahn it. Then ya ad a flannil pinned ta t' inside a your vest, ta keep it clean, an' ta keep your chest warm at same time. But t' flannil didn't keep t' stink in. T' other kids soon knew who ad camphorated oil on ther chest, an' didn't they let ya know abaht it! John Brahn's baby weren't t' awf on it.

But t' worst a t' lot were gooise greease an' brahn paper. By! That wor a torment. When t' paper got a bit rumpled it pricked, an' as sooin as anybody heard it crackle, they thumped you on your chest, just to ear it agen. They didn't ahf pester ya in t' playgrahnd when ya 'ad ta 'ave brahn paper on your chest. Ah think sometimes we 'ad a flannil on, an' all. It wor like walkin abaht i' a suit of armour.

Just for a while there wor a feshion i wearing Iodine Lockits. Does anybody else remember 'em? Ah think they were advertised in t' paper an' fowk sent up for 'em. They didn't stink like camphor, an' some o t' kids swanked a bit like, an' pulled 'em aht ta show 'em off. They were round, 'appen as big as an owld penny, or was it a ha'pny? Onnyroad, they were rahnd an' were hung rahnd yer neck on a bit o' band. They might 'ave 'ad a 'ole in t' middle, but Ah'm not sure abaht that nah.

Sometimes when we 'ad a cough, mi muther 'd put a spooinful o' blackcurrant jam in t' bottom of a mug, an' pour 'ot water on it. Nah that med a varry nice drink. We'd tek as much o' that as we got chance on. Ah got ta like rum an' butter an' all, though Ah didn't care for it at first. Mi muther melted a lump o' butter in an' owld enamel mug — Ah think she put a bit a sugar in, an' then when it were 'ot, she poured a drop o' rum in. We 'ad it from a teaspoon, as 'ot as we could tek it, an' if we wern't careful, we burnt wer lips on t' spooin.

An' then they used ta give us 'olibut liver oil, an' Scott's Emulsion — ta keep up wer strength in t' winter time, an' if we did get run dahn, there were Parrish's Liquid Chemical Food. That turned your teeath black if ya didn't cleean 'em straight away. Ah think it were t' iron in it!.

Wor it durin' t' War 'at we were towld 'at turnip jewse wor good for cowlds an' sore throats? We 'ad that an' all. Ya cut t' top off a turnip an' scooped aht some o' t' middle, an' then put some brahn sugar in, an' put t' top back on agen, like a lid. T' sugar drew t' jewse aht, an' it wont bad tastin nawther. O' course, that 'at 'ad been scooped aht o' t' middle wont thrown away — it went inta t' next dinner. Fowk 'ad ta watch points i' them days, when there were no National Health and no Fam'ly Allahance.

Muriel Shackleton (WR) (1986)

The 1986 chairman, Dr Ken Smith, with Stanley Ellis and Lynne Anderson.

YORKSHIRE DIALECT IN
CHARLOTTE BRONTË'S *SHIRLEY*
Ken Edward Smith

Among many relatively neglected aspects of *Shirley,* a novel that has only recently come into its own, is its rich and integrated use of dialect speech. It is not that Charlotte Brontë was a pioneer in this area. Not only Elizabeth Gaskell in *Mary Barton* (1848) but also her own sisters in *Agnes Grey* and *Wuthering Heights* (both 1846) had followed Sir Walter Scott's example of introducing rich dialect colouring. And, as modern linguistics has confirmed, Emily's rendering of dialect is in a class of its own in terms of its accuracy and vitality. Nevertheless, Anne and Emily had carefully restricted the range of dialect in their books: Anne's *Agnes Grey* has the warm-hearted widow Nancy Brown, while Emily has the notoriously Calvinistic servant Joseph.

What distinguishes *Shirley* is that it presents not just one or two dialect speaking characters, but a whole cast of them. Nor are these dialect characters part of a single group like Hardy's rustic chorus in *The Return of the Native.* Rather we are in a world more like that of Scott's broad historical narratives where a whole way of life is being evoked. Given this saturation in a complex historical situation surrounding the Luddite risings of 1811-12 we should not be surprised to find that we have both a wide range of dialect speakers and a diversity of functions played by dialect in the novel. It may be as well to delineate these functions before going on to characterise the variety of dialect viewpoints in the novel and the author's attitude to them.

First, and not least, among the reasons for including dialect in the novel is Charlotte Brontë's sheer interest in preserving and dramatising local words and customs, an interest shared by many antiquarian historians of the nineteenth century. In other words the writer who pored through the files of the *Leeds Mercury* for 1812-1814 and read up the details of Luddism in 1811-1812 is of a piece with the writer who ensured we heard such words as 'mimmest' (most demure), 'flayed' (frightened), 'cant' (brisk, cheerful), 'kittle' (fickle), pronunciations such as 'maister' and 'amang', and expressions such as 'took on wi' '. On this level it is delight in rendering the sheer particularity and localism of dialect that we encounter.

However, it only requires a shift of emphasis in such cases to uncover the second aspect of dialect in the novel, its rich and exotic surprisingness and vitality. Against the cool tone of the narrator *Shirley* sets a whole polyphony of voices and rejoices in the particular sound-play and imagistic power of dialect, even interspersing it with phrases from French as in this outburst of Mr Yorke against Robert Moore: 'Aye, ther it is. The lad is a mak' of an alien amang us: his father would never have talked i' that way. Go back to Antwerp where you were born and bred, mauvaise tête' (chapter 3).

Finally, there is the sense of dialect as representing the oral tradition of story-telling – with its tendency towards lateral thinking rather than logical progression, towards the twists and turns of thought in the present rather than the distanced, orderly perspective of the main narrative. Joe Scott's tale of Moses Barraclough's courtship is seen humorously but it is also rejoiced in for its rich circumstantiality:

> Howsiver, Sarah had another string to her bow: Fred Murgatroyd, one of our lads, is for her, and as women judge men by their faces — and Fred has a middling face, while Moses is none so handsome as we all knaw — the lass took on wi' Fred. A two-three months sin', Murgatroyd and Moses chanced to meet one Sunday night; they'd both come lurking about these premises wi' the notion of counselling Sarah to tak' a bit of a walk wi' them; they fell out, had a tussel, and Fred was worsted: for he's young and small, and Barraclough, for all he has only one leg, is almost as strong as Sugden there; indeed, anybody that hears him roaring at a revival or a love-feast may be sure he's no weakling.   (chapter 8)

Bringing these three functions of dialect together we can see that they all suggest a standard of authenticity, of closeness to the way things are, which serves to judge the metropolitan superiority of the curate Mr Donne: 'Wretched place this York-shire ... I could never have formed an idear of the country had I not seen it; and the people — rich and poor — what a set! How corse and uncultivated! They would be scouted in the south.' (Chapter 15.) When Shirley orders this pompous gentleman out of her garden it is not just the rudeness of what he says but the drawl in which he says it which annoys her. At this level we can see the whole novel as affirming the human centrality, seriousness and reality of the scenes of Yorkshire life it portrays and as criticising those from the metropolis who would think it peripheral. Dialect plays its part in this affirmation that Yorkshire in 1811-1812 is culturally diverse and historically significant locale.

Such an implicit claim should not be thought to suggest a uniformity of dialect speech and attitude in the West Riding speech community. In fact a whole range of ways of being 'realistic' or 'down-to-earth' are explored and a number of these are implicitly criticised by the narrator. To this range of dialect speakers we must now turn.

The most unusual and enterprising dialect creation in the book is that of the middle-class Mr Yorke, a Whig manufacturer who can switch in and out of dialect as he wishes. Here is an apparent paradox in which the author clearly delights — a connoisseur of painting and a European linguist who will deliberately use the broadest dialect. On the one side we see the anti-clerical, anti-Tory, anti-monarchical streak of radical Dissenting attitudes which he expresses directly to the Rector, Mr Helstone. His response when asked why he prefers a particular chair is typical. 'My father war afore me, and that's all t' answer I sall give thee; and it's as good a reason as Mr Helstone can give for the main feck o' his notions.' (Chapter 3.) On the other side we have the fierce, almost aristocratic pride in his family, the benevolent despotism with which he runs his mill. In fact the paradox can be resolved by seeing him as representing a distinctively Yorkshire brand of democracy which fascinates Charlotte Brontë in its imperviousness to demands for social equality combined with a no-nonsense assertion of spiritual equality and dignity which neither Robert Moore nor Mr Helstone find easy to grasp or accept. In essence, it is a classically Wesleyan view and, as such, links the Tory, Evangelical and Monarchical Charlotte Brontë to her Whig, Dissenting and Republican character. As we shall see, it is a view which she opposes to the enthusiasm and egalitarianism of the Calvinistic Primitive Methodists whom she associates with the Luddite cause.

This Wesleyan viewpoint is, accurately in socio-historical terms, most fully expressed by the loyal foreman, Joe Scott, prime representative of the worthy and improved workman in the novel. Joe, with his sense that 'a man's a man for a' that', can combine rudeness to Robert Moore with an acceptance of the social order as it is: 'But your father war Yorkshire, which maks ye a bit Yorkshire too: and onybody may see ye're akin to us, ye're so keen o' making brass, and getting forrards.' (Chapter 5.) In the light of this it is interesting to observe his attitude to the deputation which tries to persuade Robert Moore not to install cropping-frames in his mill. Although unsympathetic to the to-him-alien rhetorics of Moses Barraclough and Noah (of which more later) he is nevertheless responsive to the meditated working-class speech of the redundant cropper, William Farren. Farren, although in the author's eyes misled, represents a voice that must not be ignored:

It's out o' no ill-will that I' m here, for my part; it's just to mak' a effort to get things straightened, for they're sorely a crooked. Ye see we're ill off, — varry ill off: wer families is sore and pined. We're thrown out o' work wi' these frames: we can get nought to do: we can earn nought. What is to be done? Nay: I've no grand words at my tongue's end, Mr Moore, but I feel that it would be a low principle for a reasonable man to starve to death like a dumb cratur': I will n't do 't. (chapter 8)

William Farren's conversation with Mr Hall, the neighbouring clergyman, reinforces this idea of a necessary solidarity between the classes. On the one hand we are told that Mr Hall 'though an accomplished scholar, not only spoke with a strong northern accent, but, on occasion, used freely north-country expressions'. (Chapter 8.) On the other, we see that William Farren, though embittered, is not averse to the idea of 'getting forrards' if he can, and is thus amenable to help from the clergyman. When later employed as a gardener by Mr Yorke he articulates to Caroline Helstone the only reason that he would consider becoming a rebel, namely the need to take charity. The help of Mr Hall and Mr Yorke does not come into this category since it is his help towards working for his own sustenance and that of his family. It is left to William Farren to define a set of qualities which are clearly central to Charlotte Brontë's text, qualities that give rise neither to despair nor arrogance but to a proper sense of dignity and esteem which he sees himself as sharing with Caroline: 'Ay, I *am* proud, and so are ye; but your pride and mine is t' right mak' — what we call i' Yorkshire "clean pride" — such as Mr Malone and Mr Dome knows nought about: theirs is mucky pride.' (Chapter 18.)

There are, however, negative social characteristics — negative from the narrator's viewpoint — which can also be found among the dialect speakers of *Shirley*. Thus Joe Scott, though his social attitudes are generally endorsed, turns out to profess a male chauvinism somewhat discomforting to both Shirley and Caroline. His sense of women's inferiority clearly does not square with what we know of Caroline's stoic endurance or Shirley's organised charitable generosity. Nevertheless, the spirit is not quite that of *Jane Eyre* or *Villette,* since Joe's strictures on women are backed up with scriptural authorities that the women cannot match. In fact, the whole incident is humorously treated and is probably best seen as a piece of 'flyting': still, we are entitled to say that this is an aspect of dialect culture which Charlotte Bronte and her heroines might find amusing from a distance, but could never begin to tolerate as a limitation on their own aspirations and conduct.

Much more seriously seen as representing the unacceptable face of working-class culture to the Tory narrator are Moses Barraclough and Noah o' Tims. It is true that there is humour here, but it is the humour of satire against attitudes which are feared as well as disliked. Indeed, so over-anxious is Charlotte Brontë to make sure which side we are on that in her description of the radical preacher Moses Barraclough she seems in danger of creating sympathy for this man with a wooden leg by her animus against him: 'There was a kind of leer about his lips; he seemed laughing in his sleeve at some person or thing; his whole demeanour was anything but that of a true man.' (Chapter 8.)

The speeches of the two hit precisely those notes most at variance with the implicit paternalistic Tory Anglicanism of the narrator. Noah speaks in a mixture of dialect and high-flown rhetoric — as often in middle-class novelists this latter is seen as highly untrustworthy, though from another aspect its hyperbole might be seen as typical of pre-literate oral discourse generally. Parodied at greater length and with greater empathy is the language of Moses Barraclough: 'Or iver you set up the pole o' your tent amang us, Mr Moore, we lived i' peace and quietness; yea, I may say, in all loving-kindness. I am not myself an aged person as yet, but I can remember as far back as maybe some twenty year when hand-labour were encouraged and respected, and no mischief-maker had ventured to introduce these here machines, which is so pernicious'. (Chapter 8.) As if we might be in danger of being taken in by Moses we hear swiftly from Robert Moore that the preacher is both a drunkard and a swindler. It is arguably a pity that the novelist felt the need to load the dice so obviously since her rendering of Moses Barraclough's speech itself skilfully conveys a sense of self-conscious, deceitful rhetoric. Beyond this, of course, we might well wish to question whether the religious and social trad-itions which Moses represents are fairly embodied in him. One cannot help feeling that, admirable as the range of Charlotte Brontë's empathy is in *Shirley*, stretching across English and French-speaking cultures, Whig and Tory, Dissenter and Ang-licanism, nevertheless her imagination failed her somewhat when she tried to imagine the mentality of a radical religious preacher. But even in this case her use of dialect enables her to give us a possible, if in this case less than typical, character. When added to the range of successful portrayals we have already discussed this makes for a formidable gallery of dialect characters indeed.

In conclusion, then, dialect is almost omnipresent in the novel, associated alike with attitudes that are approved, tolerated and rejected by the implied narrator. And whether seen negatively or positively in this sense it is always positive in a broader sense, in giving a sense of richness, of human breadth and depth, to the narrative. Through the use of dialect we are made to feel both the particularity and the deep human resonance of the extensive drama played out before us. Dialect increases our sense that history consists of specific and very varied individuals attempting to work out their way in life according to such lights, and words, as they have.

There is, though, a yet further dimension. From time to time the author needs to give us a sense of the totality of her action, a sense of time, change and history which cannot be expressed in the coolness of a Monday-morning-style narration. This is seen in the middle of the novel when there is extensive quotation from the Scots ballad *Puir Mary Lee,* along with the admission that it is imprecisely relevant to the ostensible matter in hand, that is the love-lorn state of Caroline Helstone. The real reason for its inclusion would seem to be the need to universalise the love-theme of the novel and its tragic potentialities.

An even more striking example of this distancing, universalising tone is to be found at the very end of the novel, this time in the Yorkshire dialect itself. Here the narrator's elderly housekeeper Martha is given the task of summarising the sweep of historical change that has taken place between the pre-industrial age, the upheavals of 1812 and the present time of the narrative's writing. Her reply when asked 'What was the Hollow like then, Martha?' seems to have little direct relevance to the action. But what it implicitly conveys, in a manner reminiscent of Emily's Ellen Dean, is that the facts of human change and transience gain dignity in the very act of being told. The intimacy of the oral style and the dialect words, the sense of unhurried agelessness in the pace and tone, serve to give a sense of longer, larger perspectives to the novel's action:

Different to what it is now; but I can tell of it clean different again: when there was neither mill, nor cot, nor hall, except Fieldhead, within two miles of it. I can tell, one summer-evening, fifty years syne, my mother coming in just at the edge of dark, almost fleyed out of her wits, saying, she had seen a fairish [fairy] in Fieldhead Hollow; and that was the last fairish that ever was seen on this country side (though they've been heard within these forty years). A lonesome spot it was and a bonnie spot — full of oak trees and nut trees. It is altered now.'   (chapter 37)

There is no explicit moral to *Shirley*, the narrator briefly concludes. If we were to seek one it might be the need to understand a whole, complex way of life before passing judgements on human affairs: or, the need to respect the sheer individual variety of human beings, the differences between Robert Moore and Mr Yorke, between Caroline and Shirley, between Joe Scott and William Farren. Either way, it is clear that dialect plays a crucial role, whether by giving us a sense of the rich range of characters or by sharply individualising them for us.

(1988)

DIFF'RUNT

Ah wor born an' bred i' Bratford
An' Ah'm prahd o' bein' a Tyke —
But Ah'm not like other Yorksher fowk,
Ah'm sort o' diffrunt, like.

Oh Ah'm partial t' Yorksher bitter
An' Ah luv mi Yorksher pud,
An' Ah'd feight like 'ell t' lick Lancasher
As onny on us would.

But still fowk say Ah'm diffrunt,
That ther's summat not quite reight,
Almost as if their 'earin' wer
At odds wi' what's i' sight.

But Ah say Ah'm a Yorksherman
In spite o' what fowk say,
Tho mi Muther comes from Delhi
An mi Faither from Bombay.

Derek Lupton (WR)

(1988)

199

SKEUL

Wi' satchel on her back, she gans
Away doon t' laane te t' gate.
Tis fost day off ti skeul, tha knaas,
I hooape she wean't bi late.

Tis lonely Ah'll bi when she's gone,
Ah's nut afeard ti say.
An Ah'll bi watchin' tahm cum roond
Ti fower o'clock teday.

Hoo will she git on wi' her sums?
Ah wunner if t' milks pure?
These thowts cum tummlin' ti mi mahnd,
Aye, these an many more.

Ah wunner if she'll lahke all t' food?
An' wesh her hands i' t' breaks?
An' wheeall bi theer ti pick her up
If she a tummel teeaks?

Mi lahtle lassie's gan, tha knaas,
She's oot o' mah control,
An' other influences ther'll be
Ower body, mahnd, an' sowl.

Eh noo, Ah musn't think lahke this,
An' git intiv a stife,
T' owd sayin' tells me, 'Skeul days is
Best days o' all thi life'.

Ruth Harrison Dent (NR)

(1988)

NUT LET ON

Yah yeear when Tom 'n' me was bairns
'n' it cem ti Kessmass Eeave,
Wa cudn't get ti sleeap at ahll,
As weel ya maht beleeave.

I' bed wa talked aboot nex' daay
'n' ahll wa shaaped ti deea;
Wa'd 'ev a reet good tahm 'n' ahll,
O' that, ther waan't mich feear.

Then wa 'eeard oor Mam 'n' Dad i' t' stairs,
Then feeat-steps pitter-pattrin'.
'Pretend ti be asleeap', Ah ses.
'The'v cum ti stop us chatt'rin.'

Thru t' bed-room door the tip-tooaed in,
Oor ees suppooasedly shut,
Then inti t' piller-caase 'ung oot
Sum grandish things the' put.

Wa tak oor toys 'n' gaames doon-stairs
Next morn, as chuff as owt;
'Wha, Dad, noo leeak at them', says Mam,
'Wat Santa Klaws 'es browt.'

It pleeased 'em weel ti nut let on,
Sooa we gev nowt awaay,
'n' ther's neea doot ahll on us 'ed
A ''Appy Kessmass Daay!'

Geoff M Robinson (ER)

(1991)

A CELEBRATION OF YORKSHIRE DIALECT
Muriel Shackleton

(Held as part of the York Festival on Saturday the 20th June 1992 in the Central Methodist Hall, St Saviourgate, York. Organised by Arnold Kellett — title suggested by Bill Cowley).

It was a glorious June day. Members arrived in force, and citizens of York, and visitors to York, including a few from overseas, came too. The big room in the old Central Methodist Hall was full to capacity, with perhaps 150 present.

Arnold Kellett set the ball rolling by explaining the origins of Yorkshire dialect, illustrating his talk with maps and diagrams on the blackboard. If history at school had been presented in this light-hearted but factual manner, many more people would now have a better grasp of events in those far-off centuries.

Arnold set dialect in the context of the evolution of the English language which, he said, was really the story of five successive invasions — the Celts (around 500 BC), the Romans (who left us in 410 AD), the Angles (from the fifth century), mainly in the north and east, together with the Saxons, in the south and west, the Vikings (ninth century) and the Normans (eleventh century).

Stressing that dialect is not a 'rough and slovenly form of English, but, on the contrary, a survival of the original robust form of English, with its roots in the speech of the Angles and Vikings', Arnold reminded us that the Scandinavian influence was stronger in the North Riding and East Riding areas. This statement was fully illustrated by relevant examples.

A quotation from Chaucer's *Franklin's Tale* showed how, by 1400, AngloSaxon and Norman French had merged to form Middle English. Caxton's press (1476) marked the beginning of the gradual imposition of a standard (London) English, contrasting with local dialects. Describing the 'war of attrition' against dialect, Arnold emphasised four factors contributing to its decline: (1) Education: when children were taught to read they were expected to speak like all the others who could read. (2) Social mobility: as people moved around, so as not to be conspicuous, so as to make themselves understood, they modified their local speech. (3) Social advancement: aware of the prejudice against dialect people made an effort to speak Standard English. (4) The mass media: even local radio rarely uses local announcers, and illustrations were given of northern soap operas where local speech is weak or from the wrong area.

He spoke of the early champions of dialect, especially Robert Burns, who was followed in Yorkshire by David Lewis (1815). Extracts were read from *Wuthering Heights* and John Hartley to show how Yorkshire dialect was at last being taken seriously. A brief account of Joseph Wright and the founding of the YDS in 1897 followed.

Finally, Arnold turned the tables on those who dismiss Yorkshire dialect as something 'quaint and clownish' by reading his own poem *Talking Posh*, which included the lines:

> An' ter think 'at we'r mocked bi fowk same as yond
> Fer wer accent an' plain 'omely talk —
> Nay, Ah'd as lief bi awther gawmless or dumb
> As sahnd like a stiff stuck-up mawk!

In the second half he introduced speakers representing each of the three main dialect areas. From the North Riding, Ruth Dent, our chairman, and a 'real Dales-bred lass', read *On a Farm* by Muriel Carr, *Bed Ends* by Brenda English and two of her own humorous poems — *A Trip to London* and *A Roond Tooit*.

Peter Walker told some amusing true tales from his village of Ampleforth, including one about the chap who thought the 'Legal and General' would be a reliable insurance company 'cos they do t' weather forecasts'. He read some of his own poems, including *Oor Lengthman* (featured in this year's *Summer Bulletin*) and one about 'Off-comed-uns' ('Meeast on em couldn't tell a yowe frev a tup').

From the East Riding Jack Danby gave us a superb rendering of *Goodies* complete with actions — a real *tour de force*. He was followed by the inimitable Irwin Bielby, who had a wonderful rapport with his audience, ('It's grand ter see seea mony feeaks 'ere'), telling lovely stories from *Pock*, including the chap (?Geoff Robinson) who, when asked what he'd given the people coming round raising money for a swimming pool, said 'Ah gev 'em a bucket o' watter!' Austin Hyde's *A Countryman i' t' Toon* was included in the poems also read by Irwin. Geoffrey Robinson, complete with his little flat cap, gave his usual uproarious performance of very funny stories, including the one about the boss under a cartload of hay, and one of his Chulton Parva poems.

Muriel Shackleton (editor of *Summer Bulletin*) opened the battle for the West Riding. A Wibsey lass, she reminded us that although he has twice been mayor of Knaresborough, Arnold is really a Wibsey lad and therefore, like herself, 'a proper Wibsa Gawby'. Having explained that like Gowcar Lillies, Slawit Mooinrakers, Marsden Cuckoos and similar folk, Wibsa Gawbies are 'nooan soa daft as the' like ter mek aht', Muriel read one of Harold Priestley's poems from his *Rhymes of a Wibsa Gawby*. This was followed by her own anecdote *T' Owld Man's Getten a Cowd* and her 'autobiographical' (?) poem, *Noan a Reight Gooid Yorksher Ahswife*.

Arthur Kinder, recently elected as one of our vice-presidents, gave some of his comic tales now available on tape, including the one about being asked what he'd like for his 'teea' .... On replying 'Salmon', he was told 'Well, bring a tin wi thi, then!'. Finally, Stanley Ellis, our secretary, capped Arthur's tale with one about a local preacher who made sure he got two eggs for his tea .... He also read John Hartley's poem about 'lettin t' lasses alooane'.

This lively meeting was rounded off by a couple of verses of *Ilkla Moor* led by Sydney Martin on his melodeon. Sydney was also one of those who worked behind the scenes, managing to find a hall not already booked for some other festival event. Jean Maybury, too, had the difficult task of representing the society to the festival organisers who disbanded and reformed at one point. People on the platform are seen and heard. Others behind the scenes oil the wheels and enable our society to function.

After the meeting closed, the stalwarts manning the bookstall were completely hidden by the throng, not only looking, but also buying. 'Even all the ties have gone', said Stanley at the finish. That the audience had thoroughly enjoyed their couple of hours with Yorkshire dialect was clearly seen and heard. With suitable publicity it is obvious that we can attract a satisfactory audience. We have some good readers and performers, many of them also busy with council offices and already stretched to capacity. If we are to continue to produce events like that in York, we need more workers, on council, behind the scenes, and on the platform.

(1992)

MEN OF FEW WORDS ...

In the 1930s and earlier, when farmers were looking for lads to hire for the year to live in on the farms, it was something like slave-trading in small agricultural towns such as Selby and Driffield. At Driffield, where my father grew up, you might have heard something like the following during Martinmas Fair (around the 11th November):

Farmer	Lad
Did thoo want 'irin'?	Yis
Can thoo ploo?	Yis
Can thoo sow frev a 'opper?	Yis
(A hopper fastened round his waist)	
Can thoo stack? *(Build a stack)*	Yis
Can thoo slash a 'edge?	Yis
(Trim a hedge with a long-handled slasher)	
Can thoo mow? *(Mow hay with a scythe)*	Yis
Can thoo dyke? *(Clean out a dyke and make it tidy)*	Yis
Can thoo drahve 'osses?	Yis
Can thoo theeak? *(Thatch a stack)*	Yis
An' steeak? *(Stook the harvest in the fields)*	Yis
Can thoo plug muck?	Yis
(Load manure into carts for muck-leading)	
Can thoo milk coos?	Yis
Is thoo coortin'?	Yis
Can sha milk?	Yis
Could sha com' an' 'elp thoo of a Sunda?	Yis
Thoo could gan tiv 'er 'oose for thi teea?	Yis
Thoo wad 'eti be back ti fodder at neet.	Yis
Thoo's nut varry big!	Ah yance wor
Dis thoo play crecket?	Yis
Dis thoo play a straight bat?	Ah did afoor Ah met thoo. Noo Ah's ammost doubled up wiv all that wark thoo's mentioned.

Thoo's 'ired, then. Twenty pund for t' year.

Sydney Martin (ER)

(1992)

204

THE PUBLIC READINGS OF JOHN HARTLEY, BENJAMIN PRESTON AND EDWIN WAUGH

Ian Dewhirst

On Saturday night, the 30th December 1871, Benjamin Preston, familiarly known as Ben Preston, 'the Yorkshire Humorist', was billed as 'a Great Treat' at the Keighley Mechanics' Institute. Interspersed in pairs between overtures and selections from Mozart, Bellini, Rossini and Auber, played by a five-piece band, he gave a total of eight readings: Edwin Waugh's *Jamie's Frolic*, John Hartley's *Done Agean*, and his own *Short Timer, T' Creakin' Gate, Come to thy Gronny, Doy, Stand Up, Lads, an' Let's Hev a Feyt, The Oak and the Ivy* and *Natterin' Nan*. Admission prices ranged from 4d in the gallery to 1d in the area, with mechanics' institute members at half-price. Preston (who was giving his services gratuitously) attracted the largest audience in that season of 'Saturday Night Entertainments', and responded to their appreciation with encores. His humorous readings were 'irresistibly droll', his *Come to thy Gronny, Doy*, 'replete with tenderness and feeling'.

The fact that several of our best-known dialect writers gave public readings is usually mentioned in their biographical notes and obituaries, but details are rare. A proliferation of mid-Victorian local newspapers, however, provides a rich source of contemporary information — given a very great deal of time and patience!

This article should be viewed in the nature of an impression rather than a definitive study of the subject. Newspaper research is fraught with difficulties. At a practical level, most libraries make you use microfilms nowadays, which tend to be hard on the eyes. Public readings were not generally considered newsworthy at the time, and their reporting often seems to be the work of local correspondents rather than regular journalists. Many known readings were not reported at all. The prose style of the period substitutes 'the audience frequently manifested their gratification by warm plaudits' for 'they clapped', and 'he succeeded in tickling the risible faculties of the audience" for 'he made them laugh', leaning towards an unctuous verbosity which can tell us little or nothing: 'The name of this gentleman is so well known and his work so familiar in every household, that we feel we cannot do him sufficient justice in praising his readings' — that was Waugh at Ilkley in 1875!

Public readings formed part of a wider context, for mid-Victorian social life was exceedingly busy. There were lectures and entertainments, sermons and oratorios, concerts and grand concerts, balls and soirées, teas and *conversaziones*. Commenting on a series of penny readings in 1864, Keighley Mechanics' Institute congratulated itself in that 'a very considerable portion of the audience consisted

Mr. John Hartley's
PUBLIC READINGS & RECITALS.

Applications should be made as early as possible to prevent disappointments.

All applications for J. Hartley's Works should be made to W. Nicholson & Sons, 26, Paternoster Square, London, E.C., and Albion Works, Wakefield

Mr. John Hartley's Season will close on Good Friday, 1897.

Special Arrangements made for Schools & Charities.

Address :—

JOHN HARTLEY,
55, Harehills Terrace, LEEDS.

of the working classes, for whose benefit especially these readings have been established', whilst a chairman gave an address on 'recreation for the working classes'. Those Saturday Night Entertainments, of which Preston's had been a highlight, were organised through the winter of 1871-1872 'expressly for the benefit of the people, and managed with a view to their pleasure and profit'.

Nor were readings confined to the dialect. A mechanics' institute in a town like Keighley could engage 'Dramatist and Elocutionist' J M Bellew, Professor Greenbank and Arthur Sketchley, 'author of the popular *Brown Papers*'; to say nothing of such lecturers as George Grossmith, Gerald Massey, Lord William Lennox (fee £5 5s), and Miss Emily Faithfull, editor of the *Victoria Magazine*. In 1869 their minutes resolved to invite John Ruskin, though there seems to be no record of him actually coming. Truly, however, the 'pleasure and profit' of the working classes were catered for in no uncertain terms.

Edwin Waugh, the Lancashire dialect poet, would appear to have set an example on the reading platform. Late in 1863 the Bradford Saturday Half-Day Closing Association announced 'a series of popular concerts' to include the 'author of *Come Whoam to thi Childer an' Me*'. A native of Rochdale, aged forty-six at that time, Waugh had achieved a measure of fame on the strength of this poem, and had taken up full-time writing in 1860. His appearance in the Bradford Temperance Hall, whilst drawing only a 'fair audience', demonstrated what were to become standard qualities of 'touching pathos' and 'the peculiar humour of the Lancashire dialect and people'. An Orphean Party provided musical interludes.

Waugh had a following in the West Riding. Early in 1866 he drew good attendances on two successive evenings at the Saltaire Literary Institute when he read from his own work. In the British School-room at Allerton his programme included *Besom Ben*, *The Barrel Organ* and the inevitable *Come Whoam to thi Childer an' Me*. Another two evenings at Bingley Mechanics' Institute attracted 'crowded audiences, composed of his friends and admirers of all classes'. It was here that a proposer of a vote of thanks 'said that the dialects of Lancashire and Yorkshire were sufficiently closely akin to enable us to claim Edwin Waugh as pretty much our own', and drew a parallel between Waugh and Preston: 'He thought that both dialects had borne their bright consummate flowers in the two lyrics, *Come Whoam to thi Childer an' Me*, and *Ah Nivver Can Call her my Wife.*'

From Bingley's point of view, Benjamin Preston represented local talent, since in 1865 he had moved from Bradford to an allotment on Gilstead Moor (in the prose of the period he was 'the small freeholder whose spade turns its bleak, stubborn, and ill-conditioned sod'). Only a couple of years younger than Waugh, he would not attain a similar literary eminence until in 1872 his poems would be 'collected out of the newspapers and magazines in which they are scattered, revised, and published in a volume'. On the 25th February 1867, however, what the *Bradford Observer* called 'the undoubted masters of the Yorkshire and Lancashire dialects' were brought together for a prestigious double reading, under the patronage of the mayor, in St George's Hall at Bradford. Charles Dickens, possibly the most famous public reader of all, was due there the following week.

In devoting an unusually generous space to previewing this event, the *Bradford Observer* stressed the superfluousness of its accompanying musical interludes — two singers and Master Dodds, 'the Juvenile Thalberg, Solo Pianist' — and criticised its advertisements in strident tones:

> Nor can our gratitude to the promoters of the entertainment restrain us from pointing out the bad taste of heading the posters announcing the Readings with 'VR' and the Lion and Unicorn. These showy beasts are not the sort of cattle men of simple and self-respecting genius care to herd with, who are neither Court flunkies, nor Queen's tradesmen, nor recruiting sergeants, nor vendors of patent medicine; and 'Victoria Regina' could add nothing by the sanction of her initials (which she has not given) to the character or interest of a public evening with the laureates of the people ...

In the event, 'the brother bards' read to 'a large and highly respectable gathering', though Dickens's similarly large and respectable audience a few days later suggests that reporting, then as now, employed catchphrases. Interestingly, however, prices of admission to Waugh and Preston ranged from 1s 6d to 3d; those to Dickens from 4s to 1s — in other words, you could see and hear Dickens in a cheap seat for sixpence less than Waugh and Preston in a dear seat!

Bradford, however, had scooped their first double reading only by the narrowest of margins, for the pair appeared together again on the 26th and 28th February at Bingley Mechanics' Institute. 'The entertainment', reported a Bingley correspondent, 'was good' — which scarcely tallies with a comment from Keighley Mechanics' Institute where Waugh read alone on the 1st March, to the effect that his reception 'was much better than what it was at Bingley'. Apparently there was 'a marked improvement in the reading, although Mr Waugh was suffering from cold'.

Meanwhile, John Hartley too was emerging as a public reader. Some twenty years younger than Preston — he was twenty-eight in 1867 — he was to credit Waugh's *Come Whoam* with having influenced him to write poetry; his *Halifax Original Illuminated Clock Almanack* had started that year. Early in 1867 his name was repeatedly listed in the programmes of a series of Haley Hill Penny Readings. The *Halifax Guardian* called him 'our own vernacular poet'. He was also reading farther afield. At Addingham Mechanics' Institute, where he was described as 'the author of *Annie Linn*', he included 'his new tale *There's a mule i' th' garden*', whilst at Cross Hills Town Hall one of his supporting singers was 'Master Halliday', also from Halifax. Other venues were Shelf Mechanics' Institution, Hipperholme Grammar School, and the Oddfellows' Hall at Halifax, where he shared a 'Literary and Musical Entertainment' with a glee choir, a pianoforte and W Priestley, 'the popular Lancashire reciter'. At a soirée of the United Ancient Order of Druids, Hartley's programme consisted of *Waivin' Music, My Native Twang, Duffin Johnny, Hah a Deead Donkey Towt a Lesson,* and *Th' Little Black Hand.*

A fully-fledged Hartley repertoire can be glimpsed in two readings which he gave at Keighley Mechanics' Institute in January and February of 1869. In the first he read *Bite Bigger, May, Babby-Burds, That's a Fact, Hah a Deead Donkey Towt a Lesson, The Old Bachelor's Story, Waivin' Music, Time to Wakken Up, Plenty o' Brass, Th' Little Stranger* and *A Happy New Year*; in the second, *Th' Little Black Hand, Shoo's Thi Sister, Better nor Buttermilk, Silly Billy, Lily's Gooan, Plenty o' Brass, Another Babby, Duffin Johnny, Hah a Deead Donkey Towt a Lesson, A Voice from the Wood* and *That's a Fact*. Interspersed with songs, duets and glees, these were considered 'an intellectual treat', and 'highly amused and gratified' their audiences

Obviously *Hah a Deead Donkey Towt a Lesson* (a lengthy prose piece), *That's a Fact* and *Plenty o' Brass* went down particularly well, as they appear in both programmes. All are by Hartley himself. Preston, on the other hand, included works by both Hartley and Waugh in his readings. When, for example, at Pullan's Music Hall on Christmas Day 1869, he took part in an entertainment for the poor of the West Ward, Bradford ('Tickets, GRATIS, at Holden's Cooking Depot Westgate, and the Ragged School, Rebecca Street'), Preston read 'from the Dialect Authors of Yorkshire and Lancashire'.

An intriguing detail emerges from a brief note of John Hartley readings at Haworth on New Year's Eve 1870, 'interspersed with Music, when Miss Wilson of Halifax (Pupil of the celebrated Mrs Sunderland), will appear for the first time in Haworth'. This was Sophia Ann Wilson, daughter of the founder of the *Clock Almanack,* the singer and music teacher who in 1880 was to become Hartley's second wife. She accompanied him again when he paid a return visit to Haworth a year later. In March, 1872, they were in Lancaster together ('the Lancaster papers speak in the highest terms of both'), whilst on the 5th April 1872, Miss Wilson, 'now an established Halifax favourite', sang 'splendidly' at 'Mr John Hartley's Concert' before an enthusiastic audience at Halifax Mechanics' Institute.

At the time of this Halifax concert, Hartley was about to emigrate. According to his *Yorkshire Observer* obituary in 1915, his decision 'to try his fortune in America' grew from 'his literary work and his numerous engagements as a public reader', and he sailed on the 2nd May 1872. But his local popularity failed to sustain itself across the Atlantic. On arrival first at Quebec, Hartley promptly 'engaged a large hall, and advertised extensively, but the fates were against him'. In the teeth of wind and rain (common enough but little deterrent in the Pennines) 'one solitary individual managed to reach the hall in some way, and Mr Hartley went through the hour and a half entertainment to his audience of one!' Despite reports of his later achieving 'a fair success by his public readings and recitations' in the New World, Hartley's chequered career in Canada and the United States suggests that he was not the draw he might have hoped to be. By 1875 he was back in England.

By then, the heyday of the mid-Victorian public reading was beginning to wane.

That year one mechanics' institute entertainment was already being described as 'a good old-fashioned penny-reading'. When Preston appeared in Keighley that February, his pieces 'in the home dialect were read with such ease and naturalness that scarcely a single one of the many hits and puns they contain was lost'; but his audience was 'not so numerous as might have been expected' and the Old Keighley Glee Party formed 'the prominent figures in the evening'. When Waugh gave two evenings at the Ilkley College Literary and Scientific Association that October, his 'numerous audience' seems, however, to have been only 'occasionally held spellbound'. The comment 'Now and again a smile was visible on their faces' scarcely suggests a generous response to a programme which included *Besom Ben and his Donkey* and *The Dule's i' this Bonnet o' Mine*!

To be sure, Hartley resumed his readings after his return in 1894 from a second and lengthier sojourn in America. Between 1895 and 1899 his *Clock Almanack* carried advertisements for 'Mr John Hartley's Public Readings and Recitals', which reveal that he charged two guineas plus his third-class return railway fare for distances beyond a ten-mile radius of his home, first in Leeds and then at Shadwell. 'Special arrangements' were offered for schools and charities, and applications invited 'as early as possible to prevent disappointments'. Quoted reviews represent venues as far apart as Leeds, Burnley, Barnoldswick and Elsecar, and extol his usual combination of humour and pathos. His 1898-1899 season, he stressed, whilst gratefully acknowledging the liberal support accorded him, would 'positively be his Farewell to the Public Platform'.

However, the main popularity of the public reading came generally between the mid-1860s and the mid-1870s, from which period a number of conclusions can be deduced. Contemporary attempts to describe readings imply that the style of delivery tended to be more dramatic than would probably be the case nowadays. Here is Preston in full flight in 1872:

> As a reader he possesses rare versatility. There is a manly breadth and genial unction in his humour which, as we irresistibly gave way to its laughter-provoking influence, inclines us to think that the region of humour is his *forte;* but as he carries us from humour to sentiment, we find such a breadth and depth of delicate heart-sympathy in his pathos that we are, in turn, disposed to think that his talent is displayed more happily in the latter …

The implication of audience response is significant, for mid-Victorian audiences could be openly emotional. Dickens's power to make his listeners weep is well-known, but our dialect poets too were capable of a similar effect. 'Many were melted to tears', we are told, by such readings as Waugh's *Come Whoam to thi Childer an' me* and Hartley's *Who Cares?* On the other hand, audiences could be 'convulsed' with laughter, and over-enthusiastic in their applause. 'It is always gratifying to see a large and happy audience such as there was at the last entertainment', wrote an attender of a Preston reading in 1872, 'and it must be gratifying to the mechanics' committee to observe the growing success which is now aiding their efforts to entertain the people, but for the audience to insist upon *encores* in the consistent and rather inconsiderate manner indulged in last Saturday night was 'too much'.'

Robust though such gatherings may sometimes have become, they were invariably presided over by locally influential chairmen, often clergymen. The Haley Hill Penny Readings in 1867 were chaired by figures like H Akroyd Ridgway, Esq, and the Rev F Musson, Hartley's fellow-readers on those occasions including the headmaster of Hipperholme Grammar School and the Hon and Rev Philip Yorke Savile. At Saltaire in 1866, Waugh was chaired by G W Glyde; Preston at Keighley in 1871 by Dr William Dobie, a local devotee of Robert Burns — appropriately in an age of comparisons whereby Waugh was called 'the Burns of Lancashire' and Hartley 'the Yorkshire Waugh'! Waugh's chairman at Bingley in 1866 was the vicar, the Rev A P Irwine, who expressed himself to have been 'much struck with the tender beauty and noble moral lessons of *The Moorland Flower*'.

A concern for 'sound and healthy morality' lies indeed at the heart of the public-reading craze. A handbill publicising a mechanics' institute concert which included Preston in 1875 spells out, amongst its 'Reasons why you should go to the Entertainment next Saturday Night', the principles underlying this 'recreation for the working classes':

Because it is a Special Night, offering Special Pleasures.
Because the room will be warm and comfortable.
Because many of your friends will be there.
Because the charge is only 1d.
Because you can get home early.
Because these Entertainments should be encouraged.
Because they are for your own good …

Taken to extremes. that latter consideration could lead another dialect poet and reader, Tom Twisleton, as a young Winskill farmer and temperance advocate, to write such verses as *Johnny Bland, the Blacksmith* expressly to recite at the Settle Temperance Festival of Christmas 1865.

To draw one of those retrospective political conclusions so beloved by modern historians, the public readings of Hartley and Preston and Waugh, far from being an expression of radical or alternative culture, reinforced the stable values of their day as epitomised in the third line of Hartley's *Waivin' Music*, popular in his repertoire:

> Nick-a-ting, nock-a-ting;
> Wages keep pocketin';
> Workin' for little is better ner laikin';
> Twist an' twine, reel an' wind;
> Keep a contented mind;
> Troubles are oft of a body's own makin'.

(1992)

DIALECT WORDS: WHAT ARE THEY AND WHAT CAN WE DO WITH THEM?
Clive Upton

There are two basic ways of regarding the term 'dialect'. One is to make it descriptive of the *non-standard* only. The other is to allow it to embrace varieties of any kind, regional, occupational or social. Taking the first of these views, the great linguist Abercrombie wrote in 1951:

> I have used the word *dialect* for any form of English which differs from Standard English in grammar, syntax, vocabulary, and of course in pronunciation too. (Quoted in Petyt, p17.)

Taking the second, all-inclusive, view, and regarding *all* language varieties as dialects, the American dialectologist Raven McDavid sees:

> ... a *dialect* simply defined as a variety of a language, generally mutually intelligible with other varieties of that language, but set off from them by a unique complex of features of pronunciation, grammar and vocabulary. Dialect, thus used, is not a derogatory term but a descriptive one ... (Kretzschmar, p159.)

The fact that the former quotation is more than forty years old should not lead us to think that the view is outmoded: the division of British English into the standard *language* and the non-standard *dialects* would seem quite normal to many people, and it is probably the dominant reflex even amongst those such as English teachers who have an informed view of the prevailing linguistic situation. Many who intellectually align themselves with McDavid can be expected to contrast the 'standard language' with 'the dialects' without even noticing they are doing so.

Having aired this distinction, and after declaring myself to be McDavid-ite by conviction, I intend in what follows to concentrate on aspects of non-standard lexis. We are able to make certain assumptions, concerning spelling and meaning for example, about the words of our standard dialect — they are after all the stuff of the general dictionaries, whose job is to chart their progress in a changing language, and we therefore have ready access to authorities on them. Non-standard words have much less illumination cast upon them and, being largely free of prescriptive pressure, are far less rigid in form and meaning. Pinning down the non-standard dialect word is not always an easy thing to do. For the sake of simplicity I shall from this point make 'dialect' stand for what I take to be more correctly 'non-standard dialect', but I would wish the reader to accept that this dialectologist at least identifies a 'standard' dialect too.

It is of course usually easy to identify a dialect word: indeed, to mention the existence of a problem in identifying anything called a 'word' is often to induce a good deal of puzzlement in a listener. According to the *Survey of English Dialects* [*SED*] (Orton *et al* 1961-72, Upton *et al* 1994), a gull can, amongst other things, be a *black-head, petch, scouting-pewit, sea-crow, sea-mall, sea-martin* or *sea-maw*. A clumsy person can be variously *blundersome, bumblefisted, bungersome, clumbersome, clumble-fisted, clumble-fingered, pizzle-handed, skiffle-handed, thumby, ungain, unheppen* and many, many more. In none of these instances are we for a moment uncertain as to whether we are dealing with different words which, with certain allowances made for details, refer to the same objects or notions. As students of dialect words, we can pursue our research for some considerable time happily ignoring grey areas of identification and amassing a great deal of valuable information as we do so.

Sooner or later, however, a problem will be encountered, and when difficulty arises over the identification of a dialect word it is quite likely to stem from the fact that dialect is essentially a spoken medium. This is in no way to decry the work of those who engage in dialect writing, and indeed such people are among the most expert in wrestling with the problems created by the predominantly spoken form. But the student of dialect words is permanently engaged in an area where vocabulary and pronunciation abut on one another, where she or he is often uncertain whether the focus is on vocabulary or pronunciation.

Take for example the contrast between 'great' and *gert*. In a phrase such as a *gert black rat, gert* is clearly related to the standard word 'great'. Do we treat the two items as pronunciations of the same word, or are they sufficiently different to warrant individual word status? Here the dilemma is in fact quite readily resolvable. Drawing upon linguistic theory, in this particular case upon the vowel-consonant inversion concept of *metathesis* (the phenomenon which gives us 'bird' from Old English *brid*), we can with some confidence declare the two to be pronunciations of the same word and, presuming on both etymology and the particular place of the present standard dialect in matters of lexicography, we would not be unreasonable in allotting *gert* a place as a variant of 'great'.

The case of such pairs as *bridge* and *brig, ridge* and *rig* is similar, but it cannot be solved in the same way. The second form in each pair is clearly related to the first, and their differences are, as with 'great' and *gert*, essentially those of pronunciation. However, in the contrast exhibited in each pair between the 'soft' *-dge* sound and the 'hard' *-g* sound, we have a clear realisation of different word histories. As the 'Bridge' map overleaf shows (Upton *et al* 1987), *brig* is the traditional dialect form of northern and much of eastern England, the area of strongest Viking influence, and it is not surprising to note that whilst *-dge* is the English ending, *-g* is the Norse. (The 'soft/hard' English/Norse contrast can be observed with other sounds too, as for example *church/kirk* and, with an attendant difference in meaning, *shirt/skirt*.) Similar though such cases are to that of 'great', etymological considerations mean that the links within the pairs are looser, and the word status of the paired items has at the very least seriously to be considered.

There are, then, instances where we need to be wary of making easy assumptions of similarity or dissimilarity, but where a modicum of linguistic knowledge can resolve a problem with almost complete certainty. The further we move into the grey area between 'words' and 'pronunciations', however, the more difficult it becomes to decide quite what word, or words, we are dealing with.

Take, for example, a few responses to the *Survey of English Dialects* questions which asked 'How is the wheel kept on the axle [of a cart]?' A response in Herefordshire was [dɹɒʊpɪn], one in Shropshire [dɹɒppɪn], and another in Lancashire [dɹɔppɪn]. Here we have speakers making various closely-related noises to identify an object well-known to them but which they have probably never in their lives had to write down. Perhaps they are able to identify precisely what they are saying: quite likely they have never consciously thought about it. Whichever is the case, it is certainly necessary for us, as outside observers, to be able to assign recognisable values to the sounds if we wish to handle the utterances at anything other than the phonetic level. But how are we to interpret what the fieldworker heard and transcribed? The second element in each compound is unproblematical: we need not doubt that the object in each case is some kind of *pin*. But judging from pronunciation alone there must be some doubt as to whether the first element in each case is *draw* or *drop*. Perhaps, since the collecting fieldworkers in Shropshire and Lancashire heard a monophthongal sound and some explosion of a [p] before the [p] of *pin*, in those counties the word is *drop* and, probably on this evidence, the survey's editors did indeed make this interpretation. In Herefordshire (where the fieldworker was the same as that for Shropshire), a single transcribed [p], presumed to be that of *pin*, and a diphthongal vowel-transcription led the editors to infer that *draw is* the first element. This latter is certainly only an inference, however. The relatively close proximity of the Shropshire and Herefordshire localities, and the fact that it is unusual for draw to be pronounced with a diphthong in any dialect, suggest that the interpretation, though possible, is by no means certain.

If the situation just described leads to uncertainty, consider another, where the phonology and the consequent interpretation are still more complex. Among responses to the survey question 'What do you call those lines left behind by the cartwheels when the ground is soft?' were the following: [ka:ttɹɒks], ['ka:'traks], [ka:tɹaks] and [ka:tɹæks]. It is quite clear that these four forms, though differing from each other in detail, represent quite similar pronunciations. Yet how are we to interpret these pronunciations as words? Unlike the situation confronting us with the previous example, where at least the segments into which the compound word was to be divided were identifiable, here even that first step to interpretation cannot be made with any great certainty. The first element is quite likely to be *cart*, and the second element should be *tracks*. But in much of Northern England a cart is traditionally a *car*, and the evenly-stressed ['ka:'traks] in particular, record-ed in Cumbria, probably represents *car-tracks*. Perhaps those forms where two ts are articulated can with some certainty be taken to be *cart-tracks,* one [t] ending cart and the other beginning tracks. But *rack* is used in very many dialects with reference to narrow linear shape in various senses, and in Herefordshire it is actually recorded as meaning a path through a field, so that there exists a strong possibility that some forms like those listed represent not *cart-tracks* or *car-tracks* but *cart-racks*. Ultimately some of our dilemmas over such problems of

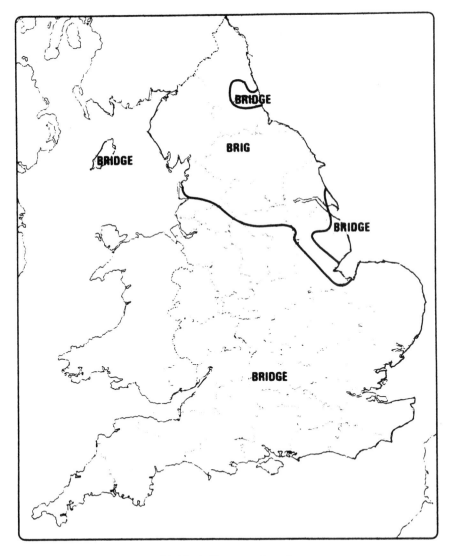

'Bridge', Upton et al, *1987.*

interpretation are insoluble. All we can do is to make the best guess possible and to signal that a problem of interpretation exists. There is perhaps some consolation to be gained from the likelihood that many speakers who use such forms, when quizzed, may admit to not knowing the answer either!

There are, therefore, areas where vocabulary is confused by pronunciation, making it impossible categorically to decide upon safe written forms. In a somewhat similar way vocabulary may be considered to overlap with that part of grammar, technically called morphology, which has to do with the way words change

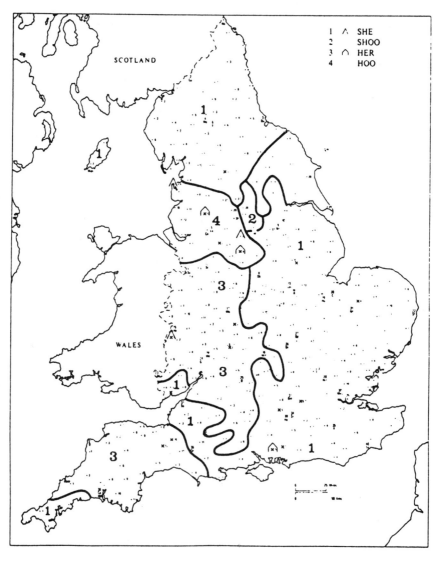

'She', Orton et al, *1978.*

in order to signal grammatical relationships. This can readily be seen in relation to variety in the system of pronouns which different speakers use.

The student could very readily suppose when studying the map opposite of dialect reflexes for *'She'*, taken from *The Linguistic Atlas of England* (Orton *et al* 1978), that whilst *her* used in place of *she* is a grammatical (or morphological) choice from the present-day standard pronoun system, *hoo* is a different word, whilst *shoo* is a blend of this with standard *she*. Seen from a purely modern perspective this would be a reasonable interpretation. An understanding of the Old English pronoun system is needed in order to see that at the historical level the distinctions are ultimately those of grammar rather than of vocabulary, all the 'words' being ultimately related. Even more of a pitfall is the simple word *'en*, for *him*, widely heard in Southern England in such phrases as 'I couldn't catch 'en'. This could variously be taken to be a quite distinct form or, more easily, as simply the rapid articulation of *him* itself, but it is in fact a modern survival of the Old English masculine object pronoun *hine,* and deserves to be regarded as such. Again what we are confronted with is an essentially grammatical variation, with different parts of the same pronoun system giving us both *him* and *'en*: the significance of this variation is diminished if we insist on seeing it at a simple word level.

To say all this, however, is to say no more than that dialect vocabulary can be complicated, rooted as it is in the history of the language and involving difficult problems of pronunciation. If the student wishes to engage deeply with such matters, that is well and good, but there is plenty of scope in the area of dialect words to satisfy everyone and to permit everyone to make an important contribution to their study, whatever their interests or level of training. No-one should be discouraged from developing an interest in dialect vocabulary because they lack training in the techniques of historical linguistic analysis.

The first level at which anyone with an interest in dialect words should be involved with them should, I quite unashamedly believe, be that of delight, delight in the richness of our varied and infinitely expressive regional vocabulary. Our regional varieties, with pedigrees often far longer than that of the standard dialect, are forms of language with which most of us identify very strongly, and the popularity of such recent works as *Basic Broad Yorkshire* and *The Yorkshire Dictionary* (Kellett 1994) are testimony to the fact that such forms are not lightly to be set aside.

Of course, a passive interest in local speech-forms is quite enough to satisfy many people, and that interest is not to be decried. For those of us who have a particular interest in things dialectal, however, is given the task of gathering up and passing on the words that are the raw material of our dialects. This is the task which members of the English Dialect Society, and the dialect glossarists before them, did so well, building for the great *English Dialect Dictionary* (Wright 1898-1905). It is the task which members of the Yorkshire Dialect Society and of other local and regional groups continue to do, and what we at Sheffield University have sought to do in compiling *Survey of English Dialects: The Dictionary and*

Grammar, published earlier this year. In this work we have drawn together the non-standard vocabulary gathered through Harold Orton's seminal survey, which began in Leeds in the 1940s and the findings of which, previously spread through many disparate works, continue to furnish data for a wide variety of linguists.

The most cursory of glances at the survey's material is enough to show the wealth of dialect lexis existing in the twentieth century — although it must be said that erosion of that lexis is inevitably taking place in those fields of activity which are themselves in decline. In a short section from the dictionary reproduced below, chosen more or less at random, we can see non-standard words, pronunciations and distributions for, amongst other notions, *sticky* and *blisters and exhausted,* and learn that *bleat* is used to describe the noise of cows as well as sheep in Suffolk and Cornwall. Also at *bleat* the user is referred to a range of non-standard dialect synonyms, at which headwords she or he will find further details of pronunciation and locality. Almost incidental to the presentation are the small additional intuitions which this new drawing together of the survey's findings brings, noticeably in this case that of the alliteration at work in dialect synonymy apparent in the set *blake/blare/blart/blay/bleak/bleat/blurt.*

This last, the possibility of making an observation which has not been made before, can be held out as an additional spur to any student of dialect words. As a

bleared up *adj* STICKY, describing a child's hands VIII.8.14. blɪ·əd ʊp Y[*old*]; **bleared up and sticky** blɪəᵈd ʊp ən stɪkɛ Y

bleat *1. vi-3prpl* [*Now tell me your words for the usual cries animals make.*] *Sheep*.... III.10.5. Eng exc. Du We Db Wa Gl O R Nf W Do Sx. ⇒ **baa.** *baa-aa* ⇒ **baa.** *bae* ⇒ **baa.** **bawl. bellow. blake. blake out. blare. blart. blate. blay. bleak.** *bleat and* **baa. blurt. cry. holler.** *hollo* ⇒ **holler. maa.** *mae* ⇒ **maa. mark. mawl**

2. vi-3prpl they MOO, describing the noise cows make during feeding time in the cow-house III.10.4(a). bliːt Sf. bɫiːt Co

3. vi-3prpl they MOO, describing the noise cows make in the fields III.10.4(b). bɫiːt Co

blebs *npl* BLISTERS VI.11.5. bɪɛbz Nb La Y[*when not burst xl*]. blɛɪbz Nb

blethered *adj* EXHAUSTED, describing a tired person VI.13.8. blɛðəd Y

Extract from Survey of English Dialects: The Dictionary and Grammar, *Upton* et al, *1994.*

young dialect student researching the English of that long-anglicised area of Pembrokeshire and Gower, often called 'Little England Beyond Wales', I 'discovered' the word *cluppit,* meaning 'broody', describing a hen. That word, apparently never previously recorded, is one of which I am justifiably proud: it is only a small discovery, but it is one which may not have come to light outside the small area in which it is — or perhaps was — used had I not recorded it. We can all hope to discover such little gems if we persevere.

We are then on a voyage of discovery each time we deliberately go into the field or, if we are sensitive enough, even when we are engaged on entirely non-linguistic business. Even when we are entirely desk-bound there are fascinating discoveries to be made. Perhaps the best known commentator on the *Survey of English Dialects* has been Martyn Wakelin, whose *English Dialects: An Introduction* (1978) is required reading for anyone interested in historical-based dialect study. In that work, under the heading 'Words of Obscure Origin' (p67), Wakelin writes, as if in challenge to those following him:

> Some [obscure words] are words which are poorly attested ... and admit of no explanation for the present, although one may be found in due course. Examples which seem to fall into this class are *cornutor*, 'donkey', found only as the second response at [SED locality number] D11, and otherwise utterly unknown.

Having read this many times, I gave the matter little thought until, while compiling the 'donkey' entries for the survey's dictionary, I encountered again the word *cornutor* and, more significantly, its pronunciation as transcribed by the Devon fieldworker, that is [kənʏːtəɹː]. Comparing written 'word' and transcribed pronunciation, it seemed that the written form given by the original survey editors could perhaps be obscuring understanding. In particular, the repeated *or* spellings bore no relation to the sounds made by the speaker, and appeared to be influenced rather by an entry of doubtful relevance in the *Oxford English Dictionary*. Returning to the only reliable record, the informant's response to the question asked, as recorded in phonetic script during the original interview, I made the noises, and the only possible solution quickly became apparent: the Devon donkey is not a *cornutor*, but a *Canuter*, taking its name from that English king with a special reputation for obstinacy.

We have revelled in the existence of a rich vein of non-standard dialect vocabulary. We may even have done something to foster an understanding of it. But our greatest service to dialect lexis, and ultimately to our fellow English speakers, will be if we *use* it. Even while urging the avoidance of 'Estuary English', the Education Secretary is said in a *Guardian* article (14th October 1994) to have 'hastened to add that she was not against dialects and local expressions, such as the Norfolk phrase for a ladybird: *bishy bishy barnabee*'. On one memorable occasion a most eminent member of the same secretary's party declared that she was not *frit*, sending political commentators scurrying to their dictionaries and making the point far more strongly than if she had held to the standard dialect.

Still more than trying to use non-standard words for effect, we should be aware that our identity is completely intertwined with the way we speak- with all the features of our pronunciation, grammar, and word-choice. Much is made today of the need to choose the types of language that are *appropriate* to different situations, and we can probably accept that, for some people, a totally standard dialect is appropriate for at least some of their speech activities. But it would be difficult to reach complete agreement on all such situations for all of us, and we should be pleased to assert our right to maintain our wealth of word-choice — and choice of other features too — which keeps English rich and us rooted as members of particular English-speaking communities.

References

Kellett, Arnold. 1992. *Basic Broad Yorkshire.* Revised edition, Smith Settle, Otley.
The Yorkshire Dictionary, 1994, Smith Settle.
Kretzschmar, W A, ed. 1979. *Dialects in Culture*: *Essays in General Dialectology* by Raven I McDavid Jr., Alabama University of Alabama Press.
Orton, Harold. 1962. *Survey of English Dialects (A): Introduction.* Leeds, E J Arnold.
Orton, Harold, *et al.* 1962-71. Survey *of English Dialects (B): The Basic Material.* Leeds, E J Arnold.
Orton, Harold, Stewart Sanderson, and John Widdowson. 1978. *The Linguistic Atlas of England.* London, Croom Helm.
Oxford English Dictionary, The. 1989. 2nd edition, prepared by J Simpson and E S C Weiner. Oxford.
Petyt, K M 1980. *Study of Dialect: An introduction to dialectology.* London, André Deutsch.
Upton, Clive, Stewart Sanderson, and John Widdowson. 1987. *Word Maps: A Dialect Atlas of England.* London, Croom Helm.
Upton, Clive, David Parry, and J D A Widdowson. 1994. *Survey of English Dialect: The Dictionary and Grammar.* London, Routledge.
Wakelin, Martyn. 1978. *English Dialects: An Introduction.* 2nd edition. London, Athlone Press.
Wright, Joseph, ed. 1898-1905. *The English Dialect Dictionary.* Oxford, Clarendon Press; reprinted 1986 by Oxford University Press.

(1994)

AN EAST RIDING DIALECT QUIZ

Jack Danby challenged visitors to the YDS day at Ryedale Folk Museum (11th June 1994) with an intriguing list of phrases to be translated, here reproduced by his kind permission.

1. Gan ower t' fauf for t' gainest waay doon.
2. Ah thowt Ah cud lowzen this 'ere knot bud Ah misdoot Ah's arrered wiv it.
3. If 'e cotches tha bod-nestin 'e's boon ti ezzle tha.
4. T' awd lad's nobbut middlin on 'is feeat. E's aboot as lingey as a steean pig trough.
5. Ah'll deea ni mair awhahle Ah've etten mi looance.
6. Ah thowt Ah'd lossen mi jag as we coom thruff t' yatsteead.
7. Ah nivver seen 'is marrer at plooin.
8. Oor Charloue wor a twin, bud marrer tiv er deead.
9. 'E sed Ah sudn't win if Ah bet of a Sundah, bud Ah tellt 'im sartinly yan on us 'd win. That naailed im!
10. Ah'd just getten t' gahrdin weel graaved an' sum ottherpooak oppened yat for t' pigs ti paddle all ower.
11. Ah can't noss tha! Tha's sike a rammocks.
12. Leeak afoor yer lowp, an' then deean't allus lowp!
13. Knaw what tha's deein afoor tha taks thi barra back.
14. Ah can't saah Ah lahke leeak on her. She's as blake as a gowlan. Etten ower monny bummelkites, 'appen.
15. 'E reckons 'e knaws all ther' is ti knaw. Is 'eead's as far roond as a broon porringer.
16. 'E's a juntous awd cuddy, is yon.
17. It'll be woth nowt. 'E got it muck cheeap i' market.
18. There 'e wor — a lahtle podgy fella up tiv 'is oxters in t' duck pond.
19. E's cum ooam awahle Rahve Kite Sundah.
20. Sha fetched 'im siken a skelp ower t' lug-'ooal.

(1994)

T' NAVVY 'AHSES

Winter-'edge, voider an' set-pot,
Posser an' sycamoor prop,
Piggin an' pitcher an' possnit,
Breead-fleyk an' 'arston an' mop,
Caw-rake an' fire-point an' ass-nook,
'Avverbreead, paarkin an' dooaf,
Frummerty, thick-seeam an' pestil,
Possit, mulled ale an' spice-looaf,
Stee-'oile an' cham'er an' nessy,
Garrit, slop-kitchin, stooane sink,
Cellar-'eead, cornish an' troughin'—
All theease owd words mak' mi think
O' t' owd days when wi wer childer
Livin' i' t' owd back-ter-backs
T' local fowk called t' Navvy 'Ahses —
Like the' wor nobbut owd shacks.
But the' wor 'ooamly an' cawsy,
All built o' Queensbury stooane,
When the' browt t' Gurt Northern Railway
Wheeare, afooare then, the' wor nooan.
T' top street wor called after Oakley,
T' Gurt Northern Chief Engineer,
Great Street wor t' next an' then Northern
(Ahr family ended up theeare),
Then Railway Street, it wor t' last un,
T' gainest o' t' three ter t' main rooad;
T' 'ahses theeare faced t' back o' t' Slave Raw,
An' it wonnt 'ardly as brooad.
T' roofs wor all stooane, wi' wood troughin',
T' winnders all 'ed gurt stooane sills;
Up t' top o' t' streets wor t' stooan nessies,
Stooan flags o' t' roofs an' nooa frills;
White-scrubbed wood seeats wi' rahnd lids on,
T' walls lime-weshed twice ivvry year,
Squares o' newspaper o' t' dooar nail,
(Summat ter read, cahrin' theear).
Then awf-way dahn ther' wor t' ginnils,
Leeadin' through inter t' next street,
T' fowk each side awned oo wor commin'

As the'r clogs clomped through at neet.
All t' ahses 'ed the'r awn cellars,
Stooane steps ter t' owd cellar'eead,
T' kitchin an' t' 'ahseplace wor stooan-flagged
An' stooan steps twisted an' reared
Up rahnd a corner ter t' cham'ers,
Then cawm another steeap stee,
A wood 'un this time, up ter t' garrit.
Through t' shut i' t' roof we could see
T' stars twinklin' dahn as we ligged theeare,
I' t' arn bed, cawsy an' snug,
An' we stepped aht when we wakkened
On tiv a gurt sheepskin rug;
Tabbed 'uns wor o' t' flooar i' t' ahseplace,
Gooatskins o' t' backs o' t' armcheers,
An' t' lang-case clock i' t' far corner
Knacked as it 'ed done for years.
T' range wor blackleeaded an' shinin',
T' kettle a-singin' on t' 'ob,
Ivvrythin' dusted an' polished,
All on us tiv us awn job.
Wark wor nooan eeasy ter come by,
T brass 'ed ter gooa a lang way,
But fowk all 'elped wun another
Mooare ner what some do ter-day.
But it's gooid mem'ries we cleave tul—
If we'd ter tell t' trewth, chewse 'ah,
Rough an' smooth ta'en all together,
'Appen we'd rayther live nah!

Harry P Brooks (WR)

(1994)

voider, clothes-basket; *piggin,* lading-can; *possnit,* small pan;
breead-fleyk, wooden rack suspended from ceiling; *fire-point,* poker;
stee, ladder, stairs; *cham'er,* bedroom; *nessy,* outside lavatory

BOTH SIDES OF THE OUSE
Jack Danby

Many people of my generation, at school in the 1920s and maybe also preparing anxiously for chapel Sunday School anniversaries, will remember learning long passages of poetry by heart, and be able, even seventy years later, to repeat some of them confidently, if not always entirely accurately. I can still manage *If* and *The Glory of the Garden*. A verse which has remained in my memory is:

> God gives all men all earth to love
> But, since our hearts are small,
> Ordains for each one spot shall prove
> Beloved over all.

For Kipling that spot was Sussex, Sussex by the sea. For most members of our society the spot is in Yorkshire, a place to which we are drawn by ties of ancestry or acquisition, a place inspiring affection and loyalty. The work of many Yorkshire writers through the years has reflected that affection but old Yorkshire is, in Sydney Martin's phrase, 'a fairish awd coonty'; the broad acres cover an area of great diversity of culture and literary tradition. J B Priestley and Phyllis Bentley were very definitely West Riding folk; Winifred Holtby was at home at Rudston on 'Anderby Wold'. John Hartley loved his Halifax, but would have felt as much out of place at Withernsea as he did in the United States. Fred Brown wrote in the shadow of the textile mills, Arthur Jarratt from the cheerful friendliness of the East Riding village chapels. Each displayed a particular fondness for his or her familiar surroundings, for their neighbours and for the local language. But there are some Yorkshire authors who have had, so to speak, a foot on both sides of the Ouse, who have written with discernment about places as different as the Holme Valley and Holderness, as Doncaster and Driffield. The characters in their work, portrayed with love and understanding, have been fishermen and farmworkers as well as weavers, miners and engineers.

Such a writer is Christabel Burniston, whose random recollections of a Yorkshire childhood, *Life in a Liberty Bodice*, have already given great pleasure to many of us. Her paternal grandparents were the Hydes of Cockmoor Hall at the head of Troutsdale, farmers who moved late last century to cultivate the fertile land near Fraisthorpe in Holderness. From Sherburn in Elmet came Christabel's lively and lovable mother whose many activities, social, cultural and political, after her marriage when she lived in Crossgates, included enrolment on one of Professor Moorman's three-year literature courses at Leeds University. So, to quote Christabel, 'she was able to profit from his intellectual stimulation and enjoy not only his standard English interpretation of literature but his wonderful stories and plays in Yorkshire dialect'. Many of us, more recently, have enjoyed Professor Moorman's dialect writing and our society owes much to his inspiration. Christabel describes visits to the Moormans' summer cottage beside the Skirfare at Hawkswick in Littondale. She describes also the widespread shock and grief caused by Professor Moorman's death by drowning in the River Skirfare in 1919, when he was only forty-seven years old.

Christabel's childhood was spent mainly in the Leeds area, but with constant contact with the farming families in the east of the county. Founder of the English Speaking Board and now its president, author of many important books, Christabel has, during all her adult life, written and lectured about our language and literature. She is as much at home with all the dialects of Yorkshire as she is with the language of Shakespeare. Recently, going through old family papers, Christabel found a dialect poem, *A Martinmas Idyll*, written by her grandmother Hyde, probably in the very early years of this century. 'My father's mother', writes Christabel, 'who left her village school at nine, brought up her large family to be healthy, kind, alert, literate, sociable, law-abiding and capable. Her letters were a joy to look at and to read, for they were written with a dip pen in copper-plate calligraphy, standard English grammar, a generous vocabulary enriched with lively dialect, accurate spelling and correct punctuation. Family and village news was interspersed with homespun philosophy and always she closed her letters with a reassurance of her love.'

She evidently also sometimes put her thoughts into dialect verse. Telling the story in Grandma Hyde's *Martinmas Idyll* is the fifteen year old hired farm lass, who has decided, after all, not to change her 'spot' at Martinmas because her mistress had recently had a new baby and, she says 'Ah ings tiv a bairn'. The waggoner's lad, she implies, was not much interested in the new baby, but was certainly concerned for the welfare of a calf born and orphaned on the baby's birthday: 'Jimmy ings tiv a cauf'. I hope that dialect society members will soon have the opportunity to hear and to read the whole of that appealing poem.

Familiar already to many of us is the name of Christabel's cousin Austin Hyde, another writer who was equally at home using the local language of West, East or North Ridings. He was born at Driffield, taught for many years in the Heavy Woollen district and later became headmaster of Lady Lumley Grammar School at Pickering. He loved the Wolds and in his poem *A Countryman in Town* wrote that he 'cared nowt for toons and would rayther grow awd where t fields stretch si wide ower Duggleby wawd'. That poem is printed by way of dedication at the beginning of the *East Yorkshire Anthology* of dialect poems, the anthology which, had he lived longer, Austin himself would have edited. His *Yorkshire Shepherd to his Dog* is a much loved contribution to the *Cleveland Anthology* and the poem *Depper Awd Meer* in the East Yorkshire collection is even more often quoted and recited. It was written in protest against the export for slaughter of horses which had reached the end of their working lives. The poem reached a wide public through the BBC Home Service broadcasts and is thought to have had some influence in ending the trade. I have no doubt that Austin Hyde would have had pertinent comment to make about crated calves and the export of live lambs if he had been alive in 1995.

One of my own treasures is a copy of *Depper* autographed by Austin, with whom on occasion I was privileged to share a platform in the 1950s. His tales of the Wolds people were a joy to hear. Here is just one sample which I remember: A waggoner's lad, returning to his living-in 'spot' after the Martinmas break, asked his colleagues what they thought of his new suit, on which a good proportion of his annual pay had been spent, and added 'I've had her made to measure'. After looking him up and down the waggoner replied, 'Thoo'd a done a deeal better if thoo'd had her made to fit'.

> Ah nivver thowt it 'ud cum ti pass;
> Oor Jackie's wedded a city lass!

Those are lines from Ruth Hedger's *London Piece* which is included in the *Cleveland Anthology*, edited by the late Bill Cowley. [*Editors' note: the poem is reproduced in full on page 80.*] Ruth Hedger was no city lass though she became well acquainted with many urban areas of the West Riding in her lifetime. She was familiar with the people of the villages in several parts of Yorkshire, living for a while in Coxwold and in Birdsall, where her father was the Vicar, and in Sowerby. She knew the East Riding well, and one of her best known stories in dialect is *Arethusa of the Wolds* first published by the society in 1944. Ruth's interest in our regional languages continued right to the end of her life in January 1976. During her last days in hospital at York she took great pleasure in listening to recordings of *Plaan Speeakin'*, a series in and about East Yorkshire dialect which I wrote for Radio Humberside a year or two earlier. The days of 'plum in the mouth' radio presenters had by then disappeared, but to 'talk like fawk on t' Wyerless diz' was still, to the older country people, an unforgivable affectation.

Through the adaptation of some of Peter Walker's (Nicholas Rhea's) stories of a police constable's life and work in the North Riding, for the television series *Heartbeat*, the village and neighbourhood of Goathland (if not the dialect) have become familiar to millions. To appreciate the point of Ruth Hedger's amusing poem *Sheep i' t' Chotchyard*, included in the *Cleveland Anthology*, you need to know that the turf beside the Goathland village roads and surrounding the church-yard was common grazing. There were sheep everywhere, wandering in their constant search for greener pastures. The poem records a supposed conversation between two permanent occupants of the graveyard after someone had left the gate open. The final ignominy for them came when the strains of *Sheep May Safely Graze* came floating from the church organ. Every time I read that poem I remember Ruth Hedger with affection.

Next in my list of writers with knowledge of Yorkshire language both sides of the Ouse comes Walter Turner, who died quite young in 1917 after just eight years as vicar of Fridaythorpe on the Wolds. He spent the early years of his working life at Dewsbury and then was curate to his father at Middleton near Pickering. Walter Turner is best known to the dialect society for the stories first published in 1912 under the title *Goodies*. He also wrote dialect poems with pertinent comment on the national and international events affecting the lives of his parishioners. He felt strongly about the difficulties faced by the families of farmworkers in Victorian times, and welcomed the improvements in their conditions early this century. In his powerful poem *The Good Awd Tahmes* [*Editors' note: see page 11*]:

> Me muther she slaaved, i' t' good awd tahmes,
> An' scratted, an' tewed, an' rahved, an' wrowt wer weeams te trig ...

That poem was chosen for the anthology *White Rose Garland*, celebrating fifty years of the Yorkshire Dialect Society's existence, published by Dent in 1949.

Turner also felt strongly about the terrible folly of the Great War:

> You ax what Ah think o' this war?
> Weel, Ah deeant think mich tiv it misen;
> Ther sudn't be neea sike a thing
> Betwixt nations o' Christian men.
> It was said, aye, when Ah was a lad,
> Iv a song 'at was sung a good bit,
> 'Nobbut them at meead quarrils sud fight';
> Bud we ain't getten up ti that yit.

Those lines are from his poem *A Wold Shepherd*, and he also chronicled the formation and the mobilisation of the Sledmere Waggoners, farm workers who were called up for the army in 1914.

Observing the frailties and peculiarities of human behaviour from a point of vantage in the pulpit of his village church, Walter Turner recorded many humorous incidents besides the well-known tale of the lady searching for a sweet to suck during the sermon. I think particularly of the parson's questions when he discovered a large sheepdog sitting on the chancel steps before a wedding ceremony. 'Wheeah's owes t' dog? Wheeah's letten t' dog in t' choch?' To which the bridegroom replied: 'Whah, ee's mahn. Ee wanted ti coomm.'

Finally I include Edward Charles Booth, musician and writer, who hailed from Doncaster but lived also for varying periods in the North Riding and in Holderness. His novel *The Treble Clef* is set in a town like Doncaster, *Bella* in Scarborough and five of his long stories in Holderness, with splendid portraits of the village characters, accurate accounts of their customs and careful presentation of their dialect. Miss Mary Macdonald of Edinburgh has recently completed research into the life and works of Edward Booth, research begun by her nephew John Munday who died in 1991. A copy of her long essay is now in the society's library.

I conclude with a brief extract from one of the Holderness novels. I should like to think that Booth's stories could be enjoyed by many more people than know about him at present. From *The Doctor's Lass*, first published in 1910, here are a few sentences from the account of Hull Fair, the annual October festival which to this day has a significant place in the calendar of many Holderness folk:

Ancient mortals who are set out by kitchen fires like armchairs and moved up and down stairs at other people's convenience, like furniture:- 'Set Father oot i porch while we get floor scrubbed' ... 'Run, Lizzie, and fetch thi grandfather in quick, it's coming on ti rain' ... 'Take Father i parlour a bit. I can't get ti oven door ...'. Ancient mortals such as these resuscitate a fragment of antiquated pride from some dusty cupboard of memory and at mention of Hunmouth Fair be heard to say 'Aye, I've had my share of Ummouth Fair i my time, you may depend. I've seed fotty on 'em and nobbut missed yan, year my Mother deed'. It is the biggest Fair in England, the Elysium for all who love noise and dust and movement. The special trains, panting between Hunmouth and all the district round, pump the soil dry of its workers during

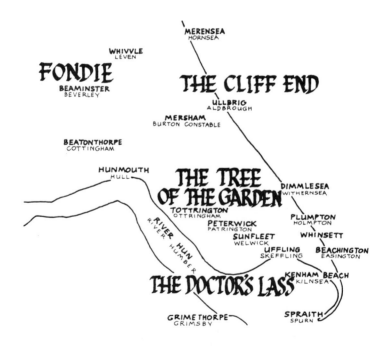

The settings of the novels of E C Booth.

the magic week. The plough lies neglected by the hedge and no ploughman's cry of 'Aaave!' — 'Whooa!' — rings melancholy under heaven. The horses group themselves inquiringly about the pasture gate, holding their heads despondently over the top rail in the direction of the farmstead, and ask if today can be Sunday …

Works by E C Booth

The Cliff End, 1908 and 1956.
The Doctor's Lass, 1910 and 1956.
Bella, 1912 (no dialect).
Fondie, 1916 and 1957.
The Tree of the Garden, 1922 and 1957
The Treble Clef, 1924 (very little dialect).
Miss Parkworth and other stories, 1934 (little dialect).
Kith and Kin, 1929 (dialect spoken by all characters).
The Brass Knocker, 1934 (by 'Edward Rathbone', no dialect).

(1995)

WHERE DO *YOU* COME FROM?
(An excursion into forensic linguistics)
Stanley Ellis

When I give an illustrated talk on the development of dialect, I often begin by showing the page from the biblical book of Judges where the Israelites challenge the Ephraimites at the ford of Jordan with a demand that they say the word for 'flowing stream'. The word they asked them to say contained a 'sh', and Ephraimites couldn't say a 'sh'. The word itself was foreign to them and contained a sound not in their own language, and they had never learned how to pronounce it; so they got it wrong:

> 4 Then Jephthah gathered together all the men of Gilead, and fought with Ephraim: and the men of Gilead smote Ephraim, because they said, Ye Gileadites are fugitives of Ephraim among the Ephraimites, and among the Manassites.
> 5 And the Gileadites took the passages of Jordan before the Ephraimites: and it was so, that when those Ephraimites which were escaped said, Let me go over; that the men of Gilead said unto him, Art thou an Ephraimite? If he said, Nay;
> 6 Then said they unto him, Say now Shibboleth: and he said Sibboleth: for he could not frame to pronounce it right. Then they took him, and slew him at the passages of Jordan: and there fell at that time of the Ephraimites forty and two thousand.
>
> (Judges, ch 12, vv4-6. Authorised Version.)

You will notice that around you are English people who can't sound a 'th' properly in either of its sounds. In 'thing' and in 'with' they don't get the tongue between the teeth to make the 'th' sound, but they put the bottom lip up against the top teeth and pronounce a 'f' or a 'v'. This is becoming more and more widespread at the present time among young people. Not long ago there was a song widely sung that was well known to be sung by a Londoner: 'fings ain't what they used to be'. American Black English was often shown in writing, or pronounced, using an 'f', for example in 'Shut yo' mouf'. I have a friend well into her eighties, a Yorkshire woman, who has never been able to pronounce her v's and f's, however much she tries, and with her that would be called a speech defect. In Northumberland at the present time you can hear across the country speakers who use an 'r' sound that comes out very differently from the 'r' sound heard in ordinary English. A

1797 edition of an encyclopaedia comments that 'The commonalty [of Northumberland] are remarkably distinguished by a kind of *shibboleth* or *whurle,* being a particular way of pronouncing the letter *R*'.

It's easy to see how, once you don't have a particular sound, it would be impossible to say a word on demand in just the right native pronunciation. We are not told how many others than Ephraimites had a speech defect preventing them from saying 'sh', but if there were any around at the time they might well have been among the slaughtered 42,000 who shed their blood that day. A gruesome thought.

The effect of that bloody tale in a book full of bloody tales has been that we have taken the word 'shibboleth' into our vocabulary — a test of language, even a thing used to identify a particular group. Even my early biblical example is not the earliest printed example of a simple voice recognition. In Genesis, when Jacob impersonated his bother Esau, his father recognises the voice of Jacob. (Genesis 27:22, 'The voice is Jacob's voice.')

It seems, though, from an examination of literature over the last two or three centuries that saying a word the wrong way could still be a matter of life and death. In a seventeenth-century work by Cleveland, *Rustick Rampant (1658)* we find on page 36, 'They had a Shibboleth to discover them, he who pronounced *Brot* and *Cawse* for *Bread* and *Cheese* had his head lopt off.'

Most people blessed with normal hearing can usually identify somebody who is not native to their own area. It's quite possible to be wrong about where a different speaker actually *does* come from — now that's another matter. Once, working with a Dutch colleague who speaks English superbly, we were together in Devon and a local man said to him: 'And what part of England do you come from?'. He knew he wasn't Devon, but he had no experience to say that my friend was not English: actually Henk was by miles the best foreign speaker of English I've ever met.

Just because I have spent so many years collecting dialect from all over England it has become a party task to identify speech, and I'm most impressed by my own reported skill in telling folk that they were born in Scotland, worked in Canada and spent an army career in South Africa before settling in Wiltshire. (It's not true, I don't believe I ever said it — or was able to say it.)

The legend seems to exist, and one of my embarrassments is to be tackled by a complete stranger with the words 'Tell me where I come from, then?' as a sort of challenge, the speaker knowing he has picked up his pronunciations from a variety of backgrounds and is sure to fool me. I have been taken to task for my gracelessness in responding 'Oh, dear. Are you lost?' to such demands.

Being known to work full time on the varieties of speech and particularly trained in the analysis of sounds gave a Hampshire solicitor in 1966 the idea that maybe I was the person to be enlisted in a type of court case that has become more and more common. A Winchester man, tired of being rebuffed in advances to a certain lady, decided to play a trick on her and call the local fire brigade to her home. The fire brigades don't very much like being called out on stunts like that. They may well be covering the wrong end of town chasing a hoax, when a real fire breaks out in the other direction that delays their arrival to put out a real fire and perhaps save life. Putting things and people at risk like that is not the work of a good citizen. The joker, if that's what he was, must have been surprised to find that the fire service had installed new equipment for the recording of all calls to the brigade. Recorded calls like his were kept, and the tape taken to the owner of a harassed home and played to see if there was any hope of pointing the finger at the owner of the voice.

Since this caller had no idea at that time that his voice might be recorded there was no attempt at disguise, and I suppose the lady in question really didn't have much doubt about it. English courts being what they are, it was not possible just to present this fact to a magistrate and have the man found guilty. English courts demand a 'qualified expert' to give an opinion before the court, and for this opinion to be tested by a defence.

At that particular time, machine research into the actual make-up of speech — all speech sounds — was being carried on vigorously in the United States, and in many states of the Union a type of machine analysis often called 'voice-prints', the supposed speech equivalent of fingerprints, was being presented and used as if they identified a particular individual. This was very controversial and articles in journals were being published, followed by rebuttals. Books were being published. Our Winchester solicitor had heard of the work and wanted a university phonetician familiar with it to become an expert witness to produce this kind of analysis and stand up in a witness box to say his piece. He got in touch with me, and with some misgivings I agreed to listen to his tapes.

Attending court is something most people are unfamiliar with and most reluctant to embark upon until they are forced to do so. Academics were reluctant to appear in public in this way to have to explain themselves. Many university people still disapprove of putting their work so clearly under scrutiny and I received a lot of opposition from professional associates. This has become much less over the years and some who at first were disapproving are themselves taking part in forensic examinations and court proceedings on phonetic matters.

I finally decided I would act. I got the tape and a specimen reading that the suspect had been prepared to make for him, still not aware, I suppose, how damning this could become. The solicitor had cleverly devised a passage apparently relating to the building of a new fire station in Winchester and containing many of the words and phrases that had appeared in the recorded call for the brigade. The fact that these phrases were being repeated so handily probably never occurred to the man, and he went ahead, saying in his normal voice all the things he had said before, not aware he was doing this, giving beautiful material for a comparison.

As an undergraduate I had become familiar with attempts to reproduce something you can see out of something you can say. An early attempt at what was called Visible Speech had been to use cathode ray tubes, essentially the same thing as a television screen, to show the sound frequencies of a voice to help deaf people. It was believed that by seeing something ever-changing, translated from something they could not hear, deaf people might quickly become familiar with the coloured shapes before them and interpret them as the words and sounds they electronically represent .

Such a process might well have worked with deaf people, but they could hardly have carried all that gear around with them all the time in ordinary life. Other ways of helping the deaf have proved equally successful and more easily portable.

The use of electronic analysis is, however, useful. It may well not be true, though some leading phoneticians in the past have declared it to be so, that no two people speak exactly alike. In order to be actually sure of this you might have to test every human being and their speaking over the whole range of speech sounds, not a seriously possible task. Frequency analysis would certainly be a tool in even beginning to do this. In general the sounds of a person's speech can be analysed by non-electronic means and shown to make up frequencies. It has long been known that a tuning fork vibrates at a certain number of vibrations per second to make a certain note and it is this 'frequency' that provides the first measurement of a spoken sound. A voice sounding a note is much less complicated than the same voice making a vowel sound and the various sounds that make up a sentence become more and more a combination of vibrations at many levels at once.

I tackled the Winchester job in two ways. One, because I had been particularly asked if it could be done, by the use of a Sonogram. The machine I had to work on produced some beautifully matching patterns from the man involved and the call to the fire service. These can be printed out in various ways. Similar words spoken by me, several Winchester policemen and others, while giving shapes that were reasonably identifiable as the same words, did not give the same matching shapes that the suspect gave. I devised a little game of about ten sheets marked A-J and 1-10 and asked people to put them together. It was not too difficult for anyone to say that the two from call and suspect gave a better match than the others when the same words were compared.

I made what I considered my most important examination by a careful phonetic analysis of the various speech sounds, using the background of training and experience I had been using for years in collecting dialectal material for the *Survey of English Dialects* and came to a pretty firm opinion.

I now know that, compared to the majority of the work that came my way in later years, this was a pretty uncomplicated case. I went to court, guided through the complexity of the legal system, and said my piece. As well as the voice evidence there was a deal of other evidence. What I gave then, and have continued to give since, was an opinion, like that of, say, a doctor suggesting a time of death, a gun expert saying whether a bullet came from a particular gun. It has always been certain for me that there were no 'voice-prints' comparable to fingerprints, that would prove the likeness of one voice to another, and give absolute proof that a certain speaker was involved.

The magistrates of Winchester very sensibly declined to be convinced by my little shuffle card game and carefully said that they had made up their minds and excluded the electronic presentation from their decision. They took close notice of the analytical evidence I gave, among the rest, and decided that the gentleman was guilty of the offence charged.

My particular involvement was apparently a 'first', and gained a mention in the court journals and magistrates' magazines (the editorial, no less), and mention by a local journalist provoked national headlines of the 'Voiceprints capture Hoaxer' style. The ballyhoo died quickly but the case was remembered, and as at that time more and more emergency services were beginning to record the telephone calls made to them, more and more improper calls were being investigated. Tape recording of all kinds underwent an enormous expansion in the late 1950s, 1960s and 1970s and it is not difficult to realise, seeing the numbers of stores with high-quality recording of sound, and now vision equipment available, how rapidly this has become common.

All 999 calls to the emergency services are now automatically recorded, often by several recorders. The police, fire and ambulance services often make their own, and British Telecom have an elaborate system of recording material and identifying the origin of every telephone call made by the operator instantly. Much of this, like the last call information obtainable by dialling 1471 on a domestic telephone, is coming into use currently. There has been an explosion of opportunity to tape record events of all kinds, business meetings, aircraft and shipping movements, face-to-face interviews of all kinds and the everyday occurrence of leaving messages at the homes of people.

As this happened, more recordings of criminal events were made. Cases kept coming to me, not too many at that time, but enough to make me familiar with the inside of magistrates and crown courts in many parts of the country. I worked on cases brought to me by defence as well as prosecution. I acted in industrial tribunals. I was also consulted by what I saw as odd people, mostly journalists, who came to bring strange recordings to disrupt my thinking. I was asked by a journalist working on what I later found was a tabloid newspaper to authenticate the voice of a man involved in what is often called the 'Jeremy Thorpe/Scott case'. The only thing that seemed to happen was that Mr Scott was handed what was then a great deal of money and the journalist went off to write up his story, confident, I suppose, that if it was then challenged he could blame me for being so certain. Looking back I can see that this was another part of my learning about life and humans.

I had always known that my experience in years going around interviewing and making friends of very ordinary and straightforward people in a search for local dialect had been very enriching. I was to learn that working with criminal voices was certainly to be a different kind of experience that might be called enlarging.

I found the work interesting, and not at that time taking up too much time. Many of the cases I was sent were quite impossible to do anything with. Some were comparisons of voices, a known and an unknown, and these gradually became the majority and the ones that could be expected to produce some kind of a result. I learned how to put together a Statement of Witness, a very serious document that is attached to one throughout a case. Mine includes nowadays a clear sentence that it is not to be taken as evidence comparable with fingerprints. It sets out how far from absolute certainty an opinion may be, and it sets out my method of work, which has itself grown and changed.

Perhaps the most dramatic case in which l was involved was the 'Yorkshire Ripper' case. When the frequent murders were being reported I was brought a tape sent to the police and was able to give an opinion on it. My own story has been published recently in the *International Journal of Speech, Language and the Law*, and the only thing perhaps worth saying here is that the man who made the tape was not the murderer, and that after a while I, along with others involved, suggested this to the police. Those who pursued the case did not take any notice, and a great deal of money was spent.

The most important event regarding the recording of criminal voices for comparison has been the Police and Criminal Evidence Act of the early 1980s which coincided with my enforced early retirement from the university, which was being severely cut in its budget. 110 members of staff aged fifty-five and over were retired from Leeds in 1983 and the resulting shortages had to be made up in many departments by the appointment of new young staff. The Institute of Dialect and Folk Life Studies was left without anyone to run it, and as under the terms of the cuts no one else could be appointed to do so, it was wound up. Only recently has any interest in local speech and work on it, including the archives so carefully put together, been possible.

Among the points in the Act of Parliament I have mentioned was that the police, for the protection of criminals who often asserted that they had been misrepresented, or even mistreated, were required to tape all the interviews held before a person was charged. It was also good for the police because it mostly showed that the suspects were not mistreated or misrepresented and this has proved quite helpful to the police side. It also proved helpful in providing what have come to be known as 'voice samples' for comparison with recorded criminal events such as telephone calls. From the time of my early retirement, therefore, the amount of material on tape coming to me for comparison by phonetic analysis began to increase. I had found a new career.

At about the same time equipment for analysing speech became available as speech laboratory programs for use in computers. This development has grown at almost bewildering speed along with the computer age. People who see computers in shop windows, and their children wanting to play games or use them for school essays, have no concept of the vast body of new things that continue to

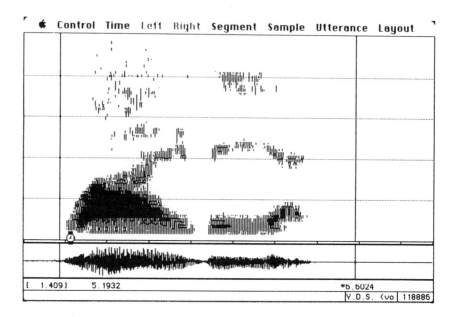

*Stanley Ellis saying 'YDS'. The screen of the computer is set for two seconds'
width. The vertical lines enclose a time of 1.409 seconds. The horizontal
lines are set at 1k intervals.*

come out, wiping out the achievements of last year, last month, in a new expansion
of storage of information and communication.

We are being presented in every newspaper with articles on the Internet, e-mail
and the World Wide Web, and assured that these will transform our lives. Maybe
they will, but much of the revolution will have to be presented to us in a much
simpler way before many of us will want anything to do with it. Members of this
society can be reminded of how nowadays they use the television set with great
ease and in adopting it how much *they* have changed. Much of the 'nuts and bolts'
of all this business can be left to those in the back rooms, but we will certainly be
involved in our homes at some time soon. Computer programmes have made it
easy to take sounds and by 'digitising' them, make it possible to copy, move them,
place them in a variety of positions side by side for comparison, take them and
analyse them for frequency, pitch, length, even nowadays things we certainly don't
think we have such as 'jitter' and 'shimmer'. You will be able to live without knowing anything about them, but they have increasingly formed part of my everyday
life over past years.

I have to confess to being what is often called a 'gadget man' and have enjoyed
playing with all the machinery I have had for my work. The business of analysing
and presenting results from all this material in a form that a judge and a jury, not

to mention solicitors and barristers, can understand has been a fascinating one.

Within all the work have been stories that form human interest and often show a great deal of human frailty and weakness. It seems that many burglars who are violent and have killed will call an ambulance in the hope that the victim may not be dead. The telephone call may be the first thing that will give them away. People who call 999 may be violently interrupted by attack, but a dangling telephone will be going on recording evidence that may eventually be used to bring someone to justice.

The brighter side is often that the increasing spate of nuisance calls can now be checked by an intelligent use of telephone answering machines and the last number recall service, leading to prosecution. Telephone call answering machines provoke a good deal of evidence that can be used later in all kinds of cases where disputes, even threats, may be clearly set out to listen to later. Fortunately most people, in spite of the hectic reporting in newspapers, do not, in fact, become involved with crime and the courts. My own involvement with this has seemed as though I have been moving over into another existence that travels alongside the everyday life. Just as I found that colleagues and friends often had no notion of what life was like in the simple villages where I collected dialect material in the 1950s, in the same way the majority are largely uninformed of a process that is going on all the time in police stations, fire stations and courts. Television programmes give a flavour, but it is entertainment for our homes, flickering non-reality that we don't have to live.

Your editor asked me to write this article about my parallel experience. My work is still about variety in speech, which is what the dialect society is all about. The work I did in dialect collection and editing, carefully classifying the elements of one dialect for comparison with another, has proved invaluable as the basis of this criminal work. The fact that Irwin Bielby has one kind of pronunciation that is a radical contrast with that of Arthur Kinder differentiates them just as much as that one lives on the East Riding plain and the other at the top of a West Riding hill. It also can be important that a recording of a telephone call to the fire brigade, that can be replayed, is spoken by a voice with different characteristics again. Factors like this may well be the first point for me to decide whether to proceed with a more detailed comparison of features within the two voices I am given on tape.

(1995)

T' PEGGIN' RUG

'Not another hoil in t' 'earthrug?!
Aye! Sithee, worn reight through!
They don't mek things ter last these days,
Not like they used ter do.
Tek 'earthrugs fer an instance,
Wi' ther fancy nylon pile,
Right posh they look when spankin' new–
But yer notice in a while
'Ow dull they've gone, an' kind o' frayed,
An' t' pile all worn an' flat,
I allus says ther's nowt can beat
T' owd-fashioned peggin mat!

When t' winter neets werc drawin' in
(No telly then, tha knows!)
Me mam 'ud start ter sooart things out,
Owd coits and worn-out clothes.
Ther'd be a job fer each of us
While some cut t' cloth in strips,
Another cut aw t' buttons off
An' t' 'ooks an' eyes an' zips.
We clipped until wer fingers ached
An' thumbs were near red raw,
By heck! it wor a stallin' job
Wi' bits all ower t' floor!

At last me mam 'ud say 'That's it!
We've getten fairish theer —
Well start ter peg termorrer neet
Whan Dad brings t' frame in here.'
She'd draw a fancy pattern
On a piece of harden sackin',
An' nail it in to t' frame ter mek
A strong an' sturdy backin'.
An' then t' best part of all began —
All seated in a row
We'd prod an' poke them clippin's in
An' watch the pattern grow.

On t' day as it were finished,
An' down bi' t' fireside,
Me mam 'ud bring all t' neighbours in
An' show 'em it wi' pride,
When yer nobbut 'ad linoleum,
Or a floor o' cow'd stone flags
They browt a touch o' luxury —
Yon mats med out o' rags.
Ah've one upstairs, still goin' strong,
Outside o' t' bathroom door
'At me dad and me were workin' on
    in 1944!
What can yer buy these days as cheap,
'Ardwearin', warm an' snug
As yon owd-fashioned work of art?
Aye! t' good owd peggin' rug!

Christine Thistlethwaite (WR)

(1996)

T' LASS THRO' BUCKDEN

She's reet, is t' lass thro' Buckden,
Reet fer me;
Thro' t' wick, nim way of her gannin'
To t' grey of her ee:
She's getten her feet on t' fellside,
Her glance in t' gill-beck's glee —
Reet, is t' lass thro' Buckden,
Reet fer me.

She's fair, is t' lass thro' Buckden,
Fair to see;
She's addled her lewks on t' moortop,
Brant an' free:
Her hair is t' birks at Autumn,
Her blush, Spring's sap in t' tree —
Fair, is t' lass thro' Buckden,
Fair to me.

She's feat, is t' lass thro' Buckden,
Feat as t' bee;
She'll laup ower t' intak' pastures
Grand to see:
Theer's t' clouder's rigg in her fraimin'
An' t' foss's glint in her ee —
Feat, is t' lass thro' Buckden,
Feat as t' bee.

She's fain, is t' lass thro' Buckden,
Fain wi' me;
She'll sing tiv a blackbird's pipin'
High on t' tree:
Her laugh is a lambkin's laikin',
Her wit is t' levret's spree —
Fain, is t' lass thro' Buckden,
Fain wi' me.

She's *mine,* is t' lass thro' Buckden,
Mine! Fer me!
Ah reckon missen a sailor
Home thro' t' sea:
She'll breeten mi farmstead's 'earthstun
An' mother mi bairns to be —
Mine, is t' lass thro' Buckden,
Mine! Fer me!

She'll be reet, when t' lass thro' Buckden
Comes to dee;
She'll fassen her lownd, grey glances
Onto Eternity:
Theer'll bi t' valley o' stars in her
thinkin'
An' t' lamp o' God in her ee,
An' t' Dale 'll bi dead wi'aht her,
Dead fer me.

Gwen Wade (Ripon)

(Published as a tribute to Gwen Wade, BEM, on her death in 1996.)

brant, steep; *feat*, lively; *foss*, waterfall; *lownd*, calm

BURNS AND BROAD YORKSHIRE
Arnold Kellett

Those of us who can still speak authentic Yorkshire dialect have always warmed to Robert Burns. How fitting it is that the bicentenary of his death in 1996 is followed so soon by the centenary of the founding of the Yorkshire Dialect Society.

The influence of Burns, as a champion of dialect, cannot be overstated. He wrote in an age when Standard English was already imposing itself on every part of the British Isles as the only acceptable form of English, both spoken and written. The contrast between this London-based language and that of the various provincial forms was seen as the contrast between the normal and the abnormal, between what was correct and what was deviant and degenerate. When Burns chose to make use of the speech of his native Ayrshire he was asserting that, far from dialect being a corrupt and inferior form of English, it often preserves valuable lexical items and idiomatic turns of phrase which have been lost from the mainstream language.

The roots of both Scots dialect and so-called 'broad Yorkshire' go deep into common ground. This is essentially the robust language of the Angles, with an additional strength provided by the Vikings. Yorkshire readers with a knowledge of their dialect only need to glance through the glossary included in any serious edition of *The Poems and Songs of Robert Burns* to find themselves immediately at home. Both Scots and Tykes have, for example, such words as *aiblins* (perhaps), *bairn* (child), *bauk* (cross-beam), *bield* (shelter), *brak* (broke), *chimla* (chimney), *claes* (clothes), *clarty* (dirty), *coble* (fishing-boat), *doited* (failing with age), *dub* (puddle), *een* (eyes), *flay* (frighten), *gang* (go), *gowk (cuckoo)*, *greet* (weep), *kist* (chest), *lug* (ear), *nieve* (fist), *mense* (decency, discretion), *oxter* (armpit), *ratten* (rat), *reek* (smoke), *shoon* (shoes), *sodger* (soldier), *telled* (told), *threeap (insist)*, *whin* (furze). There are hundreds more, if we allow for slight variations in pronunciation, and a number which sound like modern German, such as *lang, blinnd, yon* (cf *jener)*. There are also words surviving from Norman French, with their original meaning — eg, *chamer* (bedroom) and *buffit* (low stool).

The shared inheritance is particularly noticeable when the Scots of Burns is compared with the dialects of the North and East Ridings, in which you can still hear the vowels used by the Angles in the kingdom of Northumbria (ie the land north of the river Humber). For instance, 'mouse' is traditionally pronounced *'moose'*, exactly as in Scots.

However, this very example raises the question of to what extent Burns really used full-blown dialect. In his famous *To a Mouse* (1785) the printed version has *mousie* rather than *moosie, cowrin'* rather than *coorin'* and *wee-bit housie* rather than *hoosie*. But it may be that in order to reach a wider readership Burns accepted literary conventions of spelling, knowing that local dialect speakers would pronounce the words in real Scots style. It is also true that Burns interlaced his dialect verse with lines in Standard English, so that sometimes the contrast is quite marked. For example:

> But Mousie, thou art no thy lane,
> In proving foresight may be vain

The first line ('you are not on your own') might be understood only by a dialect speaker — one, indeed, who would be unlikely to express himself in the more formal English of the second line.

Though Burns does not necessarily use dialect exclusively, or perhaps always authentically, the fact remains that his best poems are richly spiced with it — so much so that English readers, even Tykes and Geordies, need the help of the glossary. Sometimes the Scots dialect predominates, as in *Tam o' Shanter* — in parts impenetrable to a Sassenach. Sometimes, as in that incomparable love-song, *A Red, Red Rose* it is a matter of accent and intonation, the only strong dialect word in the whole poem occurring in 'Till a' the seas *gang* dry'. But the effect of Burns's widespread use of local speech in his verse — notably from the countryside round Tarbolton — was that dialect now became respectable. No longer would it be seen as the quaint and common twang of country bumpkins, but as a language in its own right, capable of subtle and forceful expression.

Towards the end of the eighteenth century, soon after the death of Burns, there was a revival of interest in dialect of all kinds. In Yorkshire, antiquarians were making word-lists or writing down ancient dialect verse such as the *Lyke Wake Dirge*. The direct influence of Burns can be seen in the little-known poet David Lewis, a self-educated man who farmed near Knaresborough, North Yorkshire.

One day, as he was scything his meadow to make hay, he accidentally killed a frog — and began to philosophise over this poor creature, just as Burns had done with his mouse, addressing it directly in local dialect:

> Poor luckless frog, why com' thoo 'ere?

He expresses his compassion for the creature, describing its beauty and life-cycle — then, after a touch of humour, suddenly realises that all of us will one day be cut down by the relentless scythe of time.

This and a narrative dialect poem by David Lewis was published in 1815. During the course of the century there was a growing interest in original dialect writing, especially in verse. Some of this appeared in the rural setting of the North and East Ridings, but by far the biggest output was in the industrial parts of the West Riding, where the dialect almanacks made an ideal vehicle. William Wright of Keighley, using the pen-name of 'Bill o' th' Hoylus End', was a self-styled 'Yorkshire Burns' who wore a Scotch cap and plaid, and published his work in his

Haworth, Cowenheead and Bogthorn Olmenac. Best known of all was John Hartley (1839-1915) of Halifax, with his immensely popular *Clock Almanack* and crowd-pulling public recitations. Hartley excelled in both comic and serious verse, the latter sometimes verging on the sentimental, but at its best reminiscent of Burns in its down-to-earth portrayal of the hard life of ordinary working folk.

Those who belong neither to Scotland nor Yorkshire sometimes see an affinity between the two cultures, especially in respect of caution over brass. 'A Yorkshire-man', it has been said, 'is a Scotsman shorn of his generosity' ... But in an increasingly amorphous world they also share a sense of identity, of solidarity with those who have gone before them. Both Scots and Yorkshire folk are in general proud of their heritage — including their linguistic heritage. They know it provides something distinctive and colourful in a world that is becoming increasingly standardised and uniform, monotonously the same everywhere.

Dialect, alas, is in serious decline, hanging on by the skin of its teeth. Those of us who want to keep it alive, or at least to keep the memory of it still fresh, may well be accused of sentimental nostalgia. But as Burns showed, the very act of looking back on 'auld lang syne' helps to reinforce that crucial sense of belonging, of the worth of local, homely, human things in the impersonal electronic dustbowl we are in danger of creating.

(1996)

YDS officials present at the Centenary AGM, York, March 1997: Cedric Sellers, Arnold Kellett, Jeremy Muldowney, Walter Leach, Muriel Shackleton, Sir Marcus Worsley, Arthur Kinder, Ruth Dent, Michael Park.

APPENDIX:

The Yorkshire Dialect Society 1897-1997

The following are the principal office-holders over the first 100 years — all, incidentally, honorary and unpaid. The vice-presidents are too numerous to list in full, but amongst the distinguished names we might note Professor Joseph Wright, the Most Hon the Marquis of Zetland, Rev Canon Atkinson, Rev Professor Walter W Skeat, Rev M C F Morris, Dr J A H Murray, Sir Michael Salter, Professor I Gollanz, Dr Henry Sweet, Professor Sir W A Craigie, Major J Fairfax-Blakeborough, Rev A N Cooper, Sir Alfred E Pease, Sir J B Baillie, Profesor G C Moore-Smith, the Rt Hon Earl of Harewood, Sir Ben Turner, Sir Montague Burton, Miss Storm Jameson, J B Priestley, and three archbishops of York.

Also worthy of mention are the successive editors of our *Summer Bulletin*, started in 1954 — F W Moody, Miss G B Jones, J Waddington-Feather, B T Dyson, Jack Danby and (since 1988) Muriel Shackleton.

Presidents

1897–1908	The Most Hon the Marquis of Ripon
1909–1935	Sir William H Arthington Worsley
1936–1963	Mrs McGrigor Phillips (Dorothy Una Ratcliffe)
1964–1974	Dr Wilfrid J Halliday
1975–1983	F W Moody
1983–	Sir Marcus Worsley

Chairmen

1897–1898	Prof Charles A Federer
1898–1918	S Philip Unwin
1919	A C Coffin
1920–1922	Lionel Cresswell
1927–1935	Joseph Hambly Rowe
1936–1940	F Austin Hyde
1941–1945	Prof Bruce Dickins

1946–1964	Dr Wilfrid J Halliday
1964–1965	F W Moody
1965–1969	William Cowley
1970–1972	Stanley Ellis
1973–1975	Cedric Sellers
1976–1979	Jack Danby
1980–1982	B T Dyson
1983–1988	Dr K E Smith
1989–1990	Linda Sherwood
1991–1993	Ruth Dent
1994–	Arthur Kinder

Secretaries

1897–1906	Rev Thomas Clarke
1907–1908	William Edwards
1908–1910	John Bacchus
1911	Stephen J Gordon
1912–1913	Prof F W Moorman
1914	Robert Coventry Denby
1915–1918	A C Coffin
1919–1924	George W Cowling, Dr W J Halliday
1924–1929	Miss L H Allison
1929–1932	F Austin Hyde
1932–1937	W Day Metcalfe
1938–1943	H J L Bruff
1942–1953	A Stanley Umpleby
1953–1960	F W Moody
1961–1963	Miss G B Jones
1964–1968	J Waddington-Feather
1969–1972	Ian Dewhirst
1973–1974	P Fawcett
1975–1984	Gerald Williams
1985–1997	Stanley Ellis
1997–	Michael Park

Treasurers

1897–1914	John Clapham
1915	John Slicer

1916–1923	H Bryen Bell
1923–1929	Miss L H Allison
1929–1932	F Austin Hyde
1932–1937	W Day Metcalfe
1938	H J L Bruff
1939–1948	A Stanley Umpleby
1948–1962	J M Parker
1963–1984	Donald R Sykes
1985–1989	Lynne Anderson
1990–1992	Cedric Sellers
1993–	Walter Leach

Editors of *Transactions*

1897–1903	H E Wroot
1904–1911	(Chairman and Secretary)
1912–1917	Prof F W Moorman
1918–1922	(Chairman and Secretary)
1923–1926	George H Cowling, Dr W J Halliday
1927–1946	Dr W J Halliday
1947–1960	Prof Harold Orton, W A G Doyle-Davidson
1961–1965	Dr B R Dyson, Stanley Ellis, Dr W J Halliday
1966–1974	Stanley Ellis, Dr W J Halliday
1975	Stanley Ellis, B T Dyson
1976–1979	Stanley Ellis
1980	Stanley Ellis, Dr P M Anderson
1981–1985	Dr P M Anderson, Stanley Ellis
1986–1990	Dr Ken Edward Smith
1991–	Dr Arnold Kellett

Enquiries concerning the Yorkshire Dialect Society should be addressed to the honorary secretary, Michael Park, at 51 Stepney Avenue, Scarborough, YO12 5BW.